Sex, Laws & Stereotypes

Authentic workplace anecdotes and practical tips
for dealing with ADA, sexual harassment,
workplace violence, and beyond . . .

N. Elizabeth Fried, Ph.D.

Sex, Laws & Stereotypes

Authentic workplace anecdotes and practical tips
for dealing with ADA, sexual harassment,
workplace violence, and beyond . . .

N. Elizabeth Fried, Ph.D.

INTERMEDIARIES Press
Dublin, Ohio

An **INTERMEDIARIES Press** Book
Copyright © 1994 by N. Elizabeth Fried

All rights reserved under International and Pan American Copyright Conventions. Published and printed in the U.S.A. by **INTERMEDIARIES Press**. No parts of this book may be used or reproduced in any manner whatsoever without written permission of **INTERMEDIARIES Press** except in the case of brief quotations embodied in critical articles for reviews.

For additional information, contact:

INTERMEDIARIES Press
5590 Dumfries Court West, Suite 2000
Dublin, OH 43017

10 9 8 7 6 5 4 3 2 1

Library of Congress Catalog Card Number: 93–91792

ISBN 0-9637481-0-6

Cover design and typography by Gary A. Hoffman

Cover photography by Mike Greer
Endflap photography by Jerry Boling

To all the "deep throats" who trusted me with sensitive information. Special appreciation to "B" who provided the most complex and challenging cases.

Sex, Laws & Stereotypes

Introduction

"The anecdotes in this book are true. They are not corporate legends nor extensions of my imagination."

N. Elizabeth Fried, Ph.D.
Author

Entertainment with Substance

"Employees who catnap with cadavers? Security officers doing a line of coke in the rest room? Company-subsidized sexcapades? Things like that don't *really* happen in the workplace," you may be thinking. "You must be making this up, Elizabeth."

Well, unfortunately, they do happen and can make life a living hell for business owners, managers, and human resources professionals. The anecdotes in this book are not corporate legends nor extensions of my imagination. (I wish I *were* that creative!) So, for the record, let me state clearly that these cases are true. As part of my research, I interviewed trusted sources from across the country, including clients, business owners, human resources professionals, and employment attorneys. I promised to keep my sources confidential, and my sources agreed to share only those cases that they personally handled or resolved. In fact, many had the files in hand during our interview.

To ensure confidentiality and protect my sources, I changed the names, places, and certain other revealing aspects of the cases, but the key facts and underlying issues remain unchanged. For example, I often altered industry, geographic location, sex, or nationality of the characters if these modifications did not detract from the essence of the case.

For those of you who are familiar with my first book, *Outrageous Conduct: Bizarre Behavior at Work,* welcome back. I hope you like the additions I've made to the original format. For those of you who are new to my offbeat techniques, thanks for joining me. You're in for an interesting surprise. This is not a conventional business book. My intent with *Sex, Laws & Stereotypes* is to provide entertainment with substance.

Although I've maintained the dramatic, easy-to-read anecdotal style found in *Outrageous Conduct,* the cases I chose for *Sex, Laws & Stereotypes* have a slightly different flavor. It was tempting to select the weirdest, wackiest stories again, but I restrained myself. Instead, I required each case to meet some key criteria before being considered for inclusion in the book. Each case had to raise an important legal or management issue to make the cut. For example, during my research I uncovered at least four flasher stories. At first I thought, "Great, now I can devote a whole chapter to flashers." Then it occurred to me, "So what? What are the management or human resources implications of dealing with flashers? And, are there really any significant differences among these cases?"

Once I went through that thought process, I eliminated three of the cases and kept the one that had the most interesting nuances and challenging issues. (Although, admittedly, it was as hard for me to toss out a juicy story as it would be to throw out leftover cheesecake!)

Nevertheless, the decision resulted in more substantive cases with greater educational value. This change and others were in response to comments from *Outrageous Conduct* readers who said, "We loved the stories. . . liked the panel comments too . . . wish there were more . . . ." The need for expanded panel commentary was further substantiated by a university professor who uses the book as a supplemental text for his course on human resources management. He told me that *Outrageous Conduct* helped to make his course a real hit with students. The students found the cases fun to read and a pleasant break from their dry, traditional primary text. However, he pointed out that the panel commentary needed bolstering because the class was hungry for additional professional solutions. This was not surprising. My primary purpose when writing *Outrageous Conduct* was entertainment. Thus, after considering all the input, it seemed prudent to expand the number of panel members as well as the length of their commentary to serve a wider range of readers.

To accomplish these objectives, I invited a number of highly experienced professionals from throughout the United States and Canada to provide expert opinion. These dedicated individuals from diverse industries were excited by the project, and over 40 agreed to volunteer their services by providing thoughtful commentary on a portion of the 36 cases. I wanted to ensure that the panel members enjoyed their experience and didn't feel overburdened. Thus, I divided the entire panel into six smaller groups, each containing seven to eight members.

I used specific criteria for forming these groups. Each member came from a different industry and different geographic area. There was a minimum of two women in each group, and members had varying levels of experience and organizational stature. I assigned each group an assortment of six stories reflecting various policy or legal issues. For example, no group received all sexual harassment or all workplace violence stories. Instead, the group of cases may have included such issues as privacy, office romance, substance abuse, and defamation. However, there was one exception. I formed a unique group composed primarily of benefits specialists. To best utilize their expertise, this group reviewed only cases having benefits implications.

Once I received all the panel comments for each case, I reviewed them and looked for consistent thinking as well as differing opinions. Then I consolidated the comments into a logical, cohesive format. Throughout the book, the panel offers practical tips and wise guidance for both inexperienced as well as seasoned professionals.

I also had the good fortune to work once again with Tom Greble from the New York employment law firm of Roberts and Finger. Tom enthusiastically agreed to volunteer on this new project, and this time he included the talent of the firm's able associate, Lee Boyd. Together, they not only skillfully provided the expanded legal comments that I requested, but did so under extraordinarily tight deadlines. They raise serious issues and offer practical preventive strategies.

Managing people in today's complex world is truly an adventure. I hope you find the cases intriguing and the commentary informative as well as insightful. However, the opinions expressed by the panel and particularly, the employment law experts, are offered only as general suggestions and should not be construed in any way as formal or legal advice. Moreover, their comments reflect their *personal* opinions and not necessarily the policies and practices of their employers. *Sex, Laws & Stereotypes* is not intended to be the definitive text on human resources, but a thought-provoking, enjoyable departure from traditional professional reading.

Before I introduce you to the panel members, there are few other individuals who deserve a special recognition for the success of this project. The first is my husband, Douglas. He reviewed each story and gave me the blue-collar point of view on dialogue and other related story elements. He was also responsible for suggesting several of the colorful character names sprinkled throughout the book. The second special "hats off" goes to my trusted assistant Carole Lassak. She transcribed miles of confidential interview tapes, reviewed every case for consistency and logic, and kept a running dialogue with all the panel members to ensure they met their deadlines. Coordinating with 45 busy professionals who have other, more pressing agendas was a monumental task. I applaud her for terrific organizational skills and dedication to this project. There is no question that she helped me stay sane and on track. Finally, I am indebted to my secret sources. It's because of their confidence and trust that this book was even possible. Even though I can't acknowledge them publicly, I appreciate their generosity and willingness to make this unique professional contribution.

Now, for those whom I *can* publicly acknowledge, it's with a great deal of pleasure that I formally introduce you to my panel of professionals. They represent human resources expertise gained from a broad spectrum of organizations, ranging from non-profit and educational institutions to *Fortune 500* companies.

N. Elizabeth Fried
Dublin, Ohio
March, 1994

Panel Members

Jim Austgen is vice president and director of human resources with Motorola, Inc.–Land Mobile Products Sector in Schaumberg, Illinois. His 19 years' experience in human resources includes the insurance, manufacturing, software development, and personal care products industries. Austgen holds an undergraduate degree in psychology from Purdue University in Indiana.

C. Neal Baileys is vice president of human resources for the PMI Food Equipment Group (a division of Premark International) in Troy, Ohio. He has 20 years' experience in human resources covering the education, service, and manufacturing professional and industry sectors. Baileys received an undergraduate degree in marketing education from Bowling Green State University in Ohio and a master's in personnel from Xavier University in Cincinnati. Baileys serves on the business advisory council of the Tipp City Chamber of Commerce.

Anne Ball, CCP, is president of HR Solutions, a human resources consulting firm located in Mukilteo, Washington. Prior to opening her practice, she had over 15 years' experience in human resources for various industries and professions, including banking and finance, higher education, and health care. She earned an undergraduate degree in economics from The Ohio State University and is nearing completion of a master's degree in human resources development from Seattle Pacific University. Ball served as a founding board member of the Northwest Compensation Forum, is currently president of the Skagit-Island Human Resources Management Association, and serves as civil service commissioner for the City of Mukilteo.

Terry Bean, CCP, SPHR, is senior vice president, human resources, of Rose's Stores, Inc. in Henderson, North Carolina. He has 20 years' human resources experience in the manufacturing, transportation, and retailing industries. Bean's undergraduate degree in management and psychology is from Memphis State University in Tennessee. He has served on the steering committee for human resources and operations management issues of the International Mass Retailers Association since 1991.

J. Carolyn Bertram is regional director of human resources for the Marriott Corporation–Courtyard/Fairfield Inn Division in Washington, D.C. She has 14 years' human resources experience in the hospitality industry.

Bertram received her undergraduate degree in elementary education from Murray State University in Kentucky and a master's degree in guidance and counseling from the University of Missouri in St. Louis.

J. Barry Bingham, CCP, is director of compensation for Monsanto Company in St. Louis. He has 25 years' human resources experience in chemical and pharmaceutical manufacturing. Bingham holds an undergraduate degree in management and a master's degree in human resources management from the University of Utah in Salt Lake City. Bingham serves on the faculty of the American Compensation Association and is a member of its executive and variable pay committee.

Alice Boon-Harris is vice president for human resources at St. Louis Regional Medical Center in Missouri. She has 17 years' human resources experience in the nonprofit health care industry. Boon-Harris received her undergraduate degree in business administration from the University of Missouri—St. Louis and her master's degree in human resources development from Webster University, also in St. Louis.

Andrew Borkin is senior vice president of Meta/Mat Ltd., an Iselin, New Jersey-based human resources consulting firm, specializing in outplacement, training, human resources consulting, and search. He has 20 years' human resources experience including the education, manufacturing, and oil and gas professions and industries. Borkin received his undergraduate degree in history from the State University of New York in Fredonia and his master's degree from the State University of New York in Albany. He is past president of the Computer Industries Personnel Association.

Frank R. Bosse is vice president of human resources for the Fireman's Fund Insurance Company located in Novato, California. He has 20 years' human resources experience encompassing retail, insurance, and federal and state governments. Bosse received his undergraduate degree from the State University of New York at Buffalo and his master's degree in industrial and labor relations from The Ohio State University.

Ruth N. Bramson is vice president of human resources and administration at Charles River Laboratories (a Bausch & Lomb Company) in Wilmington, Massachusetts. Her 17 years of human resources experience includes the communications, education, manufacturing, research, retail, and biotechnology professions and industries. Bramson received her undergraduate degree from Columbia University and her master's degree in organizational development and training from Boston University. She is a published author and lecturer and has served on the board of directors of local and international human resources associations. Currently she serves on the advisory board of Suffolk University.

Robert W. Connolly is director of corporate human resources for Safeguard Business Systems, Inc. of Fort Washington, Pennsylvania. He has 15 years' experience in human resources in the manufacturing and nonprofit fields and holds an undergraduate degree in psychology from Penn State University. Connolly serves on the board of directors for the Philadelphia Regional Chapter of the Society for Human Resources Management and is a member of the General Committee for the Westown School in Westown, Pennsylvania.

Claudia D. Denaro is vice president, human resources services, for Consolidated Stores Corporation in Columbus, Ohio. She has 13 years' human resources experience covering the banking and finance, food service, and retail industries. Denaro received an undergraduate degree in business administration from the University of Akron in Ohio. She chaired the Ohio Stock Option Forum and currently serves on the board of directors for the Big Brothers/Big Sisters Association of Franklin County.

Marlene M. Dennis, CCP, CEBS, is director of human resources for McDonnell Douglas Helicopter Systems in Mesa, Arizona. She has 23 years' human resources experience in the insurance and aerospace industries. Dennis received her undergraduate degree from California State University at Long Beach and a master's degree in business administration from UCLA. She is a faculty member for the American Compensation Association's certification program and has served on ACA's education committee.

Kathleen Dole, CCP, is human resources officer for John Hancock Mutual Life Insurance Company in Hartford, Connecticut. She has 20 years' human resources experience in the insurance, investments, and finance industries. Dole earned an undergraduate degree in English and social sciences from Emmanuel College in Boston.

Sandy Fleming Dulaney, CCP, is a human resources consultant for ARCO Exploration and Production Technology in Plano, Texas. She has over 20 years' human resources experience in the oil and gas and research industries. Dulaney received her undergraduate degree from North Texas State University in Denton and her master's degree in organizational behavior and administration from Southern Methodist University in Dallas.

She currently serves on the advisory board of the Presbyterian Hospital of Plano, Texas.

Ann B. Ewers is a human resources consultant in the Washington, D.C., area. She has 15 years' human resources experience in the financial services, management consulting, and distribution industries. Ewers earned her undergraduate degree in industrial psychology from Middle Tennessee State University in Nashville. She has served in numerous leadership capacities for the American Compensation Association, including board member, president of the Southern region, and chair of the benefits committee. Ewers was also founding member and president of the Middle Tennessee Employees Benefits Council and served as vice president of the Mid-South Compensation Association.

John Faure, SPHR, is a human resources manager for Atlanta-based Medaphis Corporation. His nine years of human resources management experience covers the banking and finance, receivable management services, and transportation industries. Faure received an undergraduate degree in business administration from Illinois State University in Normal. He currently serves as president of the Greater Atlanta Chapter of SHRM, as an editorial board advisor for *HR Atlanta,* and as an instructor at Kennesaw College's continuing management education program.

Renee M. Fondacaro is a human resources manager with Microsoft Corporation in Redmond, Washington. She received her undergraduate degree in industrial and labor relations from Cornell University School of Industrial and Labor Relations in Ithaca, New York. She focused her eight years of human resources experience in the software development industry. Fondacaro also served for three years as an officer of the Society of Human Resources Management's college affiliate at Cornell.

Bob Forbes is a personnel executive for the Powertrain and Acustar Division of Chrysler Corporation in Auburn Hills, Michigan. He has 27 years' human resources experience in auto manufacturing and health care. Forbes received his undergraduate degree in marketing and economics as well as his master's degree in industrial relations from the University of Detroit. He has also served on the board of directors for Selectcare.

Ray George is employee relations manager for Camp Dresser & McKee Inc. in Cambridge, Massachusetts. He focused his 20 years of human resources experience in the environmental consulting services business. George received his associate's degree in business administration from Burdett College in Boston and is currently a member of the Society of Human Resources Management.

Glenn Gienko is vice president of human resources for Motorola General Systems Sector in Arlington Heights, Illinois. He has 18 years' human resources experience in telecommunications, research, and software development. Gienko received his undergraduate degree in biology and chemistry from St. Thomas College in St. Paul, Minnesota. His master's degree in human resources management is from Loyola University in Chicago.

Ellen Goss is vice president, administration and program development, for the Diagnostic and Rehabilitation Center in Philadelphia. She has 15 years' human resources experience in the health care and nonprofit industries. Goss received her undergraduate degree in education from Temple University and her master's degree in health care from St. Joseph's University in Philadelphia. She served as program chair for the National Institute for Alcohol Abuse and Alcoholism and board member for Life Guidance Services Mental Health/Mental Retardation Base Service Unit.

Belinda M. Griffin is vice president, manager of community relations, for Texas Commerce Bancshares. She has 11 years' human resources experience in banking and finance. She received her undergraduate degree in biology and chemistry from Texas Southern University in Houston. Griffin served on the curriculum development board for the American Bankers Association's National and Graduate Schools of Human Resources Management. She currently serves as an advisory board member of the Children's Museum of Houston, chair of the United Negro College Fund Fundraising for Delta Sigma Theta Sorority, Inc., and the education committee for Houston Urban Bankers Association.

Fred J. Grigsby, Jr., is director of human resources for Westinghouse Electric Corporation in Pittsburgh. He has 24 years' human resources experience in the manufacturing industry. Grigsby earned his undergraduate degree in business administration from Central State University in Wilberforce, Ohio, and obtained his master's through the executive program at the University of Virginia in Charlottesville. Grigsby served as a member of the board of directors for the Executive Leadership Council. He currently serves on the board of the Pittsburgh chapter of Kappa Alpha Psi Fraternity, Inc. and is trustee of the Negro Emergency Education Drive.

Lorraine Griffin Johnson is manager of employee relations with Pillsbury in Minneapolis. Her 10 years of human resources experience encompasses the communications, education, government, health care, and manufacturing professions and industries. Johnson received her undergraduate degree in sociology from Stephen F. Austin State University in Nacogdoches, Texas, and a master's degree in public administration from the University of Texas. Johnson was past president of the Tyler, Texas, chapter of Alpha Kappa Alpha Sorority, Inc., and a governor appointee to the Kansas Arts Council. Currently she serves as corresponding secretary and publicity chair for the Minneapolis/St. Paul chapter of The Links, Inc.

Kenneth D. Kostial is corporate director, employee relations, for Honeywell Inc. in Minneapolis. His 23 years of human resources experience has been in the electrical manufacturing industry. Kostial received his undergraduate degree in history from St. Olaf College in Northfield, Minnesota, and did graduate studies in industrial relations at the University of Minnesota. He has also served in leadership roles with various community and industry groups and associations.

Ken Kunkleman is vice president, human resources, of Peer Review Systems in Westerville, Ohio. His 10 years of experience in human resources has been in the banking and finance, health care, insurance, nonprofit, research, and software development industries. Kunkleman received an undergraduate degree in insurance and risk management as well as a master's degree in labor and human resources from The Ohio State University. Kunkleman served as treasurer for the Personnel Association of Central Ohio and on the board of the Scioto Superfest.

Roy Lantz, CCP, SPHR, is vice president, human resources, of Sound Advice in Dania, Florida. He has 10 years' human resources experience including the education, health care, manufacturing, wholesale, and retail professions and industries. Lantz received his undergraduate degree in psychology and sociology from Jacksonville University in Florida. His master's degree in human resources management is from Nova University in Davie, Florida. Lantz is the president elect of the Human Resources Association of Broward County and has also served as a board member and secretary.

Kathryn McKee, CCP, SPHR, is region head of human resources Americas for the Standard Chartered Bank in Los Angeles. She has over 25 years' human resources experience in the financial services, toy and auto manufacturing, and entertainment industries. McKee received her

undergraduate degree in sociology from the University of California at
Santa Barbara and has taken advanced executive course work from the
Anderson Graduate School of Business at UCLA. McKee served as past
national chair of the board for the Society for Human Resources Manage-
ment, is a past president of the International Association for Personnel
Women, and incoming president of the SHRM Foundation.

Robert H. Meehan, CCP, is director of compensation and human
resource information systems for New York Power Authority in White
Plains. Meehan has 24 years' experience in banking and utilities. He received his undergraduate degree from Montclair State College in New Jersey and his master's degree in personnel management from Fairleigh
Dickinson University in Teaneck, New Jersey. Meehan is currently pursuing a doctoral degree at Lubin Graduate School of Business at Pace University in New York City. He is an American Compensation Association
faculty member, served on the ACA board of directors, and chaired the
direct compensation committee.

Al Munholland is manager of employee relations for the Royal
Bank of Canada, whose corporate offices are located in Montreal, Quebec.
He has 25 years' human resources experience in banking and finance and
has developed innovative employee relations programs during his extensive career.

Cecil L. Murphy is director, corporate employee relations, for The
Travelers Companies in Hartford, Connecticut. He has 19 years' human
resources experience in the higher education, manufacturing, and insurance financial services professions and industries. Murphy received his
undergraduate degree in industrial and labor relations from Cornell University School of Industrial and Labor Relations in Ithaca, New York. He
also obtained a J.D. from Albany Law School in New York. He has served
on local zoning boards of appeal and several community organizations,
such as Camp Fire.

Michael C. Rivera is president of Human Resources Group, Inc., a
Kansas City-based human resources recruitment and consulting firm.
Rivera has 15 years' human resources experience covering the telecommunications, education, insurance, software development, and utilities professions and industries. He earned his undergraduate degree in
psychology and secondary education from Central Missouri State University in Warrensburg.

Brian Rourke is manager, human resources, for ARCO Petroleum Products Company in Los Angeles. He has 18 years' human resources experience in the oil and gas and retail industries. Rourke received his undergraduate degree in biology from Lafayette College in Easton, Pennsylvania, and his master's degree in business administration from Penn State University in Harrisburg.

Dallas L. Salisbury is president of the Employee Benefit Research Institute in Washington, D.C. He has 20 years' human resources experience in the banking and finance, government, and research industries. Salisbury earned his undergraduate degree in finance from the University of Washington in Seattle and a master's degree in public administration from the Maxwell School of Syracuse University. He is a member of both the Presidential Advisory Council at the Pension Benefit Guaranty Corporation and the benefits committee for the American Compensation Association and serves on the editorial advisory boards of several professional benefits and compensation journals.

Edward H. Seidler, CCP, SPHR, is classified personnel director for the Long Beach Community College in California. He has 25 years' human resources experience in education and government. Seidler received his undergraduate degree in political science from the University of Santa Clara in California and a master's degree in public administration from California State University-San Jose. Seidler has completed his course work and is pursuing a doctorate in public administration from the University of Southern California in Los Angeles. He also serves on the adjunct faculty for the School of Public Administration at the University of Southern California.

Brian C. G. Settle is vice president of personnel for The Methodist Medical Center of Illinois in Peoria and has 15 years' human resources experience in the health care industry. Settle received his undergraduate degree in personnel management from Eastern Illinois University at Charleston and is past president of the Central Illinois Society for Healthcare Human Resource Administration. He serves on various community and educational boards in the central Illinois region.

John Shamley, CCP, is vice president, human resources, for Keeler Brass Automotive in Kentwood, Michigan. His 20 years of human resources experience has been in the health care, insurance, and manufacturing industries. Shamley received both his undergraduate degree in psychology and master's degree in history from the University of Illinois in

Champaign-Urbana. He has served as a director for the Visiting Nurses Association and on the Board of Directors of the American Compensation Association. Currently, Shamley is a faculty member for ACA's certification program.

William Sumner is manager of employee relations of Bechtel Corporation in San Francisco. He has 30 years' experience in human resources in the manufacturing, nonprofit, as well as engineering and construction industries. Sumner received his undergraduate degree in sociology from Samford University in Birmingham, Alabama, and a master's degree in business from Golden State University in San Francisco.

Frederick (Rick) E. Taylor, SPHR, is vice president, human resources, for Society National Bank in Cleveland, Ohio. He has 23 years' human resources experience in the banking and finance, oil and gas, and human resources consulting industries. Taylor received his undergraduate degree in management from Capital University in Columbus, Ohio. Currently he serves on the board of trustees for Career Initiatives Center and is the chair for the All Ohio Human Resources Conference.

Richard T. Vander Laan is vice president of human resources for Vermeer Manufacturing Company in Pella, Iowa. He has 17 years' experience in human resources in the manufacturing industry. Vander Laan earned an undergraduate degree in education from Calvin College in Grand Rapids, Michigan, and a master's degree in biology from Central Michigan University in Mount Pleasant. Vander Laan has served on numerous professional boards and committees. He currently serves on the Governor's Council on Work Start–School to Work Transition, Governor's Council Subcommittee on Access for Rural Health, the Job Service Employer's Advisory Board, and the Calvin College Board of Trustees.

Charles F. Weiss, SPHR, is senior vice president, chief administrative officer, of Pacific Enterprises in Los Angeles. He has 30 years' human resources experience in the banking and finance, nonprofit, oil and gas, real estate development, utilities, retail, and entertainment industries. Weiss received a master of arts degree in psychology from Pepperdine University in Los Angeles and a master's in business administration from the University of Southern California. He currently serves on the governmental affairs committee of the American Assembly of Collegiate Schools of Business and on the board of directors and executive committee of The California Foundation for Employment and Disability, Inc.

Valerie C. Williams is vice president of human resources for GATX Capital in San Francisco. Her 20 years of experience covers the retail, finance, management consulting, and pharmaceutical industries. She earned her master's degree in business administration from Lake Forest Graduate School of Management in Illinois. Williams is past president of the Chicago Compensation Association and is on the faculty of National Training Laboratories. She most recently co-authored an American Compensation Association "Building Blocks in Total Compensation" pamphlet on documentation of job content. She serves as a faculty member as well as a course cadre committee member for ACA's certification program.

Legal Experts

Thomas C. Greble is a senior partner in the law firm of Roberts & Finger, with offices in New York City and Parsippany, New Jersey. He represents employers in a variety of industries in the areas of labor relations, equal employment opportunity, employment law, and litigation. Greble has represented employers in collective bargaining, arbitrations, judicial proceedings, appeals, and before administrative agencies throughout the nation.

Greble lectures extensively on employment-related topics to a variety of professional groups, business organizations, and trade associations. He is the author of the *Manager's Guide to Employment Law* (National Association of Temporary Services, 1992) as well as numerous monographs and articles on employment-related subjects. He also provided all legal commentary for Fried's first book, *Outrageous Conduct: Bizarre Behavior at Work* (Intermediaries Press, 1991).

Greble is a graduate of Villanova University and Fordham University School of Law, where he has served as an adjunct professor of law. He is currently an adjunct assistant professor at New York University where he teaches a graduate course in the Management Institute titled "Fair Employment Practices." Greble is also general counsel to the New York Association of Temporary Services, Inc., a trade association of employees in the temporary help industry.

Lee E. Boyd is an associate in the law firm of Roberts & Finger. An honors graduate of Seton Hall University Law School, Boyd also has a master's degree in labor relations and human resources from Rutgers University Graduate School's Institute of Management and Labor Relations. Having worked in human resources management for eight years for a *Fortune 100* company prior to beginning her practice of law, Boyd brings unique practical experience and an understanding of the corporate perspective to the problems faced by today's employers. In addition to assisting in the representation of employers in court and administrative proceedings, Boyd has worked closely with employers in developing affirmative action plans and in drafting manuals and policies. She regularly assists in preparing the annual supplements to the *Manager's Guide to Employment Law* (NATS).

The law firm of **Roberts & Finger** counsels and represents management in the areas of equal employment opportunity law, employment law, labor relations, and civil litigation. The firm has successfully represented employers in employment law litigation at the trial and appellate levels and before federal and state administrative agencies in various jurisdictions across the country.

Roberts & Finger believes that in today's litigious society, the only prudent and cost-effective employee relations philosophy for management to adopt is one of prevention, not cure. Skilled and aggressive representation in bargaining, litigation, and arbitration is, of course, very important. However, the firm believes that it is equally important for management to adopt policies and to manage individual situations in a manner designed to minimize the risk of formal proceedings and to maximize management's prospects of prevailing in those cases where formal proceedings cannot be forestalled.

Consistent with this proactive philosophy, Roberts & Finger assists employers in formulating policies and procedures, develops and conducts appropriate training programs, performs employee relations audits to identify potential problem areas, and regularly counsels management regarding the appropriate handling of complex and often sensitive employee relations problems.

A Passion for the Profession

"I joined the panel because of the realistic nature of the cases. Most business people are unaware of the skills required in human resources management. This book serves as both an excellent guide for applied reasoning and a powerful source of enlightenment."

Charles F. Weiss, SPHR
Senior Vice President, Chief Administrative Officer • Pacific Enterprises

"Volunteering to collaborate with other human resources professionals is an opportunity I wouldn't have passed up! This mentally demanding exercise proves the old adage that regardless of your experience, you haven't really heard it all!"

Terry Bean, CCP, SPHR
Senior Vice President, Human Resources • Rose's Stores, Inc.

"You could spend your lifetime in this field and still never quit learning! As a panel member I found the issues and complexities in these cases an exhilarating stretch!"

Sandy Fleming Dulaney, CCP
Human Resources Consultant • ARCO Exploration and Production Technology

"This was a complex, absorbing, career-related puzzle. Assisting on the panel gave me the ultimate human resources challenge."

Claudia D. Denaro
Vice President, Human Resources Services • Consolidated Stores Corporation

"These stories provide a window into the kinds of situations which rarely hit the business press. It was intriguing to contribute to the body of knowledge experienced by HR professionals during some of our darkest or most bizarre moments."

Valerie C. Williams
Vice President of Human Resources • GATX Capital

"It was an honor and a challenge to sit on the panel of reviewers. This book is filled with fascinating accounts that make the workaday world anything but boring."

Anne Ball, CCP
President • HR Solutions

"These stories—though unusual—demonstrate the very real range of people management issues that can confront managers and interfere with business success."

Kathleen Dole, CCP
Human Resources Officer • John Hancock Mutual Life Insurance Company

"Most managers will be confronted with unique or subtle issues whose resolution will not be found in a policy manual or previous personal experiences. It was refreshing to comprehensively examine a case without the inherent pressures of quickly reaching a decision."

Kenneth D. Kostial
Corporate Director, Employee Relations • Honeywell Inc.

"I was honored to share viewpoints and perspectives with other HR specialists in an informal forum regarding real-life workplace situations. I thoroughly enjoyed the experience."

Michael C. Rivera
President • Human Resources Group, Inc.

"This was a fun, thought-provoking professional exercise. Whether you work for a large or small organization, odds are that a manager will encounter one or more of these situations."

Edward H. Seidler, CCP, SPHR
Classified Personnel Director • Long Beach Community College

"I enjoyed sharing my expertise with others about how to handle these legally complex and emotionally laden cases. The incidents are outrageous, ridiculous, funny, and sad, but oh so *very* real."

Frederick (Rick) E. Taylor, SPHR
Vice President, Human Resources • Society National Bank

Chapter 1

Space Cadets

"A human resources professional should remain calm even when the walls are falling in."

Belinda M. Griffin
Vice President Manager Community Relations
Texas Commerce Bancshares

Lien on Me

"Max, here's your mail," Trixie said. "You might want to check out the one marked 'Registered' first," she suggested before turning to leave.

Max didn't even look up from his desk. He just motioned for Trixie to drop the mail in his "in" box. He was immersed in reviewing a major proposal. Max and his partners were feverishly trying to land the Melrose account. If they could get the business, revenues would top $1,000,000 for the year—an impressive feat for a company just rounding its three-year mark.

When Max finished rechecking the figures, he was satisfied that his competition would have a tough time stealing the business. His mind then turned to how he'd get the staff to meet the needs of the job. Right now he and his partners not only ran the business, they also worked alongside their 10-man crew.

Trixie was the only female in the company and Max's only office staff. He marveled at Trixie's ability to balance her responsibilities like a veteran juggler, never dropping a plate. She was responsible for customer service, accounting, collections, payroll, dispatching, and general office functions.

He felt lucky to have her. She had a special knack for dealing with cantankerous customers. The tougher they were, the more she liked them. Max had observed Trixie working her magic on several occasions. Trixie could not only ice down a fiery customer, but also have them thank *her* as she walked away with a new order. This kind of skill made Harvey McKay and Zig Zigler look like amateurs.

"Sometimes you just get lucky," Max would remind himself every time he thought about Trixie.

As Max scanned his mail, he grabbed the registered letter on the top. He slit it open and blinked several times after he read the first paragraph. He read it again to make sure he hadn't misinterpreted anything. The letter indicated that he owed more than $22,000 in accrued fines and interest based on unpaid state sales tax. The letter indicated they were placing a lien on his home until he satisfied the debt of back taxes plus interest and fines.

"Twenty-two thousand dollars!" he exclaimed. "That's impossible, I've signed forms and checks regularly. There's no way I could owe them this money. There must be some mistake."

Max immediately got on the phone to Garret Cline, his accountant. "Garret, I've got a whale of a problem that just beached on my desk. I need an immediate audit of my books—somebody may be embezzling from me," he said, filled with worry. He explained the circumstances, and Garret asked Max to fax him a copy of the letter from the state.

Garret arrived the next day to personally review the books. After several days he determined that the company accounts showed full payment of state sales taxes. Garret found no discrepancies or anything that appeared unusual or suspicious with the journal entries or the financial statements.

Finally, he verified the bank reconciliation statements for the checkbook. When he compared the statements to the amount listed as cash-on-hand for the month, he noticed the bank statements were higher than the amount recorded in the books. Trixie was responsible for reconciling the checkbook, so Max and Garret asked her about the discrepancy.

"Oh, I can explain that easy enough," she smiled. She opened the bottom left drawer of her desk and pulled out a stack of unmailed forms and signed checks.

"Here they are," she said matter-of-factly.

Astounded, Max asked, "Why didn't you mail them?"

"Because I hate those crumb bums," she replied.

"*What?*" Max was incredulous. Garret, standing beside him, was equally appalled.

"I just hate paying sales tax," Trixie continued. "It seems so stupid. Why should the state get the money? They didn't do anything to earn it. It just annoys me."

"Didn't you think they'd figure out that we haven't paid them?" Max asked sarcastically.

"I don't know, I figured it was worth a shot, and I could save you a ton of money," she answered innocently.

"Well you figured wrong, Trixie!" Max steamed. "Not only do I have to pay the back taxes, I have over $22,000 in interest and fines. That's $22,000 I was planning to use to buy another service truck so I can meet the demands of the Melrose account. That is, if I live long enough to work the Melrose account. I'll be lucky if your stupidity doesn't cause me to have a stroke," he railed, as he felt his blood pressure rising. "If you wanted to kill me, why didn't you just stick a knife in my heart?!"

The impact of her actions finally dawned on Trixie, and she looked frightened. "Gee, Max, I didn't realize they would fine you and make you pay interest. I suppose I'm fired and I should pack up my things."

"Frankly, I don't know what I'm going to do to you yet. I may call the police, I may fire you . . . I don't know," Max replied, his voice escalating with each phrase. "Right now I just need to figure out how I'm going to pay for this, and I'll deal with you later. In the meantime, keep working, and don't discuss this with anyone."

After some thought Max presented Trixie with an alternative. "Trixie, you have a choice. I'm turning all financial matters over to Garret. His office will handle all money matters, down to petty cash. You can continue your other assignments at no cash to you until you've worked off the $22,000. We'll continue your paychecks as usual. I'll pay your social security, medical, and everything else I normally do, except we'll deduct the net amount of your salary as if it were a loan you are paying back to the company. The way I figure it, you'll have to work for two years to satisfy the debt."

"And what's my second alternative?" Trixie asked weakly.

"I call the police and file charges against you. You hire a lawyer and take your chances against going to jail or being fined," he responded, not knowing whether this was a criminal or civil action. He just knew he was going to get his money somehow.

It didn't take Trixie long to decide. "I'll work," she said, and she continues to work for the company to this day.

 It appears that Max allowed himself to be totally reliant on a well-intentioned but naive employee. We believe that Max was negligent. He did not take reasonable steps to either personally monitor the accounting records and bank reconciliations or arrange to have his accountant do it for him. He may also want to consider switching outside accounting firms. If they had been doing their job, the accountants would have been properly auditing the bank statements.

Threatening Trixie was totally inappropriate and was, essentially, blackmail. Max should have either terminated her or kept her on board with the understanding that this was an isolated event. Initially, he should have suspended her to investigate or decide what to do with her, rather than let her continue to work. In addition, by deciding to retain her, Max set a precedent for other and future employees—they can all use poor judgment and gross misconduct, which costs the company dollars. This could come back to haunt him. The employer is responsible for actions of employees. If Trixie did not meet standards, then she should have been terminated.

Since Max chose to retain Trixie, we think he had other alternatives that were both legal and certainly less draconian, such as allowing Trixie to repay the company over a longer period of time. Admittedly, this may be less expeditious and may require some protection in the event Trixie were to leave, or worse, to die. One precaution the company could take would be to require Trixie to take out a decreasing term life insurance policy. By having her list the company as beneficiary, the company would be guaranteed payment. Another solution is for Trixie to take out a loan and pay Max in full immediately.

It astounds us that Trixie accepted his alternative. This means that she would work for nothing for about two years. Obviously, she must have other sources of income on which to live. Most people would not be able to consider such an option.

 Here is a situation where the employer thinks it has solved one problem but creates another problem for itself. Employers should always seek the advice of legal counsel before they attempt to make deductions from employees' wages that are not related to the mandatory payroll withholdings and deductions.

Most states prohibit employers from making deductions from employees' wages except for limited purposes. For example, in New York State, employers may not make any deductions from employees' wages except those made in accordance with government laws and regulations (e.g., social security) or with express written authority by the employee for deductions that are for the benefit of the employee (e.g., payments for health benefits, pensions, or insurance premiums). Thus, in states with wage deduction laws such as New York's, paying off a debt owed to the company through payroll deduction, such as Trixie's debt, would not be lawful. Indeed, it could be a criminal offense.

Employers must also be wary about threatening to file criminal charges. In many states, the threat to file criminal charges in order to obtain payment of a debt would constitute extortion.

Finally, it appears that Max's decision to withhold her salary would violate the federal and state labor laws which require the payment of minimum wage. It *would* be lawful to have a written agreement with Trixie as a condition of her continued employment that she pay x amount each week to pay off the debt after she receives her pay for that week. This would avoid violating the state wage payment laws and the minimum wage requirements.

A Bellow from the Bowels

One of Corrine's rituals was to review *The Wall Street Journal* each morning. She liked to see how the company's stock fared and to get the scoop on the company's competitors. Corrine learned early in her career that the *Journal* was her barometer for predicting executive pressure. This tool and her professional savvy helped catapult her to director of human resources more quickly than any of her predecessors.

As she scanned the headlines, she spotted her company's name. "Oh, no!" she gasped aloud. "It's going to be hell around here for the next few weeks!" The organization had been listed as one of the country's top 10 most stressful companies to work for. "Just what I need. More stress to add to my stress," she obsessed, sipping her coffee and inhaling deeply on her cigarette. Moments later her thoughts were jarred when her secretary burst into her office.

"Corrine, Corrine! Come quick!" her secretary screamed in terror. "There's someone in the ladies' rest room and I think she's gone nuts! She's in there screaming and hollering that she can't take it any more."

"Oh my God, the papers are right," Corrine thought. "The stress here is making our employees crazy. I'm going to have a suicide right here. There goes my promotion!" Corrine worried, as she saw her career fly out the window.

"Quick, call the company doctor," she directed her secretary. "I'll run to the ladies' room."

Corrine sped down the hall. As she entered the ladies' room she heard howling and moaning at deafening levels from behind a stall door. "I can't stand another minute! This is too much! I've suffered too long!" a voice shrieked.

Corrine gently tapped on the door and spoke in a reassuring tone. "Try to stay calm. We're here. We're with you and we're going to help you."

"No one can help me," she wailed. "It's my own doing!"

To Corrine's relief, Dr. Claussan arrived as the distraught woman let out another anguished scream that echoed throughout the corridors.

"Now, dear," he said calmly, "I'm Dr. Claussan. Why don't you try to tell us what's bothering you. I'm sure we can help."

"No one can help," she repeated between sobs. "The pressure is too great. I can't live with this agony any longer," she lamented. "I've been constipated for three days, and I feel like I'm going to explode!"

"Well, I can give you something that can help. I'll send a nurse right up to assist," Dr. Claussen assured the woman.

He turned to Corrine, whose cheeks burned with embarrassment. She whispered, "You think I overreacted, perhaps?"

"Overreacted? I'd say overreacted is an understatement," he remarked condescendingly. "Do me a favor. Next time, ask a few more questions before you have me hauled out of a meeting for a problem that a nurse can handle."

"Sorry, sir," she responded sheepishly. "Can . . . can we keep this just between the two of us?"

"Of course," he winked. "After all, I'm a doctor, aren't I?"

 We couldn't agree on this one. Half of us think Corrine overreacted. Perhaps she should lay off the cigarettes and switch to decaf coffee. A human resources director should remain calm even when the walls are falling in. Not only did Corrine overreact, she allowed her own anxiety and stress levels to turn a fairly minor situation into a melodrama.

While Corrine may possess some "savvy," she certainly didn't show it in this set of circumstances. She should have had another employee accompany her to the rest room, assessed the situation, and then sought the appropriate resources.

We also think her actions provide insight about her personality and leadership traits. Her immediate assumption that this was a potential suicide and the sheepish way in which she addressed the doctor after discovering her mistake reflects a lack of judgment and poor self-image. There was no need to address the doctor sheepishly. Corrine made a mistake. We suspect that the source of her embarrassment stemmed from how she thought others would perceive her. She appeared to be more self-absorbed than genuinely concerned about inconveniencing the doctor.

If Corrine's actions in this case demonstrate her standard operating practices, it is unlikely that she will make a good executive. Being unduly worried about the perceptions of others will detract from her ability to provide effective advice and counsel.

The other half of us think Corrine reacted properly in this situation. Having her company listed as one of the top 10 most stressful companies in the country is, indeed, pertinent here.

Given all the incidents of workplace violence and other stress-related actions these days, it makes much more sense to respond quickly and affirmatively than to ignore and underreact. While it turned out to be a relatively minor medical problem, it could very well have been something more serious, such as an attempted suicide. Corrine should continue to be cognizant of warning signs that might indicate problems that are stress related.

Human resources managers must take such incidents very seriously even if they later turn out to be mildly amusing, such as this one. Corrine may be a bit embarrassed by this incident, but she would be a whole lot more embarrassed if she underreacted to a real crisis.

 While Corrine may have overreacted to the bellows in the ladies' room, she was correct in being concerned about stress in the company. Stress in the workplace is increasingly being blamed as the source for workers' compensation claims in cases from California to New York. Many employers, often in consultation with their workers' compensation carriers, are developing risk management programs aimed at controlling this burgeoning area.

A Real Schlemiel

Towner Flannigan loved big, powerful engines. As he sat behind the wheel, he could feel the vibrational force of the truck's 454 engine roaring through his body. His skin prickled with excitement as he pictured himself about to begin his first lap. He threw the truck into gear, gunned the engine, and spun out with a wheelie as he leapt from his place.

There was just one problem. Towner was not at Thompson Drag Raceway. He was sitting at a traffic light at Queen and Avery Streets in the middle of town. Oh, and there was another small detail. He was driving a one-ton utility truck and forgot to lock the back doors. So when he vaulted forward, an extension ladder flew out of the back of the truck, landing in front of a Mercedes waiting behind him.

Towner never heard a thing. Still steeped in his reverie, he kept on going. Unfortunately, the Mercedes driver, Trent Lions, was not having the same fantasy. He drove right over the ladder, and raced Towner to the next light.

Trent pulled up beside Towner and honked his horn to get Towner's attention. Towner was in his own world and never looked his way. Trent was furious. He took down the license plate number, truck number, and company name and called Vance Litton, the company president.

Vance listened as Trent described the incident. Vance knew Towner Flannigan had some shortcomings, but on balance, he was a hard worker and never complained about any job they gave him. They originally hired Towner hoping to train him as a service worker. However, they found he had limited ability to retain the technical information to do the job. In fact, they found his ability to retain even simple information was limited. But they were so impressed with his desire and sincerity, they created a special job that was more suited to his capabilities. Towner's main responsibilities were to wash the trucks and keep the garage and rest rooms clean. Occasionally he delivered extra supplies to the job site if the crew ran out of materials.

"Mr. Lions," Vance said, "I apologize for Towner's negligence. How badly did he damage your car?"

"It wasn't damaged," Trent said.

"Well, then, what would you like us to do to make this right for you, Mr. Lions?" Vance asked.

"Get rid of that idiot!" he demanded.

"I'm sorry, Mr. Lions, I can't do that. We don't usually have Towner run errands. He mainly sweeps the garage floor. He'd have a hard time finding a job anywhere else. I'm sure you'd rather have him employed than on welfare, wouldn't you?"

"I guess so," Trent acquiesced. "But don't ever let him loose on the road with heavy equipment again."

"Now that's something I can guarantee you," Vance promised.

Vance talked to Towner and explained to him that he could not drive any of the company vehicles to run errands. His driving would be limited to pulling the trucks in and out of the garage so he could wash them. Vance also reminded Towner that when he washed the trucks, he was to remember to do the whole truck. It seemed that Towner was easily distracted and sometimes only washed half a truck.

The following week, Vance gave Towner a special assignment. "Towner," Vance instructed, "I need you to defrost the refrigerator in the garage. The freezer is all iced up. Unplug it and just put some hot water in there. Take everything out of it and let it sit over the weekend. When we come back on Monday, it should be all defrosted. Don't worry about it. All the water will run down the garage drain. Do you understand what I want you to do?"

"Sure, boss," Towner grinned.

As soon as Vance left the garage, Towner removed everything from the refrigerator and unplugged it. He thought he'd surprise Vance by speeding up the process. First, he went into the ladies' rest room and borrowed a hair dryer. When that wasn't fast enough, he reached for a paint scraper, screwdriver, and hammer. By the time Towner chiseled off the last piece of ice, the coils looked as if they had been sprayed by bullets from an automatic weapon.

When Vance walked out in the garage and saw that the refrigerator was riddled with holes, he lost it. "What the hell is this? Did we have a drive-by shooting here?"

"No, boss, I just wanted to get this done for you before the weekend," Towner said.

"You got it done all right! The damn refrigerator is *done for!* Didn't I tell you specifically what I wanted you to do?" Vance blasted.

"Yes, but I wanted to surprise you, boss. Look, I'm sorry. I'll pay for the refrigerator. You can take it out of my pay."

"That's not the point, Towner. First we can't let you drive anymore, now this. I just can't have it. Go see Mattie in payroll. She'll cut you a check through today. You're finished," Vance said.

Towner hung his head down, and Vance choked up. He was fond of Towner and hated having to fire him, but Vance couldn't justify keeping Towner around. Towner was beginning to be a real liability to the business, and as a fledgling operation, Vance couldn't afford to continue the risk.

That Christmas the company held a party. Somehow Towner found out about it and showed up with presents for everyone. He walked up to Vance with a big grin and a statue in his hand. The sculpture was of a man holding a little child in his arms.

"Vance, I got this for you. You know, I was really on my feet when I worked for you. The man in this statue is you and you're carrying me," Towner said, handing Vance the statue.

Vance was overwhelmed and embarrassed but pulled himself together enough to say, "Well, thanks, Towner, how thoughtful." Then Vance said, "Excuse me, Towner, I've got to get more ice," and he left the room to regain his composure.

The next Monday Vance's partners, Tom and Norm, walked in his office. "Vance," Tom began, "Norm and I were thinking about Towner Flannigan. We think we ought to hire him back. The guy needs a job and he really does try hard."

Vance was flabbergasted. "Look, I like Towner too, but we have a business to run. We can't be a bunch of bleeding hearts and give in to every sad sack that needs a job. Towner could have cost us a ton of money with that Mercedes deal, and he ruined a perfectly good refrigerator. Oh, and another thing I never told you. Right after I fired him I found out that the day before he jerry-rigged an adapter to the nitrogen tank. He used nitrogen to fill a spare tire for one of the service vehicles! He's a living lawsuit just waiting to bury us. We can't afford it."

"I still think we have a social responsibility to help him," Norm insisted. "We've all had tough times. Let's give him a second chance. We just need to make sure he receives closer supervision."

"And who has time for that?" Vance asked. "You? You're on the road half the time. If you want him back, then you'll have to supervise him. I don't want the burden."

"Look," Norm suggested, "Mary Lou, the office manager, can handle it. I've already talked to her."

"Oh, I see," Vance said angrily. "So this is one of those two-against-one; we vote, you lose; already-a-done-deal things, huh?"

"No, Vance, if you absolutely refuse, we'll go along with you. We just want you to reconsider," Norm said.

"Okay. All right," Vance conceded. "But don't expect me to take the hit for his next screw-up. That will come out of your bonuses." So, Towner was back on the payroll the next week. As Vance suspected, Towner had another mishap. Unfortunately, Vance's partners failed to tell Mary Lou that Towner was barred from running errands. She sent him on a trip out of town in a company car.

"Norm? This is Towner," said a voice barely audible above the background of highway noises.

"What's up, Towner?" Norm asked.

"Well, I ran into a little trouble here in Centerville. I kind of bumped into a lady here. We have a little fender bender," Towner said.

"Fender bender—so how much damage?" Norm asked.

"Oh, maybe $60," Towner estimated.

"Well, that's not too bad. No one was hurt, were they?"

"No, everyone's fine," Towner assured him.

"And our car?"

"Just a scratch," Towner said.

"Well, just give the lady you hit our name and number. Tell her to get an estimate and have her call us," Norm said.

The next day, the accident victim called Norm and informed him the estimate was $1,900. Norm also discovered that Towner had left the company car in Centerville because it was inoperable. After they towed it back to the office, the body shop estimated damages at $2,400. Both Norm and Tom paid for the damages out of their year-end bonuses as they had promised. Fortunately, Towner never came back to work, so they were spared the agony of having to fire him in person.

The company demonstrated good faith efforts to help Towner. Unfortunately, they were unable to structure a job that emphasized his strengths as well as provided sufficient supervision. Consequently, the results were absolutely predictable. This is a case where the best of intentions had a negative result for everyone. If an organization is unable to provide additional assistance or supervision, it should not consider individuals with disabilities as potential employees. The same would be true if the type of operation precluded the company's ability to meet those special needs (commensurate with the law).

While we all agree that Towner's skill limitations were unfortunate and the partners' demonstration of sympathy was commendable, their decision to re-employ Towner was ill-advised. A few of us, however, feel that there may be circumstances where re-employing an employee may be acceptable. For example, if attendance was the reason for the discharge, we may consider rehiring the employee if the circumstances that caused the problem have changed. Sometimes these individuals make the best employees. Often they are more appreciative of the organization after experiencing, perhaps, other less desirable working environments.

Unfortunately, Towner's situation was not a simple case of attendance problems. Companies must regularly balance their desire to show compassion with their responsibility to protect employees and the public from negligent or incompetent workers. This employee represented a dangerous liability to the company. In this case the liability far outweighs the company's obligation to show compassion. Here, the partners exposed the company to considerable liability given the employee's previous history.

 This story poses two primary legal issues. First, whether Towner would be considered disabled and, if so, what obligations did that impose on his employer. A second issue is whether the employer would be liable for its "negligence" in allowing Towner to drive a company vehicle in light of his overall shortcomings and his previous mishap with the Mercedes driver.

Given the description of Towner in this story, he may well be disabled under the Americans with Disabilities Act or under a comparable provision in state law. Mental retardation is considered an "impairment" under the ADA.

Even assuming Towner is disabled and protected under the ADA, he still must be able to perform the essential functions of the job. Although the ADA does not require employers to have written job descriptions, we often advise clients to have job descriptions in order to identify the "essential functions" of the job. In this scenario it appears that the employer continued to create special jobs for Towner—changing the job each time Towner failed to perform adequately. While the ADA does not require that an employer "create" jobs for the disabled, the employer in this case appears to have made an accommodation for Towner (changing the job duties—the essential functions).

The employer may be liable for negligence because it permitted Towner to drive one of its vehicles when it knew that Towner had limited capabilities and that he had a propensity for unsafe driving. In today's litigious climate, employers must be especially vigilant in dealing with employees who are permitted to operate vehicles. For example, Vance could have issued a written memo to managers restricting Towner's activities. Had Towner injured another person or caused property damage, the company would have had real exposure. Many employers have learned the hard way that extra care must be taken in screening, evaluating, monitoring, and appraising employees who operate motor vehicles as part of their job.

Another issue that is raised in this scenario is that the employer took no action after Towner failed to return to work. While the employer found some solace in being "spared the agony of having to fire him again," such comfort is ill-advised. A prudent employer would advise the employee and document the fact that the employment relationship has ended.

Chapter 2

Spurned Lovers

"The most dangerous liaisons are intimate relationships between supervisors and assigned staff."

Kenneth D. Kostial
Corporate Director Employee Relations
Honeywell Inc.

Unrequited Love

Jarrad couldn't contain himself any more. He had been in love with Brandon for nearly three years. It all began innocently enough. Brandon Highbridge was a new trainee, and Jarrad was providing his sales training. It was typical for Jarrad to take new trainees to dinner at the end of the week, so they stopped at a local diner and talked.

Throughout the week Jarrad had many conversations with Brandon. Their discussions ranged from sports to politics. Although Jarrad had trained a number of sales representatives throughout his years as the area manager, he never enjoyed anyone's company as much as Brandon's. During that dinner they discovered they had several other things in common. Both were married, both had children, and both were unhappy.

Jarrad had fleeting gay encounters occasionally throughout his marriage. Brandon, on the other hand, never experienced a gay relationship. He always considered himself straight. To each other's surprise, the two formed a special bond that eventually led to a lasting, consensual homosexual relationship.

They were careful to hide their relationship from the others in the company. Their clandestine meetings grew more frequent as the years passed. Finally, Jarrad decided to leave his wife and wanted Brandon to do the same.

Although Brandon continued to see Jarrad, Brandon refused to leave his wife. They began to argue about this, straining the relationship. Finally, in a desperate attempt, Jarrad called Hillary, Brandon's wife.

"Hillary, this is Jarrad Dewberry, Brandon's area manager," he began.

"What's wrong?" she gasped. "Did Brandon get into an accident? Is he all right?" she asked fearfully.

"No, no," Jarrad assured her, "Brandon is fine."

Hillary breathed a deep sigh of relief. "Thank goodness," she responded.

"Hillary, there is something I need to tell you." Jarrad paused.

"Has Brandon lost his job?" she worried, as her fears rushed back.

"No. Hillary, Brandon's job is not in jeopardy."

"Oh, well then. I guess I must sound like a real 'Nervous Nellie,'" she joked. "What did you want to tell me?"

Jarrad decided to come right out with it. "I've been in love with your husband for three years. I've left my wife, and I've begged him to leave you. He won't. Now I'm begging you to let him go," he pleaded.

"What!" Hillary exclaimed. She fell back against the wall as though a cannon had blasted her at close range.

Jarrad told her the whole story. Hillary was destroyed. She confronted Brandon when he came home that evening, and he admitted to his relationship with Jarrad. He told Hillary that he never wanted to leave her and that he would stop seeing Jarrad. However, she couldn't accept the affair and began immediate divorce proceedings.

According to Brandon, the divorce severely affected his emotional stability and eventually led to a nervous breakdown because Jarrad kept pursuing the relationship. The company put Brandon on short-term disability during his initial illness, but the reason behind the circumstances was unknown at the time.

Eventually Brandon remarried but remained on disability. Howard Costanza, corporate labor counsel, first became aware of the case when the file landed on his desk. Brandon had filed for total disability from workers' compensation, claiming the cause was mental stress from sexual harassment.

As Howard pursued his investigation, he interviewed Jarrad. "We have a claim of sexual harassment from Brandon Highbridge. He claims that although your relationship was consensual at first, you refused to end it when he asked you to."

Jarrad turned pale. "Well, we had a consensual relationship, but I never harassed him."

"Did you call his wife and tell her about the relationship?" Howard asked.

"Yes," Jarrad acknowledged.

"Did he want you to do this?"

"No," he admitted.

As Howard continued his investigation, he talked with Jarrad's manager. Howard discovered that Jarrad's performance had deteriorated. Moreover, Jarrad had been placed on progressive discipline and was, coincidentally, due that week for a final check on his performance improvement. Jarrad's manager indicated that Jarrad failed to meet the improvement goals. He planned to meet with Jarrad as indicated in the action plan and terminate him for performance that week. After carefully reviewing the documentation, Howard advised Jarrad's manager to follow through on the action plan and terminate Jarrad.

Howard conducted a thorough investigation by interviewing key individuals. However, the investigation revealed no direct evidence of sexual harassment. The company decided to dispute Brandon's claim. Currently the case is pending.

 This is a classic example of the dangers of intimate workplace relationships between supervisors and subordinates. When you throw in the extramarital ingredient, you can almost guarantee an explosion. That the men were gay has no bearing on the handling of the case. Change Brandon's name to Brenda, and we still have the same issues: consensual sex between a supervisor and subordinate where one partner has been rejected and lives of employees as well as their families have been negatively affected.

Most of us agree that Brandon's claim of sexual harassment leveled at Jarrad and the company seems thin. Brandon never claimed he felt coerced to enter and continue the relationship because of his subordinate position. This coercion would be a key factor in sustaining a *quid pro quo* sexual harassment claim. Thus Brandon, not the company, is responsible for his willing complicity in establishing the relationship as well as for the outcomes of that relationship—including the devastating consequences of his divorce.

If Brandon had sought the company's help to keep Jarrad in check, then the human resources manager would have been obligated to investigate. Once the facts were known, the human resources manager could pursue actions outlined by the company's sexual harassment policy (i.e., warning, training, and so forth). If Jarrad had persisted in his pursuit of Brandon after being warned, a sexual harassment allegation directed at the company may be sustained and potentially lead to Jarrad's termination. This was not the case. The men were apparently very discreet during the majority of their relationship. Thus, the company did not discover the facts until after the relationship was over and Brandon filed a workers' compensation claim for stress resulting from sexual harassment.

A few panel members strongly disagree with this position. Jarrad continued to pursue the relationship after Brandon's divorce. Although

Brandon never complained, silence does not equal consent. We feel a hostile environment developed, affecting Brandon's ability to continue working.

It is the responsibility of all employers to eliminate any form of workplace sexual harassment. As a form of prevention, the company should conduct periodic audits to determine if any problems exist. This activity will enable human resources representatives to test for employee knowledge and understanding of the sexual harassment policy as well as its reporting procedures. The company may also want to review its existing sexual harassment training program to assure that the program is comfortable for all employees. An employee-oriented sexual harassment training program, which openly addresses *all* types of sexual harassment (i.e., straight and gay sexual harassment) and assures confidentiality, may have encouraged Brandon to report his situation when he no longer welcomed Jarrad's advances.

Finally, because consensual relationships are difficult to control and often lead to sticky situations such as this one, the company might want to consider adopting an intimacy policy. An intimacy policy restricts romantic relationships between employees and can be narrowly or broadly defined. For example, the company may wish to develop a policy that specifically limits intimate relationships between supervisors and subordinates and would include, but not be limited to, married persons.

 Another example of an office romance that has gone sour. That the romance was a homosexual relationship is of little or no consequence under the law. Of far more significance is that this was a sexual relationship between a supervisor and his subordinate, because an employer is automatically liable for sexual harassment in such instances. (However, Jarrad's conduct does not appear to have risen to the level of *quid pro quo* harassment because he did not cause Brandon to lose any tangible job benefits.)

A consensual relationship between co-workers, regardless of their sexual preference, is not sexual harassment. However, continued unwelcome pursuit by one of the parties after the other party wants to end the relationship may become unlawful sexual harassment if the unwelcome conduct creates an offensive or hostile working environment that, among other things, unreasonably interferes with the ability to perform one's job.

Another issue raised in this story is potential risk of liability for discrimination on the basis of sexual preference or orientation. Certain state laws and local ordinances prohibit discriminating against an individual in employment on the basis of his or her sexual orientation. While the facts here indicate that Jarrad was eventually terminated for poor performance, he could file a sexual preference discrimination claim and argue that the performance issue was a pretext. This story highlights the importance of documenting performance problems and conducting follow-up action plans to maximize the company's ability to successfully defend itself in the event that he files a discrimination claim.

Obsessed

Yvonne was thrilled when the temp agency found her a long-term assignment as a second-shift computer operator with one of the town's leading computer service companies. That meant she could enroll for fall quarter, take morning classes, and get some studying done on the job.

She reported that evening to her supervisor, Alex Benson. "Nice," she mused as she looked at his ruggedly handsome face. "Nice, nice, nice. I think I'm going to like working for him."

Alex stood up from his desk and offered Yvonne a chair. "Hello, Yvonne. I understand you've accepted this opportunity for a 10-month term," he said, welcoming her as he locked on to her dancing blue eyes.

"Wow, I've had temps before, but none of them looked like this," Alex thought. "She is drop-dead gorgeous!" Alex sat down quickly, fearing he might reveal the unexpected excitement he was feeling.

While they talked, Alex watched Yvonne toss her head and smile as she told him about her college plans. The sexual tension in the room continued to escalate. "I've got to get someone else to show her around. This is ridiculous, I feel like I'm 18," Alex worried to himself.

"Excuse me, Yvonne, I'm going to have Bella show you around. She'll explain the equipment and your duties. I have a meeting in about five minutes, so I've got to dash," he lied.

Alex called in Bella and introduced her to Yvonne.

"Bella, this is Yvonne Stratton. Yvonne, this is Bella Janis, our lead operator. She'll show you the ropes, and I'll check with you in a few days to make sure everything is going okay."

Bella seemed surprised that Alex was giving her the honors. Alex always prided himself in making new employees and temps feel comfortable by spending the first few days with them himself.

Yvonne stood up and extended her hand, "Thanks, Alex, I'm very excited about working here."

"So am I!" Alex grinned enthusiastically, as he enjoyed watching her leave his office.

Alex found himself looking for every opportunity to connect with Yvonne. She was always responsive to his attentions. One evening as they were huddled over an error report, his hand touched hers. She looked at him with a welcoming smile and he kissed her. Much to his surprise she responded happily. "I wonder what took you so long?" she teased.

As the weeks passed, they arranged for stolen moments. They kissed and caressed each other freely—but always briefly. He couldn't keep his hands off her, and their activities grew more daring and heated each day.

One evening Yvonne walked into his office. She closed the door and grabbed his face tightly with her hand. "You're such a scum!" she spat. "Why didn't you tell me you were married, and that your wife *and* her sister work in the next department less than 50 feet from here!"

Alex was flustered. He loved his wife, but Yvonne made him feel young again. "Look, I'm sorry, Yvonne, it just never came up."

"Oh, right, you expect me to buy that? That doesn't sound like you, Alex," she laughed bitterly. "You're the man who is always so careful about procedures and details. Well, I'm telling you today. This is over. Find some other jerk to sucker with your charm. I don't get involved with married men."

"Look, Yvonne, I wasn't using you. I really care about you. You've got to know that. I'm sorry if I hurt you," he pleaded. "Please keep seeing me, you know what we have is special."

"No, I told you, you're married. That's immoral. I'm not even sorry for myself—I'm sorriest for your poor wife. From now on keep your hands off me and deal with me on business issues only."

"Okay, Yvonne, but it's not going to be easy," Alex said sadly.

"That's your problem," Yvonne barked, spinning on her heels and flying out the door.

Alex attempted to respect Yvonne's wishes, but whenever he got around her, he had to touch her. She slapped away his hands and spurned his kisses. Finally one evening Alex called her on the intercom.

"Yvonne, could you come in here? We need to review a new computer tape backup procedure." When she walked in his office, Alex was standing with his back to her.

"Close the door, please," Alex requested.

"Why?" she asked.

"Humor me, will you?" he replied.

Yvonne closed the door and Alex turned around. "Do you know what you do to me? I'm like this all the time—whenever I think of you," said Alex, exposing himself to her and standing at attention.

Yvonne was disgusted. "You're sick, Alex. Get help. This is the last straw."

Yvonne grabbed her purse and left the building. The next morning she reported the incident to James Kildorn in human resources. James took careful notes.

"Do you want to press charges against Alex for indecent exposure?" James asked.

"No, I just want him to leave me alone and let me do my job," Yvonne responded. "I think he needs help."

James began his investigation. He interviewed Alex. Alex basically corroborated all details of Yvonne's story, with one exception. Alex confided that he had become obsessed with Yvonne, but he denied the exposure incident. Alex also indicated that he didn't think it much mattered to the company about their relationship because Yvonne was merely a temp and not a company employee.

James interviewed other employees. None had ever observed even the slightest flirtation between Yvonne and Alex. James was not surprised because the second shift had a skeleton crew, and there were many opportunities for clandestine meetings.

Since Alex fully confirmed Yvonne's detailed explanations, except for the exposure incident, James decided that Yvonne was probably telling the truth. Alex, who was a long-term employee, told James that he was going to tell his wife about the incident, plead *mea culpa,* and go on with his life.

James explained to Alex that it wasn't that simple. Alex's continued sexual harassment of Yvonne after she ended the relationship, compounded with the exposure incident, created a very serious situation. Alex could resign or be terminated; the choice was his. Alex resigned.

As promised, Alex told his wife, Sarah, about the incident. She was angered and made an appointment with James.

"Look, James, I don't see why that little college brat gets to keep working here and my husband had to leave. He told me that he flirted with her and kissed her a few times. So what? She went along with it. Men can be seduced by young things. I've forgiven him. Why can't the company?" Sarah asked.

"Sarah, I can appreciate your concern, but I really can't discuss the details of the case with you. That's for Alex to tell you," James informed her.

"But he *has* told me. He told me everything, and I've forgiven him," she insisted. "He's always been a good employee, so why does he have to find another job? He likes it here."

"Perhaps you may want to talk to Alex again to shed more light on this," James hinted. "Alex's file is confidential and I can't discuss it with you."

"I keep telling you, he has discussed it with me. I think you guys are making a big deal out of nothing," Sarah contended.

"Sarah, company policy does not permit me to discuss individual employee cases. Talk to your husband," he replied.

"But I'm his wife," she fumed.

"That doesn't matter. You'll have to discuss this with Alex," James repeated, ending the discussion.

Sarah shook her head and looked confused. It was clear to James that Alex had left out the critical detail and probably would never tell Sarah.

Sarah and her sister were beginning to subtly stir up problems for Yvonne, causing her to feel uncomfortable. To alleviate the pressure, James moved Yvonne to another equally responsible assignment located in another building. With no opportunity for Alex's wife and sister-in-law to see Yvonne on a regular basis, the situation returned to normal.

 James handled this case extremely well with one exception. There was no need for an expanded investigation. First, Alex admitted to the allegation, except for the exposure incident. Second, there were no known witnesses to the alleged exposure incident. Thus, James had no reason to investigate further because no other facts were in dispute. By involving other employees, James unnecessarily jeopardized the confidentiality of the investigation.

James could have supported his decision to terminate on the facts, exclusive of the indecent exposure incident. The absence of Alex's admission to, or witnesses of, his alleged exposure was not a critical "missing link." There was no reason to discredit Yvonne's presentation of these facts. She had no apparent motive to misrepresent the circumstances. In fact, she demonstrated a lack of malice by indicating that Alex needed help and she did not wish to press charges.

Although we support the decision to terminate, some of us feel the company had other options. A less severe approach may have enabled the company to salvage an apparently good employee (and preserved the good will of two others, his wife and sister-in-law). Even the victim in this case acknowledged that the manager was "sick" and needed help. Perhaps probation, coupled with a mandated counseling program and reassignment of either the manager or the temporary employee (which eventually occurred anyway), might have been a more productive resolution for all concerned.

When supervisors have consensual relationships with their employees they are looking for trouble. Not only do most of these relationships deteriorate within the work environment, but they also have a negative impact on other employees as well. Co-workers begin to notice and morale inevitably suffers, potentially creating a hostile work environment.

We all agree that this case reinforces the need for a detailed, well-communicated sexual harassment policy. Most sexual harassment policies deal with harassment by or toward employees and non-employees alike. Thus, the fact that Yvonne was a temp has no bearing on the situation. Additionally, we believe the company owes Yvonne a work environment that is free from retribution from her charge of sexual harassment. Therefore, we think James should have counseled Alex's wife and sister-in-law and taken appropriate disciplinary action with them. Nevertheless, James made the right decision to transfer Yvonne away from a potentially explosive situation.

Finally, James was clearly judicious and mindful of privacy laws in his refusal to discuss the incident with Sarah, Alex's wife. Sarah shouldn't expect to get any more information from the HR manager than any other employee does about a co-worker.

 This story illustrates the problems and potential legal liability that can arise when an office romance goes sour. It is not unusual to find sexual harassment situations evolving from formerly consensual romantic relationships that have ended—at least on the part of one of the parties.

Sexual harassment generally consists of *unwelcome* sexual advances, requests for sexual favors, or other verbal or physical conduct of a sexual nature when an individual's submission to such conduct is made a condition of employment, made the basis for employment decisions, or unreasonably interferes with an individual's ability to perform, or otherwise creates an offensive or hostile working environment. Thus, a consensual relationship between co-workers is not sexual harassment; but when that relationship sours and one party to the former relationship continues to pursue the "no longer interested" other party with *unwelcome* sexual advances, then the conduct becomes unlawful sexual harassment.

The human resources manager appropriately investigated Yvonne's complaint and took swift action. However, even though the company took swift action, it is still liable for Alex's conduct. We question the wisdom of asking the harassed employee if he or she wants to press criminal charges against the harasser. Such an invitation cannot help the company. One of the primary objectives in dealing with any sexual harassment situation is to try to keep the situation in-house and to resolve the problem without the intervention of outside agencies.

Yvonne's status as a temporary employee did not relieve the company from possible liability for sexual harassment. The company and the temporary help company are most likely "joint employers" of Yvonne. "Joint employment" is a legal relationship that arises between two or more employers with each employer having actual or potential rights and duties with respect to the same employee. A joint employer relationship may be established where (a) the temporary help company pays the employee, pays and withholds payroll taxes, and provides workers' compensation coverage; and (b) the "customer" (in this case, Alex's company) supervises and directs the temporary employee's day-to-day work and activities, controls the working conditions at the worksite, and determines the length of the assignment. Since these two conditions are met in Yvonne's situation, it is arguable that a joint employment relationship exists. Thus, both the temporary service and the company could be liable for Alex's discriminatory conduct.

We commend James on not discussing details of the situation with Alex's wife. Strict adherence to company policy prohibiting disclosure of confidential employee information with other employees or "outsiders" will go a long way toward alleviating charges of invasion of privacy or defamation.

This scenario brings to the forefront another important issue that employers should consider—a nepotism policy. While it is lawful in most jurisdictions to impose restrictions on the hiring of relatives and/or having relatives working in the same department or reporting to each other, employers should familiarize themselves with the applicable law in their locality. This will ensure their policy does not create a risk of marital status discrimination. For example, under California law, an employment decision may not be based on whether an individual has a spouse presently employed by the employer, except that for business reasons, the employer may refuse to place one spouse under the supervision of the other spouse or to place both spouses in the same department, division, or facility.

Chapter 3

Jerks & Jokers

"Brandishing a firearm and setting off cherry bombs are hardly silly pranks."

Claudia D. Denaro
Vice President Human Resources Services
Consolidated Stores Corporation

Gentlemen Prefer Hanes

Dixie fished around in her purse for her keys as she stood in front of her apartment door. "Damn," she said, dropping her purse and all its contents.

She wobbled unsteadily as she grabbed her keys, scooping her make-up and belongings back into her purse. Still swaying, she finally focused long enough to penetrate the keyhole and unlock the door.

"Boy, am I exhausted," she thought, flinging her purse down on the couch. She had been out with a group of sales managers who were in town for a district meeting. Although she had a wonderful evening, she realized she had danced one too many dances and could have spared herself that last marguerita.

"I guess I'm getting too old for this," Dixie said aloud and sighed. "At 25 I could go all night; at 47, I'm beginning to feel it."

She looked in the mirror. "I've only worn this outfit for a few hours; I think I'll wear it to work tomorrow," she thought, kicking off her shoes.

As Dixie began to peel off her slacks—pantyhose and all—she quickly sat down on the side of her bed. The room began to spin and her head whirled. She sat for a few minutes until she got her bearings. Then she laid her slacks across the back of a chair, removed her blouse, and placed it on top of her slacks. The next thing she knew, she awoke to the morning sun shining in her eyes.

Her head was throbbing. She reached for her glasses to check the clock. "Ohmygosh! It's 7:45 a.m. I must've forgotten to set my alarm," she mumbled. She raced into the bathroom, grabbed some aspirin, turned on the shower, and jumped in. She filled her mouth with water from the shower head, tossed in her aspirin with one hand, while she dumped shampoo on her hair with the other.

Within 15 minutes she had showered, dried her hair, and put on make-up. "I'll get breakfast at the office," she thought, as she searched her drawers for a clean pair of pantyhose. She found a new pair and slipped them on, followed by the slacks and blouse she had worn the night before.

She arrived at the subway station with a minute to spare. On the 20-minute ride to the office, she had time to catch her breath and collect her thoughts. Dixie had been an executive secretary in the marketing department for a major consumer products company for nearly 20 years. Although she never married, she enjoyed her times with the sales force. There were always some who were loud and obnoxious, but for the most part, they were a good bunch.

Unfortunately, her new boss, Casper Nichols, was the exception. He was probably the worst manager she had ever met during her career. He seemed to enjoy finding fault with her or embarrassing her in little ways. She couldn't understand why he was so different from her other bosses.

"Maybe he hates his mother," she thought, as the subway rocked her gently. Ultimately, she knew it was only a matter of time before Casper would move on. She resigned herself to tolerating him until he would be transferred out to the field to gain more experience. "This, too, will pass," she smiled to herself as the conductor called out her stop.

When she arrived at the office, she put her purse in her drawer, picked up her cup, and walked to the coffee center. She liked her coffee strong, and today she really needed it. Although the pain in her head had subsided slightly, she was still feeling a little woozy.

On her way back to her desk, Dixie greeted the six other secretaries whose desks lined the aisle. As she continued her journey back to her desk, she heard Casper booming from the rear of the office for all to hear: "Dix, Whoa! Stop right there!"

Startled, Dixie stopped abruptly, which nearly sent her coffee whirling out of her cup and onto her blouse. "Keep cool," she assured herself, "it'll be all right."

Casper walked up to Dixie who was frozen in her spot. He squatted down and examined her ankle like an umpire dusting off home plate. Then he tugged on a section of last evening's pantyhose, whose toe was dangling from the bottom of her slacks. He slowly stood up and began to step backwards. With each step he stretched and pulled the hose until they snapped out from her trousers and into his hands.

In full view of the others, he balled them up and tossed them at her, saying, "I guess it was some night last night!" Dixie just stood there holding her pantyhose, feeling humiliated and degraded.

Although Casper's manager and the staff in the human resources department got wind of the incident through the grapevine, no one interceded on Dixie's behalf. Always the good soldier, Dixie never formally complained. She stoically endured Casper until he was transferred to another division.

All of us find Casper's behavior and the lack of action by the human resources department appalling. While one of us would have terminated Casper for gross misconduct, the rest of us view this as sexual harassment and would treat it as such. We do, however, recognize that a discharge under gross misconduct could certainly apply if there were no policy on sexual harassment.

It appears that Casper is a man whose malicious prank demonstrated a lack of humanity and poor business judgment. He not only humiliated Dixie, but he did so in front of six witnesses. The human resources department was equally culpable for ignoring the incident. Their inaction suggests that they condoned Casper's antics. We nominate them for the "Shame-on-You" award and give them an F for dismissing this as simple tomfoolery.

As soon as the human resources staff heard about this incident, they should have started an investigation by interviewing Dixie. During this process, the HR person should have let Dixie know that she was not in any trouble, but that an incident had been reported which the company was obligated to investigate. The HR representative should have encouraged Dixie to be truthful and assured her that she'd be protected from any retaliation. The representative should then have asked if any incidents involving Casper had taken place recently. If or when Dixie reported her account of the incident, the next question should have been, "Who else saw this happen?" Dixie then should have been warned against having further discussions with co-workers about this incident.

The HR representative should interview reliable onlookers as well and tell them they, too, are protected from retaliation and warn them about discussing this incident with anyone else. Finally, Casper should be presented with the allegations and should have an opportunity to respond.

Since this case had a number of witnesses, there should be sufficient evidence to sustain a sexual harassment charge. Regardless of Casper's intent, his behavior was clearly inappropriate for the workplace. If Casper has no other incidents of sexual harassment reported in his file, we'd recommend that Casper be educated on sexual harassment as part of his disciplinary action. We would also place a formal, final written warning in his file. The report would describe what happened and state that any further incidents of harassment or intimidation would lead to immediate termination. Additionally, we would warn Casper both orally and in writing that retaliation would be grounds for disciplinary action up to and including termination. This document should also indicate that Casper has been educated in sexual harassment, understands that what he did was inappropriate, and that he promises not to do it again. Casper should sign this letter and retain a copy for himself. Moreover, it may be appropriate to require Casper, in the presence of his manager, to apologize to Dixie and assure her that there will be no repetition of the behavior.

We would also examine whether or not these two individuals can continue working together. If Dixie feels the situation is untenable and requests a change in reporting structure and/or location, we should appropriately accommodate her. In doing so, we should ensure she does not lose status or pay, for example, in the process. Such an accommodation may require that we move Casper.

Finally, this incident was probably traumatic for Dixie. We would suggest referring her to the employee assistance program and/or possibly paying for some counseling if she chooses to avail herself of such services.

 Casper is one of those guys who "just doesn't get it." While he may think that his actions are "cute" and that he is just joking around, there are indications in this story that Casper is a potential liability for the company. It appears that Casper has enjoyed embarrassing Dixie on occasions other than this one. While many individuals may believe his actions are harmless, Dixie may have been able to show that Casper is guilty of sexual harassment because his actions have created an offensive or hostile working environment, had she decided to pursue a charge against the company.

The standards of evidence and types of proof necessary to prove unlawful sexual harassment are still evolving and employers are advised to stay tuned. The U. S. Supreme Court recently held that to constitute "abusive work environment" harassment, the conduct need not seriously affect the employee's psychological well being or lead the individual to "suffer injury." This case provides additional parameters in this delicate and complex area of equal employment opportunity law. Some states, such as New Jersey, have already held that the absence of a severe psychological injury to a sexual harassment victim should not bar a recovery of appropriate relief under a state's fair employment practices law.

Playing Footsie

Katherine rechecked the figures on her report, while she waited for her secretary to collate the bound copies.

"Yep, these look good," she thought.

Although making a change in a sales compensation plan is often difficult to implement, Katherine had done her homework. As an experienced compensation manager, she understood the company's marketing strategy and was confident about her data. So she was prepared for any objection the executive vice president of marketing or vice president of sales might raise during the presentation. And, with the full support of the company's chief financial officer, she knew she was golden.

Besides, Jay Cooper, the executive vice president of marketing, was not known for his smarts. A man in his late 50s with a handsome face and a twinkle in his eye, Jay was better known for his business connections and golf game than for his conceptual ability. On the other hand, the vice president of sales, Lance Dodge, was very sharp. Katherine knew she'd have to go a round or two with him before getting the nod on her program.

"Katherine, here are your four copies. They look great," Dee Dee smiled, as she handed Katherine the reports.

"Thanks, I'm on my way. I'm going up a little early," Katherine told her as she dashed off to the executive floor.

When Katherine arrived, she arranged the conference table to her liking. A few minutes later, Hal, the chief financial officer, walked in.

"Are you all set?" Hal grinned.

"All set," she returned. "I really appreciate your being here. Here's your copy of the report."

"I'm always glad to help, especially when I think it will help save the company money," he said with a wink.

A few moments later, Jay and Lance arrived. All exchanged greetings and Katherine directed them to sit across from her and Hal. She handed them copies of the report, and they went through its content in detail.

When the vice president of sales took issue with the idea of removing the guaranteed bonuses from the plan, Katherine was ready. She immediately launched into her discussion of total compensation and the purpose of variable pay programs.

"As you know, we've recently developed a new marketing strategy so we can maintain a competitive position," Katherine began. "In order to link our reward systems to that marketing strategy, we need to ensure that we only pay for performance. We simply can't afford to reward non-performance and stay in business. Unfortunately, our current sales compensation program guarantees bonuses. When we guarantee someone's bonus, there is no incentive for them to push our products. This is not . . . "

Katherine stopped abruptly. She felt a shoeless foot from under the table inching its way up her calf toward her inner thigh. She noticed Jay sitting across from her with a mischievous grin on his face as he was sinking lower and lower in his seat. She was horrified, but remained calm.

"Uh . . . This is not the message we want to communicate to our sales force," she resumed, directing her comments to Lance while she ignored Jay's intrusion under her skirt.

"Now, Kathy," Jay piped up, "don't you think it's really okay to guarantee those salespeople their bonuses? You know times are hard, and we don't want to be losing them," he said, grinning while he pushed his foot a little farther up her leg.

Katherine took a very deep breath and steadied herself. "Jay, their job is to make money. When they do that they'll get a share—not before," she said forcefully. Then she grabbed his foot and yanked it up to the table for everyone to see. In the process, Jay nearly fell out of his chair and just barely missed scraping his chin on the table as she dragged him forward.

"I think you've lost something here, and it's more than your old incentive plan!" she laughed, diffusing her own tension.

"Okay, okay, Kathy! Uncle, uncle! You win," Jay said, howling with laughter.

Katherine shook her head. "The things I have to put up with just to do my job," she thought. She went back to the human resources department and dropped in on her colleague, Webster Grant, the employee relations manager.

"You are not going to believe what Jay Cooper pulled today in a meeting," she said. She told him the whole story.

"Look, Katherine, you've got to ignore those jerks. They're just testing you to see how tough you are. You passed their test and from now on the rest is easy street," Webster commented.

"Oh, that's a bunch of malarkey, Webster," Katherine retorted. "You're just treating this casually because I'm in human resources and you think I'm not really going to do anything about it. You're lucky I'm not some female marketing or advertising manager coming down here with the same complaint. You'd be hot-footing it down there, investigating like mad."

"You're probably right, Katherine, but I know you, and I'm not worried," he smiled confidently.

Jay Cooper probably spent most of his working career "testing" female employees with unwelcome advances, comments, and other forms of behavior that smack of "good ol' boy" shenanigans. Unfortunately, Jay and others like him operate under the premise that "to get along, you must play along."

Jay will not stop "testing" Katherine or other employees until management puts him clearly on notice that his actions will not be tolerated either by the company or fellow employees. Although we don't know the culture of the organization, most of us feel Katherine should have reacted more forcefully and unequivocally. She should have let Jay know that his behavior was not amusing and that he should keep his feet and hands to himself in the future—no if, ands, or *toes* about it!

Although Katherine's actions may have momentarily stung "good ol' Jay," the results are probably only temporary. He needs some education and he needs it fast. Also, many of us think that Katherine could have racked up more points on the "toughness test" by reacting with less humor and more of a no-nonsense attitude.

If Katherine accepts Jay's game and if Webster is right about the boys and their test, then she may have earned her place on "mahogany row." However, we suspect that sooner or later the bill for Jay's behavior will come due. Although Katherine doesn't appear ready to push now, she has a legitimate complaint and may not be silent forever, particularly if her career doesn't progress as Webster predicted. If something goes wrong in the future, she might charge that her stalled career is really the result of a retaliatory response for humiliating Jay. In preparing its defense, the company would have to demonstrate it handled the incident properly. At this point it hasn't.

We think Webster was derelict in his responsibilities. He is not only deferring the day of reckoning, but also substantially increasing potential costs for the company. If the company is involved in litigation for a subsequent sexual harassment complaint, the investigation may reveal a pattern of poor and inconsistent handling of prior cases. Instead, Webster and Jay's boss should have confronted Jay with a review of the company's sexual harassment policy and provided remedial training. Webster should have also included a stern verbal and written warning stating that similar actions or behavior will not be tolerated and could result in disciplinary actions, including termination. Also, it is reasonable to demand an old-fashioned apology from Jay in this situation, such as, "I'm sorry I offended and embarrassed you, Katherine. I assure you it won't happen again."

On the other hand, we can't fully ignore Katherine's actions. While her anger was understandable, her physical maneuver could have had severe consequences. Jay could have fallen and sustained a serious injury.

Finally, as a human resources professional, Webster is responsible for safeguarding the rights of all employees. He should not use a lesser standard for colleagues than he does for the general employee population. He is obligated to assure Katherine that appropriate corrective measures will be taken and that the company is committed to maintaining a positive, non-hostile work environment.

Katherine's response to Jay's footsie game was appropriate, and we commend her ability to make it clear to Jay and the others in the meeting that his conduct toward her was unwelcome. Because Katherine is a human resources manager she may be better equipped to respond more swiftly to Jay's conduct than some other employees. But bringing public attention to and heaping some embarrassment on such offenders is sometimes the best medicine to cure unacceptable behavior. Employers, in training employees about sexual harassment, should instruct employees that the first step in combating sexual harassment in the workplace is to speak up, defend yourself, tell the harasser that the conduct is unwelcome, inappropriate, and must be stopped.

Not every incident of inappropriate workplace behavior rises to the level of sexual harassment warranting a full-fledged investigation. Some factors that need to be considered in determining how to proceed are the seriousness of the conduct at issue, whether the human resources department ever received harassment complaints about the individual in the past, the interests and wishes of the recipient of the conduct, whether there seems to be a pattern of misconduct by the individual, or whether there have been "rumors" about the individual's conduct.

Webster should have involved Katherine in his decision on how to handle the situation. At a minimum, Webster should have spoken with Jay and made it clear to him that such conduct was inappropriate. We would also suggest that Webster document the incident with the action that he took and place a copy of the documentation in Jay's personnel file, rather than simply shrugging off the episode. If a pattern of such episodes should surface, stronger action would be necessary.

Open Season

"Hey, want to see my new rifle, Opie?" Harper Johnson, the first shift supervisor, asked one of the operating technicians during a break.

"Yeah, let's look at her," Opie said, reaching over toward Harper. He picked up the rifle and peered through the scope. "She sure is a beauty." Then he tossed the rifle around in his hands. "The weight feels real good too. Where'd you get her from?"

"I saw an ad in *Guns and Ammo,*" Harper said. "I got me some shells at home that'll work just fine. This weekend I'm gonna do some target practice. I wanna be ready by the time huntin' season starts."

It was common for the crew at the small rural plant to have their guns delivered to the company. Many employees lived on rural routes where delivery on mail order items was unreliable. They could always be sure to get their packages delivered promptly at the plant.

"Hey, let's have some fun with that new guy, Wally Beemis. He seems like the nervous type who scares easy," said Harper, before spitting some tobacco juice skillfully into a rusted can several feet away. "My cousin told me this Wally fella has been datin' her daughter. Let's test him out and see if he's man enough to handle the girl," Harper added with a sinister grin. He wiped away a drop of tobacco juice still clinging to his mustache.

Harper's victim, Wally Beemis, worked at the plant as a maintenance technician. He wanted to earn enough money to go to graduate school the next year, so he worked all available overtime. Wally kept to himself mainly, reading books on his breaks.

"Hey, Wally," Harper said as he approached him, taunting with the rifle in his hands. "Ever seen one of these? It could shoot your nuts off at 100 yards."

Wally ignored him.

"I suppose not," Harper grunted. "The kick off this baby would probably send a little weakling like you back six feet," teased Harper, while he and Opie laughed raucously.

Harper attempted to rile Wally for several weeks, but Wally either left the area or ignored him. One day, Wally was standing on an eight-foot ladder to paint some overhead pipes. Harper gathered his cronies, whispering and laughing. As usual, Wally ignored them.

Suddenly, *Pop! Bang! Blam!* Smoke started to rise from beneath the ladder, where Harper had thrown several cherry bombs. Wally was so startled that he and the paint came tumbling down. Harper and Opie doubled over with laughter as they watched Wally scrape himself off the floor. Harper's laughter turned to fear when he saw a wild look cross Wally's face. Within moments Wally charged toward Harper with eyes blazing.

Harper took off running. Wally quickly began to gain on him, so Harper ducked into an office to hide. Wally spotted the maneuver, entered the office, and jumped over a desk to cut him off. Then he leaped on Harper's back and knocked him to the ground. When Opie and another technician found them, Harper was gasping for breath as Wally gripped him in a choke hold.

While Opie and the technician struggled to pry Wally's arms off Harper, someone called the plant manager, Cleve Borland. When Cleve arrived, he saw all four of them engaged in the fracas.

"What the hell is going on here?" Cleve boomed.

Upon hearing Cleve's voice, everyone stopped fighting. Harper hung his head and Wally sat down quietly. After Cleve got the facts, he immediately suspended Harper without pay for a week and sent him home. He gave Opie and the technician a verbal warning for encouraging horseplay and told Wally to clean up the spilled paint and return to work.

Things were calm for a while, at least until Harper returned. Harper, angered by his suspension, continued to harass Wally with crude comments and threats.

Two weeks later, Wally went to see a psychiatrist and told the doctor about the harassment at work. Wally claimed that his stress was so severe that he could not return to the plant. The doctor certified that Wally should be off work based on stress-related workers' compensation for up to six weeks.

When Wally's six weeks expired, he did not return to work. He informed Cleve's secretary that he was still too stressed to deal with the situation and could not return. Cleve's secretary told Wally that he needed to have a doctor's excuse to remain off work and that his workers' compensation benefit had expired. Wally would need to get new certification to receive continued benefits under workers' compensation. Wally indicated that his attorney said that state law didn't require another doctor's excuse.

When Wally refused to provide another doctor's excuse, Cleve asked the outside agency that handles the company's employee assistance program to help. The staff attempted to work with Wally to facilitate his recovery. Nevertheless, based on the advice of his attorney, Wally continued his refusal to obtain a physician's excuse.

Since Wally didn't return to work or acquire a doctor's excuse, the company terminated his employment for excessive absenteeism. Wally countered with a lawsuit. It was at this point that Alexandra Marcus, the regional human resources representative, and Russell Morris, corporate legal counsel, first became aware of the situation.

"Oh, for crying out loud!" Alexandra exclaimed. "Why do I always have to mop up Cleve's messes? I cover 25 plants in the area, and Cleve is the only plant manager who refuses to call human resources for help until it's too late. He must have some kind of an ego problem or something. It's damn annoying."

"From my initial discussion with Cleve, this one's got some bad facts, Alexandra," Russell informed her. "It sounds like a bad termination, and I'm afraid we're going to get nailed. I think we'd better fly down and investigate."

They investigated the case and learned that no one from the office had ever told Wally directly the consequences of failing to provide a doctor's excuse. Neither Cleve nor his secretary ever said to Wally, "Look, Wally, you're getting some bad advice. We have a policy that says you need to have a doctor's excuse to take advantage of our sick leave policy. If you need more time, perhaps we can move you over to our disability plan. However, if you don't follow this procedure, you have two choices: either quit or you're fired." Instead, Cleve directed his secretary to handle the communication and only retained limited documentation. The only items Cleve documented to the file were Harper's suspension for setting off firecrackers and the verbal warnings given to Opie and the other technician.

"I'm afraid this is a real loser," Russell told Alexandra when they had completed the investigation. "As you know, these cases get jury trials. All we need to do is have a jury hear that Harper attempted to intimidate Wally with a rifle and threw firecrackers under the ladder. We're better off trying to settle this one."

"I agree," Alexandra said. "I just wish it were coming out of Cleve's pocket. You can be sure the division president will hear about this one."

After meeting with Wally's attorney, they settled for $35,000 and offered Wally his job back. Wally accepted the settlement but declined the job. He entered graduate school that September.

Harassing employees is never acceptable, and brandishing a firearm and lighting cherry bombs are hardly pranks. This is a case of pathetic management, lousy supervision, and inadequate human resources involvement. This plant needs a complete people and policy overhaul.

First, while the rural nature of the operation may have made receipt of mail at the plant acceptable, the company needs better control over the disbursement of personal mail. Under no circumstances should an employee unpack a firearm at the worksite. Simply keeping all mail in the office until quitting time would have helped.

Second, Wally's harassment by several co-workers continued for a number of weeks. Where was Cleve? Even a slightly aware or interested manager could have observed and eliminated this problem.

Third, more aggressive and specific discipline of all parties after the altercation would no doubt have helped quell further activity. Along with suspending Harper and warning Opie and the technician, Cleve should have indicated that additional harassment or horseplay would result in further discipline up to and including termination. He also should have followed up with Wally to ensure the harassment had stopped. This action may have put a stop to things at that stage and/or made Wally feel more supported and less motivated to go out on workers' compensation. While Cleve may not have felt a need for active supervision before this event, a better manager would have been compelled to be more observant and "on the floor" after the incident.

Although we aren't privy to the company's specific policies and procedures, some of us feel that this incident involved more than simple horseplay. Most companies do not tolerate any type of fighting and would have terminated both Harper and Wally for engaging in a physical altercation, irrespective of the circumstances. Also, the company needed to do a better job communicating its policy on harassment and procedures for reporting it. If Wally knew that he would be protected against retaliation, he may have come forward to report the harassment, thus avoiding the whole incident.

On the other hand, we all agree that Wally's termination was grossly mishandled. It is essential that a company maintain a policy that clearly states the requirements to obtain and remain on leave of absence. In this case, it appears that such a policy existed but that management did not tell the employee that termination was the consequence of failure to comply. An employee handbook that explains such policies would be useful.

Additionally, the company should establish firm procedures for all cases that involve any triggering of a benefits situation. These procedures must include notification of appropriate corporate personnel and specific forms that must be completed for the personnel file of each individual. We also recommend scripts for the most common types of situations for use in talking with individuals on such policy issues.

Cleve shirked his responsibility by having the secretary act as a go-between and inadequately warning Wally of the potential for termination. At a minimum, Cleve should have sent a certified letter to Wally. It should have clearly stated the company's policy requiring additional documentation from the doctor for re-certification and the consequences of termination if Wally did not meet the request.

However, the most inexcusable management failure belongs to the regional human resources representative. Her tolerance and cover up for Cleve's past inadequacies only perpetuated poor management at the plant. She should have known it was only a matter of time before a serious problem occurred. If she couldn't convince Cleve to voluntarily follow her guidance, she should have long before apprised the division president of the problem. Clearly, she failed in her responsibility as well.

 Employers may require appropriate medical documentation regarding an individual's need to be on leave from work whether for workers' compensation, disability leave, sick leave, or family/medical leave pursuant to federal or state law. To reduce an employer's risk of liability for wrongful terminations, such policies need to be communicated to employees either through an employee handbook, a posting on the bulletin board, or in a letter to the individual on leave, and

should advise employees of the consequences of failing to provide such medical documentation.

Another serious issue raised by this story is the possession of a firearm on company premises. With the alarming increase in workplace violence, we recommend that employers establish—and enforce—a strict policy forbidding the possession of firearms on the company premises. We also note that Harper received delivery of his rifle at the company. It is unwise for employers to permit employees to use the company's address to receive personal mail or packages.

The facts of the story raise some questions surrounding Wally's termination. It appears that the plant manager's secretary was the only one communicating with Wally regarding his return to work and his ultimate termination. Considering the risk of liabilities associated with employee termination, such responsibility should probably not be delegated to a clerical employee.

Most state workers' compensation laws recognize that employers do not have to keep an employee's job open indefinitely or to continually hire temporary employees to fill in for the absent employee who has suffered an on-the-job injury. Many jobs cannot be staffed on such an ad hoc basis without causing undue hardship.

We suggest that employers establish a policy which states that positions can be held open only for a specific period of time due to operational concerns, and that employees who are absent for a certain designated time period will have to be replaced. The policy should identify the specific jobs or class of jobs that require consistent staffing and which cannot be filled with temporaries because of the nature of the position. The policy may be drafted in such a manner that displaced absent employees are given the opportunity to apply for the first available vacancy when the employee is able to return to work. The controlling factor is that a person's unavailability to work—not the underlying reason for that unavailability—cannot be tolerated indefinitely.

Chapter 4

Petty Plaintiffs

"No amount of formal education prepares you for these real life human resources challenges."

C. Neal Baileys
Vice President of Human Resources
PMI Food Equipment Group
(A division of Premark International)

The Queen Bee

"Sexually harassing her? That's preposterous!" Arch protested. "I have never so much as had a sexual *thought* about Eloise Duquesne, let alone harass her! Just what exactly did she say I supposedly did?" he asked, totally flabbergasted.

"Eloise claims that you were fondling yourself and leering at her while she was filing," Veronica informed him. Veronica was the regional human resources manager. She had received a call from Eloise a few days earlier and had flown in from regional headquarters for the investigation.

"Well, she's nuts," Arch insisted.

Although Veronica was not surprised that Arch denied the allegation, this was the first time she had ever heard him speak with such conviction or force. Normally, Arch was very mild-mannered and had a reputation for staying cool in a crisis.

"Look, Arch, we've been put on notice. As a result, I've got to conduct a full investigation. It's clear that you deny the allegations. Eloise's claim is that you've harassed her to the point that she's too mentally stressed to work. She wants workers' compensation for a stress-related disability," Veronica said.

"That's such a bunch of bull, Veronica," Arch scoffed, then regained his composure. "Okay, do what you have to do. I understand; it's part of the drill. But I can promise you this: you won't find a soul who'll substantiate this nonsense."

"I hope you're right, Arch," Veronica replied.

Veronica was perplexed. Eloise's allegation seemed far afield. Arch was a 15-year employee with an unblemished record. Nevertheless, Veronica recognized she could not allow her biases to shortcut the investigation. She talked with every employee in the office who would have an opportunity to observe any possible inappropriate behavior. As Arch predicted, she came up dry.

Since Veronica could not support Eloise's allegation, she decided to protest the workers' compensation claim. Part of the strategy was to have Eloise undergo a psychiatric evaluation. Among the items in Dr. Kampmeir's report, Veronica was most interested in the following portions:

Mrs. Duquesne is prone to fantasizing. She admitted that she fantasizes on a regular basis about many things in her life. She stated that she sexually fantasized about her husband; her supervisor, Arch Lanfried; as well as other male co-workers . . . . Mrs. Duquesne also stated that she was angry with Mr. Lanfried. She claimed that he recently reduced her responsibilities by delegating some of her duties to others. She felt betrayed and demoralized over this change . . . . We recommend she be denied disability for stress caused by sexual harassment.

After reviewing the report, Veronica met with Arch to follow up. She told him that there was no direct evidence to the sexual harassment charge. Then she gave him a copy of the sexual harassment policy.

"Arch, it's in your best interest to review the policy. Make sure that you don't put yourself in any situations in the future that may lay cause for another claim—this is for your own protection," she advised him.

"But I know the policy," he responded. "You know Eloise's claim was nothing but smoke."

"Even so, Arch," she repeated, "please review the policy, and if you have any questions, let me know," she said, smiling warmly.

"Okay," Arch shrugged.

"Now, Arch, I have just one other thing I need to check on. The psychiatrist's report indicated that Eloise was angered over the changes you made in her job. Can you tell me about that?"

"Sure," Arch began, "the volume of work in our department has increased dramatically. Although Eloise is good, no human being could possibly keep up with the work. I explained to her that I was going to get her some help so that we could meet the volume demands. She kept insisting that she would be able to get a handle on it if I gave her a couple of weeks. I agreed, but after the two weeks were up, she was still behind. So I had to give some of her duties to Lois. But I assure you, Veronica, I never suggested to her that the removal of these duties had anything to do with her competence. Unfortunately, I think she suffers from the "Queen Bee" syndrome and just didn't want to give anything up," Arch said.

Veronica was satisfied that Arch had not created any additional problems that might come back to haunt her. Then Veronica met with Eloise.

"Eloise, based on our internal investigation and the psychiatric evaluation, your workers' compensation claim has been denied. We would be happy to transfer you to another department, if you would be more comfortable," Veronica suggested.

"Forget it. I can't work here. I'm not coming back. Consider this my resignation," Eloise barked.

Veronica suspected Eloise might react negatively, so she had armed herself with the appropriate documents. "I regret that you feel this way, but if you insist, I'll process your paperwork," Veronica said dispassionately.

"Well, I do. I insist!" Eloise declared.

As though on cue, Veronica slid one of the forms across the table toward Eloise. "Well then, we'll certainly respect your wishes. Now, if you'll review this and sign at the bottom," Veronica said, with the composure of a seasoned poker player in a high-stakes game.

As Eloise signed the last document, Veronica wanted to shout "Hallelujah!" But instead, she called Arch to inform him of Eloise's decision. Then Veronica escorted Eloise to her worksite and supervised the removal of her personal belongings from her desk.

Superficially, this appears to be a well-handled case. Veronica conducted a prompt, thorough investigation concerning the sexual harassment allegation. She apparently followed policy by properly notifying and counseling Arch. Also, Eloise's voluntary resignation seemingly ended any prospects of further problems.

Despite the ultimate outcome, the panel disagreed on one critical procedure—Veronica's overeagerness to accept Eloise's resignation. A few panel members who support Veronica's quick actions believe it is good employee relations practice to "always accept a resignation" when supported by the facts. We feel that Veronica did her homework and came to a reasonable conclusion that Eloise was either mistaken, unbalanced, or unethical. Accepting Eloise's resignation with grace and charm was a clean and simple approach toward severing an untenable employee-employer relationship. The loss of Eloise probably left the company no worse off.

Even in the unlikely event that new evidence developed suggesting there was some substance to Eloise's story, it would be easier to resolve than dealing with her performance and possible mental problems. While there are no obvious facts to suggest Eloise will be back to haunt them, our group thinks the company should consider itself lucky. We argue that employees like Eloise are usually harder than this to lose.

The majority of the panel took a different position. We believe that Veronica's preparations to process an immediate resignation seemed a bit too pat. Conceivably, Eloise could claim her resignation was nothing more than a "constructive discharge." She could allege that the company, by creating a hostile work environment and inadequately addressing her concerns, gave her little choice except to resign. In this context, the company's apparent eagerness to accept and process Eloise's resignation could be interpreted as further evidence of an outcome it had maliciously conspired to achieve. To avoid this perception, we would have suggested to Eloise that she reconsider. We also would have referred her to an employee assistance program for help.

One member from this group also pointed out other issues worthy of consideration. Although Eloise may not have had a case for *sexual harassment,* she may have had a sustainable complaint based on sex *discrimination*. There is no evidence in the text that Veronica examined whether gender had an influence on Eloise's change in duties. Arch's actions regarding Eloise's assignment are not typical of those taken with male employees under similar circumstances. His casual reference to Eloise as a "Queen Bee" could be symptomatic of some deeper attitude problems.

Despite no finding of illegal harassment or discrimination, in certain jurisdictions, Eloise's claim for workers' compensation may be upheld. She may be able to make a case that her work environment (including supervisory actions) induced an unusually high level of stress, which impaired her ability to perform her job functions.

The number of workers' compensation claims in this country has reached staggering proportions. While most such claims are legitimate, an alarming number are false—causing burdensome insurance premiums for the employers, excessive absenteeism, and loss of productivity in the workplace.

It is gratifying to see that Veronica took steps to oppose a claim that her investigation showed to be meritless. While it is unlawful to retaliate against an individual who has filed a workers' compensation claim, an employer has a right to oppose a claim that it believes is a sham or is frivolous. Opposition to meritless claims should not be confused with unlawful retaliation.

This story also illustrates that a sexual harassment investigation sometimes results in finding that the harassment allegations are false and the alleged harasser is vindicated. Because some harassment claims are meritless, it is important to keep investigations as confidential as possible so as not to run the risk of liability by defaming—ruining the reputation or career of—the alleged harasser.

In a situation such as this, where an employee chooses to resign, the company should require the employee to submit a resignation letter. A voluntarily submitted resignation letter signed by the employee would assist the company in defending itself against an unemployment insurance claim.

The Czar of Harassment

Norbert Dodge breathed a sigh of relief. The interview was easy. He expected to be grilled on accounting procedures, but Al Leonard mainly talked about himself and football.

Now, football was a subject Norbert could discuss in detail. He and Al sealed their bond when they did a play-by-play account of last Sunday's Jets game. Both had been at Meadowlands Stadium cheering their team. So before Norbert knew it, Al was offering him the job and Norbert accepted on the spot.

Norbert wasn't exactly sure what to expect, but he figured he'd muddle his way through. Al mentioned something about supervising a group of three women. Although Norbert had never supervised anyone, and he didn't relate well to women, he wasn't worried. He didn't have to like these people—just tolerate them.

Al also said something about a computer system. Norbert's experience was primarily simple record-keeping, using a manual system. How hard could it be? Norbert figured he'd worry about that later.

During the first week, Al introduced Norbert to his group. First, there was Mimi, the group leader and most tenured employee. Mimi was about five years from retirement and an outstanding performer. Next there was Lettie, a middle-aged Jewish woman who had been with the company for about six years. She was a solid, reliable worker, whose sense of humor always kept the group on an even keel. Finally, there was Marsha. Marsha, also a competent performer, was in her late 20s. Marsha was Caucasian and had married a man from Kenya after a three-year courtship during college. She and her husband, Iman, were excited about having their first child, which was due in two months.

"Mimi, I'd appreciate it if you'd show Norbie, here, the ropes. Walk him through the procedure books, and acquaint him with our equipment," Al requested.

"Sure, Big Al," Mimi smiled. "I'll get right on it."

Mimi spent the week with Norbert. Each time she'd show him a new procedure, his eyes would glaze over in a trance-like state. She wasn't sure if she was helping the Dalai Lama or an outpatient from the St. Matthews Mental Hospital. When Mimi would review material, Norbert would wave her off with a "Yeah, yeah, yeah, you told me that. So what else do you have to show me?"

Despite his assurances, it was clear to Mimi that Norbert had no inkling of what was going on. Finally, when she tried to pin him down on a technical matter, he snapped, "What's an old bag like you doing still working anyway?"

Mimi was hurt and offended and kept to herself after that. "Fine, go hang yourself, you jerk. Try to figure out the error reports on your own," she thought, as the pile on his desk mushroomed past eye level.

When Lettie informed Norbert she would be taking a personal day for Yom Kippur, Norbert sneered, "I think we have too many kikes working here. With all of you out for your stupid holiday, we'll only have a skeleton crew. We might as well shut down. It's no wonder I can't get my work done!"

Lettie was so appalled that she immediately told Mimi. Mimi shared her "old bag" experience and assured Lettie, "Listen, honey, it's only a matter of time. He'll work himself out of a job. Just ignore him."

Al began to realize that Norbert was not performing to expectation when reports were late and other department heads complained about poor service. He counseled Norbert on several occasions, but Norbert didn't seem to improve. Each day grew progressively worse, and Norbert's incompetence became increasingly evident. Every time Al would bring up reports that required certain formulas, Norbert would turn the conversation to point spreads on the next football game.

During his third week, Norbert noticed the women heading out for lunch with presents in their hands. Several women from other departments were joining them. "Where's the party?" he asked.

"Oh, we're giving Marsha a shower. Her baby is due in about a month," Lettie smiled warmly as she glanced toward Marsha.

Norbert shuddered and shook his head at Marsha. "I don't know how you could let that slimy African touch you. Ughhh!" he bellowed, contorting his face and shaking all over. The women just stared at him in disbelief until Lettie gently suggested they be on their way.

Al realized Norbert was beyond saving. He did some after-the-fact checking with Norbert's former employers and realized Norbert was in way over his head. Al decided that Norbert had to go before he could do any more damage. He called the human resources manager, Marianne Metheny, for help.

"Marianne, I've made a huge mistake. I know it's only been 30 days, but I need to cut my losses. I've hired an incompetent guy, and I need to get rid of him right now," he informed her.

"Have you been counseling him on performance?" she asked.

"Yes," Al sighed, "and he gets worse instead of better."

"In what areas?"

"Technical. He's just plain technically incompetent," Al said sadly.

"How come you're finding that out now? Didn't you identify his competence during the interview process and follow up with reference checks?" Marianne probed.

Al was redfaced. "Marianne, I got snowed."

"How? You've been through interview training. You know all the traps."

"I know, but somehow we got off track. We got to talking about football. I have no excuses. I guess I've been so lucky with all the other employees in the group. I just liked him and thought he would work out great," Al admitted with embarrassment.

"How about his supervisory skills?" Marianne asked.

"I don't know. I haven't talked to his group and no one has come to me."

"Maybe you'd better check on that as well before you do anything else. I know one of them applied for his job. I just want to be sure there is no attempt to sabotage," Marianne explained.

"They aren't the types," Al said, defending his troops. "They're all good, loyal employees."

"Fine, but let's just investigate."

"Okay, I'll talk with them," Al agreed.

Later that afternoon Al spoke with each one of the women separately. He was shocked to learn about Norbert's crass, derogatory statements. He informed Marianne, who verified the stories with the women.

"Well, even if we didn't have him on performance," Marianne said, "this alone would do it. I don't want him here another day. He's gone."

They terminated Norbert that day, and everyone in the department celebrated. The following week Marianne received a letter from the Newark Equal Employment Opportunity Commission (EEOC) charging age discrimination on Norbert's behalf. "What!" Marianne exclaimed as she read the claim. "He's only 39. There's no age discrimination. They must be having a slow month with nothing else to do but harass us," she thought, shaking her head.

She called the local office and pointed out that he was too young for an age discrimination suit. They apologized for the error and withdrew the claim.

Norbert's next move was a letter-writing campaign. First he wrote to the chairman of the board and then to all the board members. He claimed he was unfairly treated and discriminated against because of his age. Marianne notified the board that his claims were unsubstantiated.

Marianne thought she had rid herself of Norbert, but two years later, Norbert reappeared like a recurring nightmare. She received a letter from the Tulsa EEOC. The letter stated that Norbert was willing to settle if the company gave him his old job back, paid his way back to New Jersey, and provided back pay for the past two years.

"Boy, these folks really must be bored to take this case," Marianne thought. When she called the EEOC officer, she attempted to explain why the case lacked substance, but the officer was intent on pursuing the case.

She realized the officer was an overzealous neophyte and asked to speak to his supervisor. Instead of complying with her request, the officer attempted to flex his muscles by saying, "I'm going to come in there and turn your facility upside down. You'd better take this guy back or else."

"Or else what?" she countered just as strongly.

"You don't know what I can do!" he insisted.

"Have at it, sonny boy," she challenged, "but let me talk to your supervisor."

Once the officer realized his intimidation tactics were ineffective with Marianne, he relinquished his authority. Marianne explained the case to the supervisor, who assured her the whole mess would dry up and blow away.

Now that she was free of Norbert, Marianne began her traditional file-closing ritual, which she reserved only for the most severe cases. She picked up Norbert's personnel file and reached in her desk for her lighter. She struck the flint and placed the flame at an angle, nearly touching the corner of the file. She held the lighter until the heat from the flame left a small scorch mark on the file. Satisfied that she had branded Norbert's file as officially closed, she put her lighter away. Then she leaned back in her chair, took a deep breath, and enjoyed the next few minutes of peace and quiet knowing he was out of her life.

They say that you hire your own problems. Sure enough, here's a sad but all-too-common tale of a poor hire. The company should have structured its hiring process to screen out candidates such as Norbert. Multiple interviews including human resources, peers, subordinates, and supervisors would have undoubtedly revealed Norbert's many flaws. Additionally, an assessment center would have been extremely pertinent to the selection of an inexperienced candidate for a supervisory position.

A careless hiring process can be very expensive for a company, both in absolute dollars and lost productivity. In this case, the worst consequences—possible legal fines if an employee filed discrimination charges—were avoided. Nevertheless, lost productivity, inefficiency, and the time spent by the HR manager to resolve the situation were considerable.

Al's manager in this instance should have penalized Al for failure to follow an appropriate selection process with verification of references before hiring. And, although the human resources department should not be in the business of *policing* managers, perhaps it could provide a hiring checklist for managers as part of the paperwork for establishing employment. This would at least make the manager think about steps that may have been overlooked.

This situation also points out the need for an effective employee complaint procedure that bypasses an immediate supervisor when the supervisor violates the person's human rights. We would hope that this company has a policy guideline on appropriate employee conduct indicating that sexual harassment and other types of harassment, including racial and ethnic slurs, are prohibited. Many large organizations have new employee orientation programs that demonstrate appropriate conduct toward customers as well as employees. Further, a person hired as a manager cannot be expected to just absorb the culture through osmosis, but needs a management orientation as well.

The company's action of terminating Norbert was fully defensible. Additionally, Norbert had no grounds for an age discrimination claim, as demonstrated by the Newark EEOC office's admission of error. Even if there had been grounds, the Tulsa EEOC had no jurisdiction over Norbert's case since the incident occurred in Newark two years earlier. However, the company should have written documentation that clearly outlines the issues in Norbert's termination, so that any third party could get a sense of the problems that occurred during his employment. Terminations without documentation during probationary periods are more suspect than those for which a file has been *built* through progressive discipline.

Nevertheless, Al did receive good advice from Marianne once he brought Norbert's situation to her attention. It was particularly wise to interview the employees before implementing a decision to terminate Norbert. Unfortunately, Marianne's handling of the EEOC was flawed by her indiscreet reference to the overzealous neophyte officer in Tulsa as "sonny boy." Furthermore, she should have requested a second letter from the Tulsa EEOC office withdrawing its request to enter into settlement discussions. Get it in writing!

 The primary issue here is whether Norbert's comments somehow created liability for his employer. The story also illustrates that liability for harassment in the workplace is not limited solely to sexual harassment. Rather, as Norbert unceremoniously demonstrated, it can be found in the form of racial, religious, and age harassment. While one stray racial, religious, or age-related slur will not always rise to the level of harassment, Norbert appeared to be well on his way to creating a harassing "hostile environment" liability for his employer. Norbert was a ticking time bomb. Given enough time, Norbert's bigotry may have exploded with his staff filing harassment charges against him and the company. Fortunately for the employer, Norbert's technical incompetence outshone even his bigotry.

This scenario also highlights the importance of doing reference checks on employees before they are hired and developing procedures to ensure that interviewers actually base their recommendations/decisions on job-related criteria.

A strong cautionary note: it is not good tactics to slur EEOC investigators, or any other investigatory agency. Marianne's "sonny boy" comment will not win her any points and may be, as a matter of law, discriminatory.

Marianne may think her torching ceremony officially closes Norbert's file, but that is not necessarily the case. Employers need to be mindful that each federal fair-employment practice law has its own record-keeping and retention requirements. For example, the Age Discrimination in Employment Act regulations require that employers keep records on employees for a period of three years. Another word of caution: even if the required retention period has passed, *never* destroy personnel records of employees who have filed a charge or lawsuit until after the final disposition of the charge or action. Even then, there may be strong policy considerations in favor of retaining such records indefinitely, for example, to show how similarly situated employees were treated in the same manner or to show that the company has been exonerated of discriminatory allegations.

Chapter 5

Loose Cannons & Exploding Volcanoes

"*As employers we have an obligation to provide employees with a work environment that is free from harassment, intimidation, and physical danger*"

Renee M. Fondacaro
Human Resources Manager
Microsoft Corporation

A Tussle Over Tinkle

Dana flew out of her office in a rage. "Just what is this $500 bill to repaint a wall at the Civic Center all about?" she demanded of her accounts payable supervisor.

"You'll have to talk to Fluke Doogan about that," Pat replied. "He was the supervisor on that job. I don't know the details—something about a scuffle with Dwight Jones. Fluke told me he was going to discuss it with you. Didn't he?"

"No," Dana said angrily.

"Well, I thought he had. It happened a couple months ago, so I pretty much forgot about it. I really wasn't trying to slip something by you," Pat responded sincerely.

"Well, I hope not," Dana huffed. As a small business owner, she signed every check personally and investigated every oddity. If Fluke was trying to buffalo her, she'd have his hide.

"Tell the dispatcher to raise Doogan and Jones on the radio," Dana told Pat. "I want them both in here before they go home tonight."

"Sure, Dana," Pat responded.

Both Fluke Doogan and Dwight Jones showed up in Dana's office as requested. "Sit down, fellows. It seems you've got some explaining to do about a mysterious $500 paint job at the Civic Center. Since when does our work require that we hire painters?" she asked, raising her eyebrows in anticipation of their response.

Dwight deferred to Fluke, since Fluke was his supervisor. "Well, Dana, it really was all a misunderstanding . . . ," Fluke answered. He paused and shifted in his chair.

Dana smirked. "Good, then maybe you can make this bill go away."

"I, uh . . . don't mean about the bill itself," Fluke hedged. "I mean between Dwight and me." He paused again.

"I'm waiting," Dana prompted.

"Well," Fluke continued, "you know how when we're working out on the crew and we have to hook up to a box in the field?"

"Yes," she nodded in encouragement for him to explain.

"You see, when . . ." Fluke paused to clear his throat. "When it isn't convenient for us to get to a john, we usually just open a truck door and use it as a screen so we can take a leak out in the field. But Dwight, here, doesn't like to do it that way, I guess."

Dana sighed to herself, thinking, "Great. It's not enough I had to help my daughter toilet train my grandson, now I get to listen to tinkle talk from two grown men on the fine art of roadside watering."

"So on the day we had the Civic Center job," Fluke proceeded, "Dwight whizzed into an empty paint can and then set the can in the back of the truck."

Dana let out a deep sigh of exasperation. "Fluke, do you think you can give me the *Reader's Digest* version here? I'm losing patience," she interrupted.

"I'm getting there, Dana, trust me."

"I hope so," she responded impatiently.

"Okay, so when we took off, I didn't know that the can of pee fell over and spilled on my jacket," Fluke explained. "You see, my jacket was in the back of the truck along with some other gear. Then, when we got to the job site, I picked up my jacket and it was all wet. So I said, 'How the hell did my jacket get all wet?' That's when one of the other boys told me about Dwight whizzing in the can."

"So naturally I was pretty hot at him for being so stupid," Fluke continued, "and I went lookin' for him inside the Center. When I found him I kind of lost it and started callin' him a dumb ass and a few other things. Well, then he got mad and grabbed his crotch and said, 'Yo' mama!' And that's when all hell broke loose. You see, Dana, at the time Dwight didn't know it, but my mother had died just three weeks before. So I hauled off and smacked him upside the head," Fluke confessed.

"This happened in public? In the Civic Center?" Dana's eyes widened.

"Well, yes," Fluke admitted, sheepishly looking at the floor.

"So why did they have to paint the wall?" she asked. "I don't understand."

"Because of all the blood," said Fluke. "You see, after I hit him, he came back swingin' and bloodied my nose. Well, I couldn't have that, so I split his lip. Then we were down on the floor rolling along this hall that had a big white wall. Fortunately, the other boys broke us apart by the time the Civic Center security people got there. We explained it was a misunderstanding and told them to send us the bill to repaint the wall."

"And you expect me to pay for it?"

"I was going to tell you sooner, Dana, but that happened on a Friday, and then we got that emergency call on Sunday, so me and my crew all trucked down to South Carolina and ended up staying there for three weeks. So we didn't see you. I got involved in solving the problem and just kind of forgot about the Civic Center mess. I'm sorry; it wasn't on purpose," Fluke apologized.

Dana was in a quandary. She never condoned fighting, but Fluke and Dwight were two of her best men, and training their replacements could take months. Normally she'd either fire them or at least suspend them without pay for three days, depending on the case. However, the company was so swamped with work, she couldn't afford to have them off for even a day of suspension. On the other hand, she couldn't let them off scot-free either. As a woman running a small construction business, she had an image to maintain. Her mind raced for a solution.

They all sat silently for a few moments. She wanted to make them squirm and worry that they might get suspended or fired. "Do you guys intend to settle your future disagreements by bashing each other's heads in?" she needled.

Both shook their heads no.

"Well, I'm glad to hear that, because you know I won't tolerate fighting. So consider this a formal reprimand. If anything like this ever happens again and either of you is involved, you're gone, do you understand?" she admonished.

They both nodded.

"Now that that's resolved, let's talk about the bill. How do you want to settle it?" Dana asked.

"How about payroll deduction—say $25 a paycheck from each of us?" Fluke suggested. "That would be about $50 a month. Is that okay with you, Dwight?"

"That's fair," Dwight agreed.

"What do you think, Dana?" Fluke asked.

"Done. I'll have payroll prepare the papers for you to sign tomorrow," she said, smiling. Dana stood up from her desk, walked her employees to the door, and shook their hands as they left.

She returned to her desk, inhaled deeply, and sighed, "I wish they were all this easy."

When you make bad decisions, they *are* this easy. It appears that Dana gave Fluke and Dwight a mixed message. Although she would normally fire or suspend them for fighting, instead, she simply gave them a verbal rap on the knuckles. While she threatened dismissal if it happened again, her departure from normal practice probably left her employees somewhat confused about where she really stands. It appears her view of fighting varies depending on other factors, such as how busy the company is at the time and how she perceives the employees' work performance.

Rather than having her mind race for a solution, we think Dana had other options. Perhaps it would have been better for Dana to tell the employees that she would like to give the matter some thought and arrange a follow-up meeting with them. This approach would give her some time to consider other alternatives. For example, she could decide to follow her normal practice and impose three-day suspensions without pay. However, she also had the option to advise Dwight and Fluke that they would serve their suspension later because of the current work volumes. This would have allowed her to schedule the suspensions to minimize negative impact on company productivity.

A few of us believe that termination was appropriate action, while most of us support a suspension as the minimum penalty. However, some of us do not support the use of a suspension *without pay* to discipline an employee. This practice tends to create ill will because of its severity. We prefer a non-punitive approach to dealing with workplace problems. We suggest using a three-tiered system. This consists of a verbal warning, written warning, and final written warning, coupled with a brief decision-making leave (paid suspension) to reinforce the seriousness of the situation. Had this type of procedure been in place in Dana's company, the situation would have been easier to deal with in a consistent manner.

Most of us believe that Dana had the right to demand full financial restitution for the repainting of the wall. However, we question the legality of her use of payroll deduction. She should have arranged other forms of repayment.

Needless to say, fighting has no place in the workplace. One of the legal issues illustrated in this story is the potential liability that an employer may face for injuries that employees may inflict upon each other—for example, workers' compensation liability. Although it appears that neither of the employees filed an accident report regarding their injuries, the employer is still on "constructive notice" that injuries have occurred on the job (i.e., the employees are telling their manager about the fight and the injuries that they received). Depending upon state law, it is also possible that if one of these employees harms or injures another employee in the future, or some non-employee who happens to be at one of the public worksites, the employer may be liable for "negligent retention" because the employer knew the employee had a propensity for violence.

Dana should memorialize her "last chance" agreement with Fluke and Dwight in the form of written documents which each man should sign, acknowledging that he understands that any further such conduct is grounds for dismissal. In the event that either man is terminated in the future for fighting, the employer will have documentary defense minimizing its legal exposure against possible claims.

As we discussed in *Lien On Me*, employers should seek the advice of legal counsel before they attempt to make deductions from employees' wages that are not related to mandatory payroll withholdings, etc. Most states with wage deduction laws prohibit employers from making deductions from an employee's wages to pay off the employee's debt to the company. But remember, an agreement to repay on a weekly basis is not the same as a deduction from a paycheck. The former is legal; the latter is probably not.

Deadbeat Dad

"Gordon," Maxine said nervously over the intercom, "the Wichita police are here. They have a warrant."

"A warrant? For who?" Gordon asked.

"The officer didn't say. He just said he wanted to talk to you about one of our employees," she answered.

"Great," Gordon thought. "I just love surprises."

He pressed the intercom button. "Maxine, find out who the warrant is for and pull the employee's file. Tell the officers I'll be right with them."

"Okay," Maxine said.

Gordon drummed his fingers on the desk as he waited for Maxine. His day was jammed with meetings. He had scheduled two presentations to roll out a new employee benefits program. The first one began in less than two hours, and he still had to attend to some last-minute details. Now this.

Maxine walked in with the file. "Officers Cranston and Miljus want to see Hank Risen. Here's the warrant. Apparently Hank's quite a bit behind on his child support," she said, waiting for further direction.

As Gordon flipped through Hank Risen's file, he noticed Hank had joined the company about four years ago. He had a vague recollection of hiring Hank as a graphic artist, but nothing stood out.

"Hmmm . . . ," Gordon mused, "Hank's performance reviews are satisfactory. No attendance problems. Seems pretty much like 'Joe Average.' Maybe this won't be such a big deal."

"Maxine, tell Officers Cranston and Miljus to come in."

Officer Cranston entered the room. He held his cap under his left arm as he extended his right to greet Gordon, and he then introduced his partner, Officer Miljus. Both men were in their mid-to-late 20s.

"Sorry to have to disturb you, sir," Officer Cranston said, "but we've been looking for Hank Risen for three years. He's been ducking us."

"Three years?" Gordon questioned. "But he's been here all along."

"I don't know why we lost him; we just did. Someone screwed up our computer records on his file. But he's behind three years on child support, and we have to take him down to county jail."

Gordon had never received a visit from the police before and wanted to cooperate. "Okay, I don't see that you should have any problem. But let me get our chief of security, Mark Kello, and another guard to meet us. I'll escort you to the floor, and we'll assist. I'll also need to give Hank's manager a call to let her know we're coming."

Gordon punched in Mark Kello's extension. "Mark, I have some officers here with a warrant to pick up Hank Risen for nonpayment of child support. Could you and one of your guards meet us at the fifth floor elevators, say in about 10 minutes?"

"Sure, I'll bring Norton with me," replied Mark.

Gordon then called Janet Marx, Hank's manager. "Janet, we need your help. I'm going to be arriving with some police officers . . . ."

"Police officers!" she interrupted. "What for?"

"It's not that big of a deal, Janet. It seems that Hank Risen is behind in his child support, and they need to take him to county jail."

"Oh, dear," Janet sighed. "Do you have to come up here? That could be very embarrassing for him, he's such a shy guy anyway."

Gordon thought a moment. Showing up on the floor could be embarrassing, but they might have to trump up a story to get Hank downstairs. Gordon didn't like the idea of fabricating a story. And if Janet told Hank the truth, Hank might try to give them the slip.

"I realize it could be embarrassing, Janet, but we don't have very much choice here. We have to comply with the warrant. I'm also sending Mark Kello and Norton along. Plus, I'll be there to make sure everything goes okay."

"I don't like this, Gordon," she replied. "It's going to upset everyone else on the floor and humiliate Hank. How do you think he'll feel when he has to return to work? Look, I could understand if we were dealing with an ax murderer or a rapist."

"Trust me, Janet, we'll be in and out of there in a flash. No one will even notice," Gordon assured her.

"Oh, right . . . two armed officers and security guards. Why don't you just call in the SWAT team while you're at it?" Janet snapped.

"Look, Janet, please cooperate. We'll be up in five minutes."

Gordon hung up the phone, grabbed his file, and walked out of the office with Officers Cranston and Miljus. As they rode up the elevator to the fifth floor, Officer Cranston nervously stroked his nightstick. Gordon noticed and started to get an uneasy feeling in his stomach.

"Are you concerned about this at all?" Gordon asked.

"Not really," Officer Cranston responded. "We do this all the time. These guys are generally angry that they got caught, and they may grouse a bit, but mostly they're pretty cooperative. Usually they're so embarrassed in front of their co-workers, they don't want to create a scene. It kind of works to our advantage in that case," Cranston chuckled.

Gordon didn't find Officer Cranston's humor very comforting. He was beginning to have second thoughts, when the elevator doors opened. As they walked off they were greeted by Mark Kello, chief of security, and his assistant, Norton. Gordon made some perfunctory introductions and the group strolled down the long hall to the graphics department.

The graphics department was a large room filled with computers and printers. All the artists were deeply involved with their projects. All were transfixed to their screens as they clicked their respective "mice" and busily worked on their assignments. Janet, Hank's manager, was pacing outside the door of the department.

"Look, I don't want you guys coming onto the floor. I think it looks bad. Can't you wait out here in the hallway, and let me ask Hank to come out here?" Janet implored.

Gordon considered this as he reflected on Officer Cranston's comment. He really didn't want to humiliate Hank. "Maybe you're right, Janet. Go ahead and ask him to join us in the hall."

Janet walked up to Hank. Hank was a wiry guy who kept pretty much to himself. He exercised in the fitness center every day at noon but he didn't socialize with the others.

Hank was deep in thought. Janet quietly approached and cleared her throat. "Excuse me, Hank, can I see you for a moment?"

Hank's eyes were glued to his screen. "Sure, Jan, but can it wait about 15 secs? I just need to save this file and send it to the printer," Hank responded.

"Fine, I'll wait for you out in the hall," she smiled.

"The hall?" Hank asked, looking up from his screen. "Why the hall?"

"Gordon from human resources needs to see you, and he's waiting in the hall."

"What does he want?"

Janet started to get uncomfortable. "I'm . . . I'm not exactly sure, Hank . . . Look, just save your file and meet me outside in the hall," she said hurriedly.

"I'm blowing it," Janet thought. She felt sick. She had never misled her staff. They knew her as a straight shooter, and she knew that Hank must have found her behavior out of character. She held her breath as she started to walk toward the door to the hall.

Hank was on her heels and she could feel his breath behind her. When they reached the hall, Hank spotted the officers. Before Janet could turn around to explain, Hank demanded, "Hey, what's this all about?"

"Mr. Risen?" Officer Cranston queried.

"Yeah, I'm Risen," Hank spewed.

"Mr. Risen, I have a warrant for your arrest for nonpayment of child support. Could you please face the wall, sir; we're going to need to place you in handcuffs and then take you to the county jail," Officer Cranston politely explained.

"No way! Who the hell does my ex-wife think she is, sending me to jail!" Hank fumed.

"Please calm down, Mr. Risen. I'm sure you can work this out with your attorney."

"Work this out with my attorney?! Who has money for an attorney after that bloodsucking vampire squeezes you for every dime. Stay away from me," Hank yelled, pushing Officer Cranston away.

Officer Miljus reached for his nightstick, but Hank lunged forward and let out a howl. Before Miljus could do anything, Hank spun around, and with a snapping kick, he split the officer's leg in two.

Officer Miljus, wrenching in pain, fell to the ground as Hank ran back into the department, closely pursued by Officer Cranston and the security guards.

Gordon's heart raced as he ran to the phone and called 911. "I have an officer hurt. One of our employees here just broke the officer's leg. Please send paramedics and backup quickly to the Banger Building, fifth floor."

"Is your employee armed, sir?" the 911 operator asked.

"No, but he must know karate, and they can't get him to calm down," Gordon said, craning to keep his eye on the chase.

"Is there anyone else with you?"

"Our internal security guards and one of your officers, Officer Cranston," Gordon responded.

"Don't worry, sir, backup and the paramedics are on their way," the 911 operator assured him.

The security guards and Officer Cranston chased Hank into the department. Hank's co-workers sat stunned as they watched Hank run into a small glassed-in office as the officers followed him. Cornered, Hank did what he knew best and applied his black belt techniques on the chief of security, throwing him through the door and onto a co-worker's desk. Norton realized he was ill-equipped to deal with Hank's physical abilities, and ran to help the chief. Officer Cranston tried to restrain Hank with his nightstick, but Hank kicked it out of his hand.

Moments later several other police officers arrived and charged forcefully toward Hank with nightsticks poised. Hank's co-workers stared in horror. They watched the four police officers wrestle with Hank and blast thunderous blows with their clubs to finally contain him. Exhausted and defeated, Hank dropped to his knees, covered his head with his hands, and finally fell to the floor.

They cuffed his hands and shackled his feet, dragging him out of the building as Janet, Gordon, and the others stood in disbelief. Meanwhile, the paramedics worked on Officer Miljus's shattered leg and rolled him out on a gurney. Mark Kello only suffered minor bruises.

After Hank was taken out and the paramedics left, Janet told her staff to take an early lunch. Gordon raced down to his office and told Maxine to cancel his benefits presentations.

Still shaking, he called corporate counsel, John Essex, and spilled the story. John advised Gordon to immediately arrange for security to clean out Hank's desk and send Hank's belongings to his home. Then John provided verbiage for a letter to Hank, telling him that he was being terminated for fighting.

Gordon took detailed notes and complied with John's counsel. Although the company never heard from Hank again, his co-workers, Janet, and Gordon were deeply affected. Over time, each of them left the company and tried to forget the events of that day.

Gordon was *too* eager to cooperate with the police and allowed the situation to escalate into a major confrontation. We like to cooperate—but it is not the HR manager's responsibility to assist in the law enforcement process. There was no reason for Gordon or the security force to be active in the arrest, nor for Gordon to reveal the specific reason for the warrant to Hank's supervisor.

In general, we believe that a company should take no action that has the potential of disrupting the workplace or worker productivity, even if it means saying "no" to an outside agency. Gordon's imprudent decision exposed other employees to potential harm. Gordon should have given the police Hank's schedule and suggested they try to serve the warrant away from work. If for some reason that was not possible, Gordon should have contacted legal or security to make sure the warrant was legitimate. Next, he should have met with Hank one-on-one and given him a chance to explain his side of the story. Afterward, Gordon could bring in the police officers. They would indicate that Hank had violated the local laws regarding child support, handcuff him, and take him away discreetly. In this way Hank could have maintained his dignity and probably his job.

The attrition of Hank's work group following his departure makes it clear that there was a need for post-trauma counseling to put Hank's situation in proper perspective. The employees' early dismissal for lunch was a poor decision. Both Gordon and Janet as well as the others in the work unit might have benefited from group and/or individual counseling immediately after the event. We give Gordon an F on this one.

 This story illustrates today's ever-increasing dilemma facing employers: employees' personal problems spilling over into the workplace.

Generally, employers are not required by law to permit police bearing arrest warrants to enter the employer's premises in order to reach employees. The fiasco that ensued after Gordon and the police approached Hank as if he were one of *America's Ten Most Wanted* illustrates one reason why an employer should not mix business with police action.

We advise clients to have a policy in place to address this type of situation before it happens. Here, the company was fortunate that the police came to the human resources department rather than going straight to the department head.

Employers need to avoid appearing to be an "agent" of the police or the government or they may be held liable as "government actors." For example, normally, a private employer could not be implicated for an individual's false arrest, but if the employer participated closely with the police on its premises and provided security guard backup, it is possible that the employer could be implicated in a false-arrest situation.

Employers should be mindful of the distinction between arrest warrants and search warrants. If police arrive on the employer's premises with a search warrant, check with legal counsel. Most likely you will be required to cooperate with a valid search warrant.

However, if an employer wishes to be a "good citizen" and permit police with warrants on its premises, it certainly can be done in a much calmer and more private way. From a privacy standpoint, Gordon broke the general rule of thumb: private and confidential information about one's employees should only be disclosed on a need-to-know basis—otherwise the company may be setting itself up for an invasion of privacy claim.

Gordon called corporate counsel too late. A word to the wise: no human resources official ever got into trouble for seeking legal advice up front; many have by delaying.

Beware of Flying Objects

Logan was particularly preoccupied that morning when he walked into his office at 7:30 a.m. There was a noon deadline for a payroll report, and he wanted to get an early start to check some figures before authorizing the computer run. When he entered his office, he never noticed Tanesia Martin and her supervisor, Charlotte James, sitting at the small, round conference table on the left. Instead he turned right, headed toward his desk, and began to slip off his jacket.

"Ahem," Charlotte coughed politely to let Logan know that she and Tanesia were present. "Excuse me, Logan."

Startled, Logan wheeled around, knocking over the coat tree as he tried to regain his balance. "Oh, gosh, Charlotte, it's you. I was so deep in thought, I didn't even see anyone sitting there."

"I'm sorry, Logan. I wasn't planning to ambush you," she smiled, and then took a serious tone. "We have a problem."

"What's up?" Logan asked, as he leaned over to pick up the coat tree and hang up his jacket.

"Logan, this is Tanesia Martin, a member of the assembly team," Charlotte said.

Logan walked over and extended his hand to Tanesia. "Hello, Tanesia," he greeted her as they shook hands. Then Logan pulled out a chair from the table and joined them.

"We had an incident this morning in the cafeteria," Charlotte began. "Tanesia claims her ex-boyfriend tried to assault her with an ashtray."

Logan surveyed Tanesia. She didn't appear to have any bruises. "Tell me what happened, Tanesia," he said.

"Well, I used to date Adam Franklin, who works out in shipping," Tanesia responded. "We went out together for about six months. Then I decided I wasn't interested anymore and told him we should stop seeing each other. He seemed okay about it, but last night when he found out I went out with someone else, he sort of lost it."

"Lost it? How? What exactly happened?"

"Well, usually Adam is pretty reasonable, but when he saw me in the cafeteria, he started yelling and screaming at me. I think he must've been drinking or something."

"What did he say?"

"He said, 'How could you do this to me? How could you humiliate me like this? Why don't you just rub my face in it? Of all the people to go out with, why did you have to pick a damn white boy?'" As Tanesia spoke, her eyes began to moisten. "But I wouldn't look up from my coffee, I was just so embarrassed. Everyone heard him. It was awful," she flushed.

"Then, because I wouldn't look at him," Tanesia continued, "he got so mad, he sent this ashtray whizzing right past my face. He only missed me by this much," she cried, lifting her hand to show about a quarter-inch distance between her thumb and index finger. "He could have put my eye out or knocked me unconscious!"

"I'm sorry this happened to you, Tanesia," Logan responded sympathetically. "Who else was present in the cafetcria?"

Tanesia gave him a list of other individuals, and he wrote down all their names. "How large a man is Adam?" Logan asked next, attempting to "size up" the extent of the problem.

"Just medium height and weight," Tanesia responded.

Logan relaxed slightly. "Do you want to press charges?"

"No, I just don't ever want him to humiliate or hurt me," Tanesia said. "I'm afraid."

"We'll make sure you feel safe in the plant," Logan assured her and asked her if she wanted to go home. Tanesia declined the offer and returned to work. Logan promised to investigate the matter.

Logan immediatcly pulled Adam's file and then called Matt Johnson, the shipping department supervisor, and briefed him on the cafeteria incident.

"I can't believe Adam would do something like that, it's totally out of character," Matt informed Logan. "Adam has always been a terrific employee with a positive attitude. Look, I've known him for five years, and we've got a good relationship—let me talk with him first and see what I can find out. I'll get right back to you once I can get to the bottom of things."

Matt invited Adam to his office for a private conversation. He could tell by Adam's behavior and the strong smell of alcohol that Adam had been drinking. Matt got right to the point. "I just got a disturbing call from the human resources department about an incident in the cafeteria. Do you want to tell me about it?"

"I'm sorry, Matt, I just lost my head. I was so upset about Tanesia going out with someone else that I started drinking last night and never went home. Before I knew it, it was dawn, so I just came to work. When I saw her at breakfast, I was just so hurt that I couldn't stand it and blew my cool. I know what I did was wrong," Adam said, looking at the floor.

"I understand how you must have felt, but I can't condone your actions," Matt said. "Right now, however, I think it's best that you leave the plant and get some rest. We'll arrange for a cab to drive you home safely. Then I'd like you to get some sleep and sober up. I'll need to call human resources and take care of the particulars. Are you comfortable with that?"

"Yes, I guess so," Adam said quietly. "I really am sorry, Matt. Am I going to lose my job?"

"I don't know the answer to that right now. It's not completely my decision. Let's just take things one step at a time," Matt said calmly.

Matt called Logan and told him that Adam admitted to the incident and may still be intoxicated. Logan arranged for a cab and met with Matt and a security officer to escort Adam discreetly out of the building. After a full investigation, Matt and Logan agreed to suspend Adam without pay for five days. Adam willingly accepted the consequences of his actions and returned to work without further incident.

Obviously, the organization's policies and past practices directed Logan's handling of this case. Nevertheless, being drunk or violent are conditions rarely accepted by most companies. Regardless of the outside issues that precipitated the incident, Logan should treat Adam's behavior as a workplace action for which he is fully accountable.

A few of us contend that suspension without pay was acceptable because this was Adam's first offense. We would, however, have also required him to undergo any treatment and follow-up counseling recommended by the employee assistance program.

Conversely, most of us feel that Logan was too lenient. To permit this type of incident to occur without severe penalties limits the company's ability to maintain control of conduct in its work environment and sets a bad precedent. The next drunk employee who throws an ashtray might not be a "good guy." What does the company plan to do about him or her?

Adam freely admitted throwing the ashtray at Tanesia. He also acknowledged that his conduct was wrong and very dangerous. Furthermore, he confessed to drinking the evening prior and appeared intoxicated during his meeting with his supervisor, which raises another issue. Logan should have considered getting a measurement of Adam's blood alcohol content (BAC) immediately as an extra precaution. This action would prove whether or not Adam was truly intoxicated and, if so, would prevent him from denying it later. We would expect that a BAC would be allowable because there was strong reason to believe (i.e., his confession) that he was drunk.

Rather than immediate suspension without pay, we recommend that Logan should have sent Adam home, with pay, until the investigation was completed. This would include interviewing all reliable witnesses. These procedures would have allowed Logan time to make a careful decision about the appropriate disciplinary action. We applaud Logan's decision to send Adam home in a taxi. Even if the fare was $100, it would have been a potentially tragic mistake to let Adam drive and possibly hurt himself or someone else. This was a small investment with a big payoff.

The case states that there were no further incidents between Adam and Tanesia, but there could have been. If Tanesia were injured, that could leave the company vulnerable to a negligent retention claim since they were aware of Adam's propensity for violence. (See legal comments in *A Tussle Over Tinkle*.)

We would also have followed up with Tanesia to make sure she felt safe. As employers, we have an obligation to provide employees with a work environment that is free from harassment, intimidation, and physical danger. We don't believe the company fully met its obligation in this case.

 This story highlights two troublesome problems that employers are faced with today: workplace violence and alcohol impairment on the job.

By all reports, workplace violence is on the rise—domestic and romantic relationship problems are spilling over into the workplace, disgruntled and distraught employees who have lost a job or promotion are seeking revenge on managers and co-employees, and that's just to name a few. One first step that employers can take is to conduct reference checks and criminal conviction records on applicants being considered for employment. Moreover, employers need to establish policies and procedures for disciplinary action, up to and including discharge from employment, to deal with violent conduct on the job.

Violent outbursts on the job may raise issues under the Americans with Disabilities Act. A person may be suffering from an emotional or mental impairment that manifests itself in violent outbursts—thus, such an individual may be disabled under the ADA and an employer's treatment of that individual must be responsive to ADA requirements. However, personality traits such as poor judgment, a quick temper, or irresponsible behavior are not considered impairments under the ADA. Likewise, if an individual is suffering from general stress because of his or her job or personal life, he or she will generally not be considered to have an emotional or mental impairment under the ADA.

Based on the information provided about Adam, it would appear that he does not meet the definition of mentally impaired under the ADA. And, although there is no indication that Adam is an alcoholic, this story warrants a brief discussion on another ADA issue: alcoholism.

While an employee (or an applicant) who is currently engaging in the illegal use of drugs is *not* disabled under the ADA, a current *alcoholic* is a person with a disability under the ADA. However, the ADA does not require that an employer excuse an alcoholic's behavior nor entitle the alcoholic to less stringent work rules. Nor does the ADA prohibit employers from establishing policies requiring employees not to be under the influence of alcohol (or illegal drugs) while at work. Thus, if a company has such a policy, it would not be unlawful under the ADA to take disciplinary action against an individual who was drunk on the job, even if that individual was an alcoholic. Such disciplinary action would be based on the employee's conduct and not on the basis of his or her disability. Moreover, an alcoholic person who cannot perform his or her job duties or whose employment presents a threat to the health or safety of others is *not* protected under the ADA.

However, because alcoholism is a disability under the ADA, an alcoholic may be entitled to an accommodation if he or she is qualified to perform the essential functions of a job; for example, allowing the employee to leave work early two days a week to attend AA meetings where the time can be made up on other days or providing the employee with a leave of absence to obtain treatment.

Chapter 6

Pests, Brutes & Bullies

"Raising awareness to issues of harassment and discrimination is the responsibility of all human resources professionals."

Ruth N. Bramson
Vice President of Human Resources and Administration
Charles River Laboratories
(A Bausch & Lomb Company)

Shower Power

Angeline's honey-blond hair bounced as she breezed through the revolving door of the downtown Westin Hotel. Its peach-marbled floors lining the lobby and dazzling chandeliers soaring overhead were impressive. "I'm sure glad I don't have to dust those monstrosities," she chuckled as she gazed at the sparkling fixtures.

Angeline searched for the ladies' room and located one near the house phones. "Need to check for last minute touch-ups," she thought. "After all, this is one of the top cosmetic companies; everything has to look perfect—I can't afford to blow this interview on something as silly as a run in my hose."

She gave herself a once-over glance. Her navy designer suit was perfectly tailored, falling just above the knee. Her hose were intact, her blouse lay flat, and her hair was in place. A last-minute check for lipstick on her teeth revealed a slight smudge on her left front tooth. "Whoops! Sure glad I caught that," she thought, quickly wiping away the excess color.

She walked out of the ladies' room toward the bank of house phones. Lifting the receiver, Angeline asked the operator to connect her with Jim McReardon. As the phone rang, her heart beat with anticipation.

"Jim McReardon," a voice answered.

"Hello, this is Angeline Lawrence. I'm here for my 9 o'clock interview. Where would you like me to meet you?"

"Oh, hello, Angeline," Jim's friendly voice responded. "Please come up to the suite. I have coffee waiting and I'm all ready to get started. It's room 1302."

"I'll be right up," Angeline chirped.

Angeline currently worked for a competitor, but she felt her opportunities were limited. The ad for this position sounded promising, and she was eager to interview.

Jim greeted her with a warm handshake and offered her a chair. The suite was surprisingly formal. The furnishings were traditional mahogany, and Jim seated her at a table with Queen Anne chairs.

Hotel interviews were generally uncomfortable for Angeline. But somehow, the formality of the suite made the environment seem more like an office. She subtly breathed a sigh of relief.

Jim skillfully engaged her in small talk to put her at ease and then reviewed her resume in detail. He asked her about her current employer and why she wanted to leave. She was impressed with how thoroughly he covered her background and how knowledgeable he was about her company. Next he focused on her selling skills.

"Tell me, Angeline, you've been selling cosmetics for a while now. How would you persuade a customer to buy our soaps and bath oils?"

Angeline thought for a moment. "Well, since the soaps and oils complement your perfumes," she said, "I would point out how they help provide a consistent fragrance and sustain your cologne or perfume throughout the day."

"And how would you tell them to use the soaps and lotions, Angeline?" Jim asked, coaxing her on with a raised eyebrow and a smile.

"I would tell them to prepare their bath water with the bath oil and use the soap for bathing. When they're through bathing, towel off and generously apply the body lotion. Finally, spray on their cologne," Angeline responded.

Jim looked disappointed. "Angeline, it sounds like you're selling me a vacuum cleaner, not hopes and dreams. Remember, these women want to feel romance in their lives. Our product offers romance, not just cleanliness and *smell goods*. Tell me specifically, how do you bathe?"

"How do *I* bathe?" she asked, slightly clearing her throat and stalling for time. She was hardly prepared for such a personal question.

"Yes, walk me through the motions," Jim encouraged her.

"Well, I um . . . fill up the tub with bubbling bath oil, and I soak for a few minutes and relax. Next, I soap up a washcloth and wash my body," she replied, trying to remain matter-of-fact.

"Do you lift your breasts to make sure you get underneath?" Jim asked in an equally matter-of-fact tone.

"*What?*" she asked, flushing slightly.

"You know that you perspire there. It's important to cleanse that area," he advised.

Angeline was speechless. She sat glued to her chair, trying to get a fix on the situation. "What's with this guy?" she thought, looking around for a hidden camera. "This can't be for real, I must be on *Candid Camera.*"

Jim broke the silence. "Perhaps you're having a difficult time explaining it in words. Let me show you one of our newest products. It's designed to give women an allover glow when they don't have the time to take a full bath. It's called *Shower Power*. Perhaps I could demonstrate the product for you. We could take a shower together, and I could show you how to wash all those delicate areas. Then you'd have a real understanding of the beauty of our product. Would you like a demonstration?" Jim asked earnestly.

Angeline was dumbfounded. She kept looking around the room for some clue that she was having a dream—that he wasn't really asking her these questions or suggesting they shower together. She wanted to race out of the room as fast as she could, but she felt immobilized. She kept telling herself that this wasn't real, that any moment she would wake up from this nightmare.

Finally, Angeline realized she had to do something fast so she could escape gracefully. "Gee, Jim, I don't think I can fit it into my schedule. My husband is waiting for me downstairs and I'm expected at the office in an hour," she lied. "What I would like, however, is your card, and then we can pursue discussions at a later time. How long are you going to be in town?"

"For two more days," Jim answered.

"Oh, that's too bad, I'm scheduled to be out of town the next five days. But do give me your card. I'd like to stay in touch," she said, using all her resources to hold herself together and remain calm.

Angeline remained composed, thanked him for the interview, and slowly walked to the elevator as Jim stood at the door and waved farewell as though their exchange had been perfectly normal. It seemed like an eternity before Angeline reached the lobby floor. When the doors opened, she raced for the ladies' room. Once inside, she grabbed the cool porcelain of the sink and stared at her crimson, angry expression. Her image began to fade as the steam from her cheeks clouded her glasses. She felt humiliated and angry. To clear her thoughts, she splashed cool water on her wrists and cheeks.

Angeline left the ladies' room and headed for the nearest pay phone. She fished out Jim's business card from her purse and called the corporate number listed on the card.

"Please connect me with your vice president of human resources. It's an emergency," she instructed the operator.

The operator connected Angeline to Doreen Brown. As soon as Doreen answered, Angeline hurled out her story without taking a breath. Doreen's teeth clenched and her body stiffened as she listened intently.

She knew the sales force was a fun-loving group, but this behavior was preposterous. Doreen assured Angeline that the company did not condone Jim's behavior. Then, she told Angeline that she would investigate her claim and inform her of the resolution.

Doreen immediately contacted Jim's boss, the vice president of sales, Skip Carrouthers. She told him that Jim was conducting some questionable interviewing activities and asked for a list of all Jim's direct reports and his schedule of interviews that week. Skip was shocked; he had been unaware of Jim's activities.

When Doreen talked to several women Jim had hired recently, they all confirmed Jim's bizarre interview tactics. Many repeated the statement he made about selling romance, while others said he told them they were selling lust and love. None of them actually took Jim up on his offer to demonstrate the product. However, they gave various accounts of his intimate line of questioning regarding their bathing techniques, followed by graphically lurid discussions. All the interviews revealed variations on the same sexually offensive theme. Each woman managed to keep Jim at bay during the interview. Once they got their jobs and started producing sales, they no longer had contact with him.

Doreen discussed her findings with Skip and then interviewed Jim to hear his side of the story. When Skip brought Jim to Doreen's office, she got right to the point.

"Jim, it's come to our attention that your interviewing techniques are rather unconventional. Several interviewees have reported that you asked them sexually intimate questions and requested they take a shower with you. Is that true?"

"What's wrong with asking the applicant to take a shower together so I can demonstrate the proper use and application of our soap bar?" he asked, smirking and winking at Skip.

Jim's flippancy infuriated Doreen. "I get the impression that you think this is a joke. It's not a joke. First of all, it's against the law. Secondly, it's immoral. The company does not condone this behavior. We are selling a soap product to cleanse the body. We are not selling *your* sexual fantasies," she said evenly.

"Well, don't you believe in learning by doing?" Jim sneered.

Doreen felt a compelling desire to leap across the desk and dig her newly manicured nails deeply into his throat as she throttled him into a lifeless state. Fortunately, her professional training restrained her. "There is nowhere in any training manual that even remotely suggests this type of demonstration is acceptable. Furthermore, you have never heard any executive in the company suggest that you indulge in this type of interviewing. It was totally inappropriate and well beyond the range of normal business behavior. Your actions have placed the company in serious jeopardy for a sexual harassment lawsuit. We will not tolerate your behavior. You are out the door as of today. We will not capitulate on this. You should have known better," she replied, rising from her seat. "Skip will arrange for your personal belongings to be sent to your home, and your final paycheck is ready now."

After Jim and Skip departed, Doreen contacted Angeline and informed her that Jim was no longer with the company. She explained that Jim's behavior was not typical and asked her if she would consider another interview with Jim's replacement. This time the company would fly her to corporate headquarters for a formal interview. Angeline agreed and eventually was hired.

Doreen was superb. She responded promptly and took the complaint seriously. The first thing she did was contact Jim's boss, but she retained control of the investigation. Our only criticism of her action was her characterization of Jim's behavior as immoral. Revealing that type of bias muddies the waters and could come back to haunt her. However, we fully support her decision to terminate Jim. (We suspect Jim was out of the country during the Clarence Thomas hearings, missed his sexual harassment training, or just doesn't get it.)

We were also pleased that Doreen followed up promptly with Angeline. Calling Angeline to let her know of the corrective measures taken and inviting her to engage in a legitimate interview was a good decision. Angeline may be less likely to take further steps against the company knowing that they have sound policies and practices.

This incident points out that the company probably should have done a better job communicating its sexual harassment and proper conduct policy guidelines. Training the company's managers on both sexual harassment and interviewing techniques should have prevented Jim's offensive interviewing style. The company was fortunate it did not face legal action from the current or past episodes. Employers are generally responsible for sexually harassing behavior whether they are aware of it or not.

The company should protect itself in the future by changing its interviewing practices. The least expensive way would be to mandate that interviews be held in public places, such as hotel lobby areas or restaurants. Alternatively, the company could arrange to have at least two members of corporate staff participate in each interview. Another option is to conduct initial interviews over the telephone and then invite truly viable candidates to corporate headquarters for a final interview.

 This story emphasizes why we counsel our clients to develop sexual harassment training for their managers and employees. With all the recent press about sexual harassment, many managers and employees are concerned about what is appropriate or inappropriate behavior between the sexes on the job.

Doreen acted appropriately in this situation. Once a complaint of sexual harassment has been made, an employer should investigate the allegation by interviewing the alleged victim, the alleged harasser's supervisor, other persons who may have knowledge of the harassment, and the alleged harasser. Under the circumstances, considering Jim's conduct and attitude, terminating Jim seemed to be the sensible thing to do. While there is no legal requirement to do so, it makes practical sense to communicate the result of the investigation to the complainant. Such feedback signals to the complainant that the company takes the complaint seriously and is doing something about it. It gives the company some credibility and often decreases the possibility that an unhappy or distraught employee will take his or her complaint to an outside agency. Doreen also diffused the situation by giving Angeline another opportunity to interview for the sales position—this time not in a hotel room.

Sexual harassment is not confined to the classic *quid pro quo* "sleep with me if you want the job or if you want the promotion." As in this scenario, sexual harassment, in the form of unwelcome, pervasive sexual and lewd comments, may take place during an interview with an applicant. That some of the women who were subjected to Jim's interviewing ritual were in fact hired and not subjected to any other harassment does not diminish the unlawfulness of his actions or the employer's risk of liability.

Sexual harassment may occur even though a complaining individual did not lose any tangible job benefits.

In addition to liability under federal law, employers may also be subject to liability for sexual harassment under state laws—with the state laws sometimes having different standards of liability. For example, the New Jersey Supreme Court recently held that when a supervisory employee engages in hostile environment sexual harassment, the employer will be strictly liable for all equitable remedies (including back pay, front pay, reinstatement, and other injunctive relief) regardless of whether the employer knew or even could have known that the sexual harassment had occurred.

The Vile Vendor

"Look out, here he comes again, Trudy!" her co-worker warned.

Trudy felt her stomach turn. Once a week she tolerated incessant subtle advances and wisecracks from the linen deliverer, Emil Evans. Trudy was responsible for checking in the supply orders for the company's cafeteria and had come to dread Emil's visits.

"Hi, Toots! You got some extra dirty linen you want to wash around me?" he laughed.

Trudy was not amused. "I'll take my standard order," she responded, ignoring his comments.

Before he left, Emil asked, "Say, I'm kind of hungry. Do you take orders to go?"

"Certainly," she said.

"Then go get your coat," he winked, "I'm waiting!"

"That does it, you weasel!" she shouted, and marched up to Frank McCurdy's office in human resources.

Trudy unloaded on Frank and told him about the continuous annoyance she had endured from Emil, such as his asking her co-workers about her marital status and continually making comments laced with sexual innuendo.

"Look, Frank, I have no interest in this man. He may think his conversation is harmless banter, but I think it's offensive. I've done nothing to encourage him. Probably the reverse is true. But it's to the point where every Tuesday I start getting nauseous because I'm going to have to deal with him. He's a sleaze, and I'm sick of him. Please do something!" Trudy pleaded.

Frank gathered all the details from Trudy and verified her story by investigating with her co-workers, who substantiated her claims. Although Emil did not physically threaten Trudy, Frank established that Emil's behavior was inappropriate and intolerable. Frank contacted the vendor's human resources manager and explained the situation. The human resources manager arranged to immediately reassign Emil and began her own investigation.

Subsequently, Frank met with Trudy. "Trudy, you'll be glad to know that you won't have to deal with Emil anymore. He's been reassigned."

"How about rehabilitated?" she quipped. "He needs that as well."

"I don't disagree with you," Frank said. "In fact, we're looking into drafting a policy that discusses what we expect of our vendors and their behavior toward our employees . . . maybe we'll even develop a training orientation video. Would you like to serve on the committee and provide some input?"

"Count me in!" Trudy affirmed.

 We give Frank high marks for his swift and appropriate actions. We can't speak for the vendor's human resources manager. On the surface, it appears she has simply avoided addressing the issue (Emil's behavior) by moving the problem elsewhere (to another customer, perhaps). We hope she has a sexual harassment policy in place and plans to educate Emil as well.

Clearly, Frank needs to strengthen his existing sexual harassment training. The story states, "Once a week she *tolerated . . .*" Women need to let men know directly and unequivocally when their behavior is unacceptable. Passivity does not resolve this type of problem. In most instances, the harasser will stop.

There is an increasing use of supplemental, temporary, and contingent employees as well as vendors, subcontractors, and consultants who may work alongside or have day-to-day contact with "regular" employees. Thus, it is vital for such workers to understand and be held to the same standards of conduct and behavior expected of regular employees.

We applaud Frank's "committee" approach to developing a training video. This strategy will provide him with an excellent source of information. The members can help him identify other harassment-related issues or suspect behavior within the facility as well as provide the necessary raw material for the tape. This is an ideal opportunity for Frank to develop a first-rate training video. He can use the video to educate vendors as well as new employees on the high standards of behavior expected in the plant.

Although this case turned out well, one panel member raised some interesting possibilities. What would happen if the vendor was less accommodating? Would the company go so far as to change vendors if appropriate action weren't taken? What if the vendor came back claiming Trudy had flirted with him?

 This story illustrates a subtle wrinkle in the sexual harassment arena. Depending on the circumstances, an employer may be liable for sexual harassment of its employees by its customers, vendors, contractors, salespersons, or other nonemployees.

Generally, an employer will be liable for sexual harassment by nonemployees when the employer knew or should have known of the harassment, the employer was in a position to control the offensive conduct, and the employer failed to take immediate and corrective action. What constitutes immediate and appropriate corrective action must be determined on a case-by-case basis. Corrective action is not limited to stopping the current sexual harassment but includes ensuring against a recurrence.

Frank should be commended for his handling of Trudy's complaint. He acted expeditiously and after an investigation sought corrective action from the vendor's human resources manager.

In certain situations where an employer is not in a position to control the offensive conduct of the nonemployee, the employer may offer the harassed employee a position where the employee would not have contact with the offender. However, the employer must ensure that such a transfer would not impair the employee's job benefits or opportunities or be perceived as some sort of punishment.

A Playboy's Dream

"We've spent so much time together these past two years, Fred, I feel like I ought to be buying your kids birthday presents and having them call me Aunt Gloria," Gloria laughed.

Fred nodded in agreement. "I must say, I have spent more time investigating cases here than in any other company in the city. Tell me, did your employees attend a seminar with a hypnotist who told them to file age discrimination claims on a monthly basis—or is your management really that bad?" he joked.

Fred was a local civil rights officer whom Gloria had worked with on a series of age discrimination cases in her company. Together they discovered that some cases were valid, while others were unsubstantiated. Over time, the two grew to trust each other during negotiations. If Gloria felt the company was clearly in the wrong, she avoided protracted negotiations and settled with a fair deal. On the other hand, when she could demonstrate that the case was someone's personal vendetta, which had no factual basis, Fred usually dropped the charges without argument. Their relationship was one of mutual respect.

A recent age discrimination complaint filed by Monique Letac, a 42-year-old former employee, prompted Fred's current visit with Gloria. Monique's boss, Armin Gettles, dismissed her for poor performance. Armin claimed that Monique spent most of her time studying for her real estate license, which had nothing to do with her job and provided no benefit to the company. She also yakked constantly with personal friends on the phone. Monique didn't complete her work assignments on time and continued to make errors.

Armin repeatedly requested that Monique refrain from studying on the job and focus on improving her performance. Monique ignored his requests, so Armin fired her. Monique, however, claimed Armin had more compelling reasons for discharging her. She insisted he was looking for an excuse to hire a younger, more attractive woman, so Monique filed an age discrimination suit.

"So what's the deal here, Gloria?" Fred asked.

"It's trumped-up nonsense," Gloria responded. "Yes, Armin hired a replacement that's younger than Monique, but look at Monique's history. Here's her rap sheet," Gloria said, handing Fred Monique's performance reviews and incident file. It listed every occasion where Armin coached and counseled her as well as Monique's failure to improve.

Fred reviewed the papers. "Okay, Gloria, you've sold me, but I have a favor to ask," he added.

"Uh, oh—what's the hitch, Fred?" she said.

"Well, Monique told me that her replacement is a dead ringer for Raquel Welch. How about if I just go through a perfunctory interview with her? I'm curious to see if she's really that gorgeous."

"I think that can be arranged," Gloria conceded, rising from her seat and thinking, "Geez, why are all men alike?!"

Gloria gave Armin's new assistant, Lauren, a call to let her know they were on their way. She and Fred trekked down the hall and caught an elevator to the marketing department located on the eighth floor. When the door opened, a willowy, attractive blonde woman was waiting for an elevator. Gloria noticed Fred giving the blonde a rear-view head-to-toe glance as she stepped into the elevator car beside theirs. When Gloria and Fred arrived at Lauren's desk, Gloria introduced herself and Fred to Lauren. Lauren was gracious and indicated that they would be meeting in Conference Room A for their interview.

"I don't think she's that hot," Gloria thought to herself. "Yeah, she's certainly pretty, but not movie-star quality or anything like that. The only way I can figure the Raquel Welch thing is that maybe her nostrils are a little flared," Gloria observed.

Fred, on the other hand, clearly disagreed with Gloria's assessment. He was grinning from ear to ear. Gloria just chuckled to herself.

As the trio walked to the other end of the department floor toward Conference Room A, Gloria started looking around. "Boy, the women in this department *are* pretty young," she thought. "But, I guess I knew that. Before Fred arrived, I ran the numbers out on average age, which was 23," she reminded herself. "However, I didn't realize these women were all so attractive," she thought, continuing to scan the faces of the women working busily at their desks.

"I'll be darned, there isn't a 'Plain Jane' in sight," Gloria observed, and then thought, "What's wrong with this picture?"

Suddenly Gloria felt her antennae rise. "Something is not right here. There is not one overweight person wearing polyester stretch pants and an overblouse on the entire floor. I feel like I just walked on the movie set of *Return of the Stepford Wives*—these women do not look like a normal group of department support staff," she realized.

She wasn't about to say anything to Fred and possibly give him further reason for camping out on her doorstep. So she kept her own counsel. After Fred satisfied his curiosity about Lauren by conducting his interview, he agreed to dismiss the case. Gloria quickly escorted him back across the department floor. He attempted to slow down so he could again enjoy the beautiful scenery, but Gloria subtly whisked him onto the elevator. When they reached the lobby, Gloria thanked Fred for his consideration as she walked him to the lobby door.

When Gloria returned to her office, she immediately called Lauren. "Lauren, could you set up a series of interviews with all the secretaries in the department for tomorrow? Make them approximately 30 minutes each."

"Sure. How should I tell them to prepare?" Lauren asked.

"Nothing special, just tell them we are continuing our investigation of age discrimination and need to get their views," she responded.

Then Gloria prepared a series of questions to probe into the discrimination issue.

The following day she conducted her interviews. When she questioned the women they all provided similar, sugary-sweet non-answer responses. This behavior set off more alarm bells in Gloria's head. A typical interview went something like this:

Gloria: Monique claimed that people had to be young and attractive to work in the department. Do you think that's true?

Woman: Gee, I thought Monique was attractive—so did everyone else.

Gloria: Is there any undue pressure on you here?

Woman: It's just great working here. I love it.

Gloria: Do you feel that people have to be attractive to work on this floor?

Woman: Well, I certainly try to look my best.

Gloria: Has anyone you know of been turned down?

Woman: I don't know. I don't do the hiring.

Gloria: Has anyone transferred out?

Woman: I can't imagine why—unless of course they've moved. It's such a terrific place to work!

None of this made sense, which fueled Gloria's suspicions. Undaunted, she held a second round of interviews and decided to apply a little pressure. This time she met with Jenny Welschot first.

"Yesterday I interviewed you and every secretary on this floor," Gloria began. "I'm not sure what's going on here, but I don't have a good feeling about it. What I want you to understand is that if there is a problem here, I will protect you. I can only do this if I know what's going on, otherwise I can't help you."

Jenny sat quietly for a moment. Finally, she said, "They told me I'd lose my job if I didn't cooperate. I don't really like it, but I've been going along. I know some of the girls like it, but I only do it because I need my job."

"Do what, Jenny?" Gloria asked.

"Well, every Saturday, the department rents out a room at the Sunnyside Court on Route 1—it's the one that has the nine-hole golf course and clay tennis courts. Three of us have to be available for a three-hour shift. Anyhow, usually I'll be there from about 9 o'clock until noon on rotating Saturdays. So, since there are 12 of us, I only have to go once every four weeks. The fellows in the department work it out among themselves and schedule their times with us. The girls' schedules are usually set several months in advance, although if one of us has a family emergency or something special comes up, we can trade dates with each other—but that doesn't happen very often," Jenny explained calmly, as though she were discussing a process flow chart.

"Could you be a little clearer about how they schedule their times?" Gloria asked, not believing what she was hearing.

"Well, like, if it's summer and one of the guys wants to see me, he'll act like he has to mow the lawn," Jenny said.

"Mow the lawn? What does mowing the lawn have to do with you?" Gloria was totally lost.

"Well, they try to work it out so they can tell their wives they have to run up to the gas station and get gas for the mower, or pick up some stuff from the hardware store. Then they drop by for an hour or so, and go back home to cut the grass," she explained.

"What's involved in these visits?" Gloria asked, afraid of what she was about to hear.

"We have sex," Jenny said, blushing.

Gloria was starting to feel nauseous. "Just how many people are involved?"

"Like I said before, 12 secretaries and at least 20 guys from the department."

"Was Monique Letac involved in this?"

"No, she was never asked," Jenny said.

"How long has this been going on?"

"About a year and a half."

"Why didn't anyone ever complain?" Gloria probed.

"Well, as I mentioned before, some of the girls enjoyed it and thought it was fun. Then some of us were afraid we'd lose our jobs," Jenny responded.

Gloria talked to the rest of the women to verify the information. Through similar procedures, she extracted four voluntary admissions to the Saturday "sexcapades." Since the vice president in the department was a key player in the scandal, Gloria immediately reported the incident to the president. The president called in legal counsel. They confronted the vice president and fired him on the spot. Next, the president demanded a full review of the department, its personnel, and its practices. He called in the internal auditors who conducted a comprehensive investigation.

Once the auditors began their investigation, they found that the Saturday rendezvous were mere ripples in a tidal wave of corruption. They discovered that the vice president maintained a "mystery mistress" on the payroll. No one had ever seen or heard of this woman, yet she received a regular paycheck, which naturally was delivered by the vice president. Additionally, the vice president's signature was documented as approval for the direct billing of the Saturday rendezvous hotel room charges. As the auditors delved further and further into accounting issues, they uncovered profit skimming and other devious forms of embezzlement.

Their investigation revealed that each manager was guilty of varying levels of improprieties. Consequently, each was disciplined according to the severity of his actions. Some were prosecuted, some terminated, and some merely reprimanded. However, all the secretaries retained their jobs and were given the option to remain in the department or be transferred elsewhere.

Thanks to her sharp instincts and persistence, Gloria led the way for thwarting a series of unspeakable management practices. Probably the thing that amazed her the most was that several secretaries had legitimate sexual harassment cases against the company, but not one ever filed a charge.

 It is difficult to believe that this type of pervasive corruption could take place in any organization, especially for such an extended period. In our experience, most instances of workplace sexual harassment are isolated or only involve a limited number of employees. Nevertheless, we aren't surprised that many of the women in this case truly believed that they would lose their jobs or thought they had to participate to "get along." Prior to the recent media coverage of the Anita Hill and Tailhook scandals, many investigations of sexual harassment cases that involve young women often revealed similar responses. These women were simply unaware of their rights. Today, however, forward-thinking companies provide training to ensure that management not only understands the personal and financial liabilities of sexual harassment but also that employees understand their rights.

In this case Gloria demonstrated strong instincts, one of the hallmarks of an effective human resources manager. When she discovered that the marketing department orchestrated regular weekend "sexcapades," she acted correctly by immediately informing the president. She also handled the situation well in her subsequent dealings with the culpable males. She neglected, however, to properly address the issues with the females and bring true closure to the case.

Gloria should have informed those women who believed that their jobs were in jeopardy of the company's procedures for handling sexual harassment complaints. Moreover, she should have told those women who willingly engaged in the weekend frolics that the company did not condone such behavior.

Furthermore, Gloria should consider sending every remaining manager through a sexual harassment course designed for management. She should also arrange for all other employees to attend an employee-oriented sexual harassment program.

Gloria's astonishment that no lawsuits had been filed by any of the women involved in their escapades is well taken. This story gives new meaning to the phrase "dodging the bullet." For those young women, including Jenny, who participated in the Saturday rendezvous out of fear for their jobs, the company—and the managers—would almost certainly be liable. An employer will be automatically liable for *quid pro quo* sexual harassment (i.e., sex for the job) by their supervisory personnel. This means that an employer will be responsible for unlawful sexual harassment by a manager or supervisor, even though the employer may not have been aware of such conduct, and even though such conduct violated company policy.

Sexual harassment suits can be extremely costly for employers (aside from unwelcome negative publicity). In addition to trial by jury, make-whole relief (reinstatement, back pay, and front pay), and attorneys' fees, victims of sexual harassment are now entitled to compensatory and punitive damages under the Civil Rights Act of 1991. While there are "caps" on compensatory and punitive awards, they are still substantial, ranging from $50,000 for employers of 100 employees or less to $300,000 for employers of more than 500 employees.

There is no indication in this story that the company had a sexual harassment policy or had conducted training on sexual harassment for its managers and employees. While a policy may not always stop sexual harassment, if it had existed here, it may have encouraged Jenny or one of the other victims to come forward—thus allowing the company to address the problem sooner and reducing the risk of a costly legal battle. A sexual harassment policy should have an internal complaint procedure. This procedure should encourage prompt reporting of sexual harassment claims and assure confidentiality to the extent possible, with employees having an option of reporting an incident of sexual harassment to someone other than his or her own supervisor if the immediate supervisor is the harasser.

Supervisors and managers should be made aware of their critical roles in effectuating the company's sexual harassment policy and in minimizing the company's exposure to liability. Sexual harassment training should emphasize that individual managers who sexually harass others face potential *personal* liability. Not surprisingly, when managers learn that sexual harassment can dip into their personal pockets, they generally pay closer attention to the issue. In some cases, such as with sexual harassment, where an individual manager presumably is not acting for the benefit of the employer or in its behalf, courts may even preclude the employer from indemnifying the individual manager for damages assessed against him or her. In addition to incurring individual liability for sexual harassment, the vice president who signed his approval for the hotel bills could be sued by the company for violating his duty of loyalty.

Washing Away the Evidence

"Mom, the phone's for you," Chloe's daughter yelled out the back door.

"Find out who it is and tell them I'll call them back," Chloe responded, as she patted down the soil around her new Bird of Paradise plant.

A few minutes later, her daughter was back at the door. "Mom, it's your work. They say it's an emergency. They need to talk to you now," her daughter said.

"An emergency? On a Saturday?" Chloe thought, brushing the dirt off her hands. "Okay, I'll be right there," she yelled back. Chloe was the human resources manager for a large publishing warehouse and distribution center.

When she got into the house, her daughter handed her the phone. "This is Chloe," she said into the receiver.

"Chloe, oh Chloe!" an excited voice answered. "We've got trouble with Eva Cassis. Morris Albroton . . . he hurt her last night," Rosita, the warehouse supervisor, stammered.

"Hurt her? Hurt her, how?" Chloe asked, while she rinsed her hands in the sink and searched for a pen.

"Her mother says he raped Eva last night in the warehouse," Rosita said.

"Oh no," Chloe gasped. "How did this happen?"

"I don't know, exactly, but I tell you, Chloe, I knew something was wrong when I saw Eva last night. She was acting strange . . . like, fidgety. When I asked her if she had a problem, she said that she was just feeling weird. I thought maybe she was getting sick, so I sent her home early. I had no idea he did this to her. I want to strangle that Morris when I see him," Rosita fumed.

"Rosita, let's not jump to conclusions. We don't have all the facts yet," Chloe said, realizing that Rosita was upset. "Do you have her mother's name and number handy?"

"Yes. Her name is Mrs. Brighton. The number is 555-1001."

Chloe knew Eva. She had hired Eva through a social service agency in a pilot program to broaden employment opportunities for the mentally disabled. Eva was about 27 years old, but had an intellectual ability of a

10-year-old. Despite her mental limitations, she was a wonderful, dependable employee.

She worked in the warehouse. Each day, hundreds of packages entered and left the facility. The company distributed everything from books on how to patch drywall and fix your toilet to educational videos on creative lovemaking strategies for the '90s. Eva's job was to restock all returns according to their stock number.

Chloe also knew Morris Albroton, a retired army officer about 50 years old, who worked as a part-time warehouser evenings and weekends. There was nothing particularly memorable about Morris. He arrived on time and did his job satisfactorily.

When Chloe called Eva's mother, Mrs. Brighton, Chloe got more information. Mrs. Brighton told Chloe that her first clue that something was wrong was when Eva came home a half-hour early from work. When she asked Eva why she was home so early, Eva said she wasn't feeling well. She walked around the house acting agitated and nervous, shaking her hands and pacing.

Shortly afterward, Mrs. Brighton said that she observed Eva go into the bathroom and take a bath. When Eva was done, she picked up her clothes in a very odd manner. Instead of bundling them up in her arms and putting them in the hamper, she pinched them together with her fingers at a corner and held them about a foot from her body. It was as though she didn't want to touch them. Next, she almost ritualistically walked to the laundry room and tossed them in the washing machine and turned it on.

When Eva finally seemed to calm down, Mrs. Brighton decided to talk to her to find out what was going on. Eva acted very guilty at first, as if she had done something wrong. Then Eva told Mrs. Brighton that during the middle of her shift, Morris had lured her into a room in the warehouse that was normally kept locked. He told her that he had some of her favorite candy there. Then, he locked her in and raped her. After he was done, he left Eva in the room by herself. She didn't know what to do, so she just went back to work until her supervisor told her to go home.

Chloe got Mrs. Brighton's address and drove there immediately. When she arrived, she saw Eva sitting limply in a chair. Chloe hugged her and assured her that she had done nothing wrong. Then she turned to Mrs. Brighton.

"Have you called the police?" Chloe asked.

"Well, no. It happened at work, so I didn't think I was supposed to call the police," Mrs. Brighton said, surprised.

"Mrs. Brighton, this is a crime. We need to report it as such. I'll stay with you the whole time. Would you like me to call or do you want to?" Chloe offered.

Mrs. Brighton called, and the police took the report. They went through all the questioning with Eva, as Chloe held her hand and encouraged her. Then Chloe drove Eva and her mother to the hospital so they could take the necessary tests for evidence. Unfortunately, the hospital exam was of limited use. Morris had allegedly used a condom, so there was no evidence of semen. Since Eva did not fight, there was no skin under her fingernails. Additionally, she washed away any possible remaining evidence when she bathed and washed her clothes, so there were no hairs or fibers.

The police went to Morris's home to question him. He refused to go down to the station since they did not have a warrant. In the meantime, Chloe called her boss and filled him in. They realized they had to keep an open mind, and planned a strategy accordingly. The first thing they did was to investigate the case as though it were a conventional case of sexual harassment.

When Chloe interviewed Eva, she asked, "Did Morris ever approach you for sex before this incident?"

"Well, he'd show me some of the books we stock. They had bad things in them, like naked people kissing and touching each other," Eva said, making a face. "Once he asked me to watch a tape that someone returned. He told me it was a cartoon. But when I watched it, it had naked people on it, doing nasty things, so I left the room."

After Chloe completed the interview, she obtained a signed complaint from Eva regarding the sexual harassment.

Morris arrived at work the next day as usual. Chloe and her boss called him into the office. "Morris, there have been some accusations about your actions that require us to conduct an investigation for sexual harassment," Chloe stated.

"I'm not surprised," Morris responded coolly. "I got a visit from the police last night. The whole thing is ludicrous. You couldn't possibly believe anything like that from someone as mentally deficient as Eva."

"Despite your feelings about Eva's mental capacity, we're obligated by law to investigate any claim of sexual harassment. Given the nature of the situation, we are going to suspend you with pay during the internal investigation," Chloe said, just as coolly.

"Fine, suit yourself," Morris replied in a blasé manner.

Chloe arranged for Morris to be escorted from the building and began her investigation. She learned from the other warehouse workers that they had observed him showing lewd pictures to Eva and joking with her. They overheard such comments as, "Eva, look at this picture, what do you think?" Morris had attempted similar tactics with other stock clerks. They responded to his behavior with a straightforward "Bug off."

Based on the investigation, they discharged Morris for sexual harassment. Unfortunately, the district attorney did not feel he had sufficient evidence to prosecute Morris on the rape charge or any lesser charge.

To help Eva deal with the trauma, Chloe made arrangements with the social service agency who originally placed Eva. They provided ongoing counseling to Eva for an extended period. After nearly a year of counseling, Eva fully recovered and continues to be an excellent worker.

PANEL COMMENTS This is a tragic situation. Eva's case unfortunately adds to the international statistics on reported crime and violence in the workplace. The saddest part is that the incident could have been prevented.

If the social service agency had educated Eva to recognize unacceptable workplace behavior, she may have responded differently to Morris's overtures. Her understanding of sexual harassment could have been reinforced if the company provided training that illustrated appropriate and inappropriate workplace behaviors. Moreover, if the training outlined reporting procedures for such incidents, Eva would have known where to go for help. She probably wouldn't have remained silent about Morris's repeated attempts to engage her attention with X-rated movies and lurid photographs.

Under the circumstances, Chloe handled the situation well. Rape is a crime and should be investigated by the police. She acted appropriately by contacting them immediately and offering support to Eva and her mother throughout the investigation process.

Chloe was also correct to suspend Morris during the investigation. She fulfilled her obligation to the employees by ensuring a safe workplace until she could gather all the facts. We support her decision to discharge

Morris after obtaining sufficient evidence about his inappropriate conduct. The fact that the district attorney had insufficient evidence to prosecute Morris for rape does not absolve Morris of his acts of sexual harassment.

Chloe's follow-up in this case was also excellent. We applaud her for arranging Eva's ongoing counseling with the social service agency that placed her with the company. We suggest, however, that the company arrange a more extensive orientation and closer supervision for future employees who are mentally disabled. Chloe should ensure that these employees fully understand which behaviors are inappropriate as well as when and to whom such incidents should be reported. Chloe might also consider developing a mentor program by appointing a "big brother or sister" to help these employees deal with difficult situations.

Although our last suggestion is minor, it merits attention. It probably wasn't appropriate for Chloe to hug Eva. While we recognize that Eva was vulnerable and needed some reassurance, this was a business situation, and Chloe had not heard all the facts. It was possible that Eva's allegations were false. Hugging someone in such a situation might lead the employee to believe that the company is on his or her side 100 percent.

As the official human resources representative in a sexual harassment case, Chloe should remain unbiased and swayed only by facts. However, given the overall circumstances of this situation and Eva's fragile condition, this was a very minor transgression and does not detract from the overall excellent handling of the situation.

To say this story illustrates the extreme of sexual harassment would be an understatement. This case highlights the importance of training employees to heighten their awareness and sensitivity regarding sexual harassment in the workplace. While a sexual harassment policy and training programs may not have prevented Morris's assault against Eva, it may have encouraged other employees to come forward earlier to report Morris's conduct toward Eva and other stock clerks.

With the success of the ADA, many capable individuals with mental disabilities, such as Eva, will be entering the workforce in greater numbers. Human resources managers, as well as all employees, need to develop an understanding and awareness that some individuals will be more vulnerable to certain situations and appropriate safeguards for their welfare must be taken. Since Chloe knew that Eva had an intellect of a 10-year-old, she or a supervisor should have "kept an eye out for her." Placing Eva in a warehouse at night and on weekends where there appeared to be insufficient supervision was inappropriate. The company could be liable for negligence for failing to provide a safe and secure workplace.

While employers should always do reference checks on applicants who are being considered for employment, it is especially important to conduct a criminal conviction records check on any applicant or employee being considered for a position in which there will be little or no supervision, such as a night shift.

A Rogue's Ranking

"Yes, sir, I'll schedule that with our driver for a Tuesday delivery," Fran said to the customer on the line, making a note of the request on her pad. "You're welcome," she responded to the customer's appreciative thank you.

But before she could put the phone in the cradle, another line began flashing. "Customer service, Fran speaking," her voice sang into the receiver. "How can I help you?"

While Fran was busy listening to the customer's request, Pete, the district sales manager, tiptoed up behind her. He dropped a piece of paper on her desk and scurried away quietly, as his shoulders shook with laughter. Fran sensed Pete's presence and wheeled around in her chair to respond to him when the customer put her on hold. Pete was gone, but his one-page delivery lay on the corner of her desk.

Fran recognized the paper as the company's standard performance appraisal. The scale ran from one to five, with one representing "unacceptable" and five designating "exceeds expectation." In the section where Pete was to fill in the key duties for her job and rank them accordingly, he had scrawled the following:

1. Face   =   3
2. Breasts   =   1
3. Butt   =   5
4. Legs   =   3

Fran's face turned as red as the evening Tennessee sun. She felt her teeth clench in anger as she tried to maintain her composure. When the customer came back on the line, she strained to keep a smile in her voice. Then she called her lawyer.

Three weeks later Donald Denny, the company's corporate counsel, flew to the regional office to meet with Pete and his boss.

"What the hell were you thinking when you did this, Pete?" he scolded.

"Well, we were due for a performance appraisal, so I thought it would be funny to start on a light note," Pete shrugged.

"More like a sour note," Donald groused. "Because of your idiotic behavior, we don't have a leg to stand on, and she'll get a nice little nest egg compliments of the company. Next time you decide to assess someone's butt, make it your own, because right now it's in a sling."

Donald viewed Pete as a continued liability and tried his best to persuade the regional operations manager to fire Pete for his behavior. Despite Donald's protests, the operations manager insisted on retaining Pete but negotiated an alternative solution. He agreed to freeze Pete's bonus for three years as retribution for the incident and to enroll him in a sexual harassment course.

 Pete's behavior is reprehensible. Both punishment and training are essential to prevent a repeat performance. The company also needs to communicate to everyone it will not tolerate such behavior. Since this was Pete's first offense and it did not involve intimidation or coercion, termination is not necessary. A repetition of his action, however, would justify termination.

The company must evaluate Pete's punishment in the context of its sexual harassment policy. If the company had no formal policy and never communicated to managers and staff that such behavior is wrong and unacceptable, the firm is partly at fault. On the other hand, if such a policy existed and was clearly communicated, Pete's penalty should be severe. This includes a public apology and acknowledgment that the behavior was wrong and hurtful.

The three-year loss of bonus may have significant monetary value, but the punishment takes too long and drags the issue out. Furthermore, this type of financial penalty may cause Pete to feel bitter and resentful toward Fran, making it more difficult than ever for them to continue an acceptable working relationship. The point is to change behavior and prevent recurrences.

Let's assume that Pete was really just an insensitive dolt who did not know how hurtful his actions were. If that was the case and the company rehabilitates him quickly and completely, a public apology, loss of one year's bonus, and participation in training (perhaps helping to develop a policy and training sessions if none exist) are probably sufficient. We feel it does not make sense to continue the punishment after the offending behavior has stopped and been replaced by appropriate behavior.

We also think it's important to get Fran's perspective. How did she want to see the problem dealt with? Was she prepared to continue working for Pete or had the work atmosphere been so badly damaged that it would be intolerable for her to continue working there? In the latter case, an appropriate action would be to transfer Pete or Fran (if she wanted) to a different location or position.

 This story is a prime example of why we advise clients to have a sexual harassment policy that is published in an employee handbook and/or otherwise disseminated to its employees. First, had the company had a sexual harassment policy, (hopefully) Pete would have had a heightened awareness that such conduct was not only inappropriate but also unlawful.

In determining whether conduct or statements are sufficiently severe to rise to the level of unlawful sexual harassment, some state courts have relied upon a "reasonable woman" standard. Under federal law, however, an objective standard, the "reasonable person" standard, as well as the victim's subjective perception are applied to determine whether a hostile or abusive work environment exists. Here, where the woman's supervisor was rating her *performance* based on his assessment of her body parts, it would be hard to imagine a jury not finding that a reasonable person or reasonable woman would find this conduct creating a hostile, abusive environment. After all, a performance appraisal is at the heart of the employee/employer relationship.

One of the employer's primary objectives in handling a sexual harassment situation should be to keep the investigation in-house without the intervention of any government agency. A company-disseminated sexual harassment policy may assist the employer in meeting this objective. A well-written policy will advise employees who believe they have been harassed to report the harassment to a designated individual in the company. Because an employee's supervisor is often the harasser, the policy should give the employee an option of reporting the incident to someone other than his or her supervisor. For example, employees may be told to report the incident to the human resources manager. Often times a victim of harassment determines that there is no need to go outside the company for relief when he or she sees that the company takes the complaint seriously and acts decisively to remedy the problem.

Depending on the circumstances, it is not always necessary to terminate an individual who has been found to have acted inappropriately. Often other disciplinary action, such as suspension, probation, or wage freeze, may be more appropriate. The employer should also document for the record what corrective action was taken. Sexual harassment training and monitoring of the individual's behavior in the future would be prudent. Most important, however, the employer must demonstrate that a hostile or abusive environment will not be tolerated in the workplace.

Strange Bedfellows

Hamilton Garramond III sat in his mahogany-walled office surrounded by rich leather chairs, reading his copy of *Forbes*. As president of a national pharmacy chain, he was pleased to receive the recent media coverage of the company's marketing coup. While he was immersed in thought, Amanda, his executive secretary, approached.

"Excuse me, Mr. Garramond," she said politely, "I think you better look at this right away." She handed him a four-page handwritten letter from James Varanzet.

Hamilton put his magazine aside and began to read:

> *Dear Mr. Garramond:*
>
> *I've been employed as a pharmacist at Garramond Retail Enterprises for the past three years. During that time, I have performed well and enjoyed my experience. However, recently my district manager counseled me for performance problems, and, unfortunately, I'm continuing to decline. I was too ashamed to tell my manager what was really causing my problems, but now things have escalated to the point that I need to reveal all that has happened. I have nowhere to turn and need your help.*
>
> *I am gay and have been open about my sexual preference from the time that I began working for the company. For the first couple years, I had no problems with any member of management or my co-workers. However, Rod Bendellen, your security auditor who has been assigned to monitor inventories at the store during the past year, has been sexually harassing me for the last eight months.*
>
> *It all started when he asked me to have dinner with him after we completed the store's inventory one evening. He asked me questions about my gay lifestyle and wanted to know how I had discovered my sexuality. Then he asked me how I got dates. Eventually, each time he'd visit the district, he'd ask me to dinner, and his questions became more and more intimate. Next, he started revealing things about himself. He told me he was having difficulty with his wife and wanted to explore his sexuality with me. Before I knew it, he asked me to go to bed with him.*

Naturally I refused because I'm involved in a committed relationship, but Rod kept persisting. Initially his persistence came in the form of repeated requests. He kept telling me how he liked my looks and various parts of my body. Then he came right out and asked if he could perform oral gratification for me. When I refused, he used other tactics. He started fondling me at the store in the evening when we'd go over inventory and no other employees were around. I asked him to refrain from this behavior, but he kept hassling me. Frankly, I didn't know where to turn, so I just kept silent.

Ultimately he became verbally aggressive, saying he didn't understand why I refused. Then he threatened me with my job and said he would set me up for criminal charges by finding shortages in the pharmacy if I didn't cooperate. He said that he could get me thrown in jail for theft and drug charges and that once I was there, I would be everyone's sexual play toy. Mr. Garramond, I was so scared that I finally gave in and went to his hotel. Now, he insists that I have sex with him every week when he's in the district. He calls me in the middle of the night and tells me that he needs to be with me—that he's sexually frustrated. I'm sick of being frightened all the time. I find him repulsive and the whole situation unbearable.

Mr. Garramond, this has caused me both mental and physical problems. I am seeing a doctor for ulcers, and I have difficulty concentrating on my work. As a pharmacist, I can't afford to make mistakes. I haven't told anyone about this because I'm afraid of Rod. He's an ex-Marine MP and could easily break me in two. I also don't want to lose my job over this. Please, protect me and make him stop sexually harassing me. I trust my letter will remain confidential.

Sincerely,
James Varanzet

"Holy Moly!" Hamilton paled. "Get a hold of Stanton Fieldcrest at our law firm, and tell Zack to come up here immediately," he directed Amanda, who was standing by for directions.

"Yes, sir," she answered.

Zack Horvaniz was the vice president of human resources. When he arrived, he spotted Hamilton clutching his stomach. Zack rushed over to Hamilton's desk. "Amanda sent me your red alert. Gosh, Ham, you look sick. Should I call Doc Mankoff or do you need 911?"

"No, no. Sit down," Hamilton instructed, waving the letter toward him. "Read this." He flipped the letter frisbee-style across the desk to Zack.

Zack caught the letter in midair. As he finished the first page, Zack looked up at Hamilton. "I know this guy. I've worked on several cases with him. Rod's a big, burly fellow."

"Read on," Hamilton said, "it gets worse."

When Zack finished, he shook his head in disbelief. "I can't imagine that any of this is true. It just doesn't fit with his profile. You'd have to see this guy!"

"What if it is true?" Hamilton asked, clearly horrified.

"Well, whether it is or it isn't, we still have to treat it like any sexual harassment case," Zack informed him.

"It makes me sick," Hamilton frowned. "It's one thing to be gay; it's another thing to have to hear about it."

"To tell you the truth, Ham, I'm not looking forward to the gory details myself," Zack admitted.

"Look, I've got a call into Stanton at legal. I'll brief him, and then the two of you can get together if this thing escalates. I don't want the press down my throat. With all this business about gays in the military, I don't need to blemish all the great PR we've just received. Do me a favor, just make this one go away, will you?" Hamilton insisted.

"I'll do my best," Zack said, feigning optimism.

Zack contacted James at Store 578 and set up an appointment for a conference at the district office. "I am dreading this," Zack thought, feeling squeamish. This was his first gay harassment case, and he knew he had to be extra careful with his investigation procedures. Zack braced himself as he listened to James recount the graphic details of the events that occurred. Although James provided specific dates and times, he couldn't produce any witnesses to corroborate the incidents. It was clear to Zack that James found the process painful, so Zack did his best to listen objectively and take detailed notes.

"Well, the worst is behind me," Zack thought. Meeting with Rod would be another kind of challenge. Zack contacted Rod Bendellen's manager, the vice president of risk management, and briefed him. Together they decided that it would be best if Zack talked with Rod alone.

Zack played mental tennis as he served up alternatives in an attempt to find the right strategy. "Should I approach him delicately and tap dance around this or hit him right between the eyes with the allegation and watch for a reaction?" Zack considered. Zack decided on the direct approach, but carefully selected his language.

Since Zack and Rod had worked together before, when he got a call from Zack to come to human resources, Rod assumed Zack needed his help on a case. The two exchanged greetings and Zack got right to the point in an attempt to catch Rod off guard.

"Rod, you know that we investigate things as they come up. There's a male member of the management in the company who has made an allegation. He claims that you've had a sexual relationship with him," Zack said, intentionally using the generic terms "male member of management." He wanted to protect James, so he did not say "store manager" or "pharmacist."

Rod did not respond immediately. He looked away toward the window, took a long pause as though gathering his thoughts, and then turned his head back toward Zack in delayed protest. "*What?* I can't believe that! Who made that allegation? I'm a married guy. I've been married for 17 years!"

Zack listened and observed. There was something in Rod's manner that didn't ring true. The lack of spontaneity, the long pause, and then what seemed like contrived anger didn't fit. As Zack was assessing the situation, Rod added, "Look, I've never even gone out on my wife. The only time anything ever happened to me was when I got drunk with three of my Marine buddies one night. We were all out on leave, and I wound up getting it on with some hooker."

Zack just sat there, staring at him and saying nothing. Rod's drunken Marine anecdote was not only inappropriate but irrelevant to the discussion. The more Rod protested, the more Zack was inclined to discredit him. However, despite Zack's gut reaction, he had no proof of Rod's guilt. Without concrete evidence it boiled down to James's word against Rod's.

To ensure that James was protected against further harassment or retaliation, Zack informed Rod, "Look, Rod, I'm going to take your word for it and assume you didn't do this. On the other hand, if I were in your shoes, I'd probably be wondering who made this accusation and trying to figure out who the gay men are in the company."

Zack paused for a moment and observed Rod. Rod nodded in agreement.

"Rod, although that would be a natural thing for you to assume, the complainant doesn't necessarily have to be a gay man. And, the *worst* thing you could do is go back and talk to whomever you suspect and then tell him that you were accused of this. For your own sake, don't try to take this out on anyone. If you do, we will consider that retaliation, and you could lose your job—even though you may be totally innocent of these allegations.

"It's important for you to remember, Rod," Zack continued, "that you're in a role where you have to be above that. You have to personally remove yourself from the situation and deal with it for what it is. Somebody came forward and complained. When that happens we're obligated to investigate. We have an open-door policy, and they wanted to use it. So we have to respect that and move on. Do you understand?"

"Yes," Rod responded.

"Okay, so let's forget it then," Zack said.

Rod left the office and Zack informed Rod's manager of the outcome of his investigation. Zack told him he didn't have adequate proof of Rod's guilt, so he had to assume his innocence.

Zack followed up with James to inform him that they had investigated the situation and that Rod had denied his allegations. However, Zack told James that if he experienced any further harassment, he should let Zack know immediately. Zack followed up with James again several months later, and asked if he had any more problems. James indicated that everything was fine.

About a year later, James was fired for poor performance and filed a sex discrimination suit against the company. He raised the issue of his prior sexual harassment complaint. Zack conferred with the Equal Employment Opportunity Commission investigator and indicated that the company had treated James's sexual harassment case appropriately. Zack demonstrated through his investigation procedures and follow-up that James was treated no differently than a female would have been treated under similar circumstances. When the EEOC reviewed Zack's documentation, they ruled that there was no sex discrimination and held James's termination as valid.

PANEL COMMENTS

We had mixed reactions to this one. Half of us think Zack handled the situation fairly and systematically. The other half feels that the company was lucky to get off so easily. Despite the outcome of the EEOC review, we argue that Zack's handling of the investigation and follow-up missed some key ingredients.

Although Zack began his investigation properly by holding a private meeting with James and taking copious notes of the allegations, he sidestepped a few precautionary procedures. For example, Zack should have specifically informed James that the company takes harassment seriously and that he appreciated James's willingness to come forward with the complaint.

Also, during this initial meeting, Zack should have been very clear to James that the company would not tolerate retaliation, and, if any occurred, James should immediately report the incident directly to him. Moreover, Zack needed to indicate both verbally and in writing that it would be inappropriate for James to discuss this issue with anyone in the company other than Zack. Alternatively, if James was for any reason uncomfortable with Zack, then he could discuss the matter with the president of the company.

Finally, James should have been informed that Zack was required to discuss this claim with Rod. In sexual harassment cases, if a manager knows or has reason to know that harassment may have taken place, he or she has an obligation to investigate the situation. This involves discussing the situation thoroughly with both sides, using specific detail, including names. Rod has a right to know what he has been accused of and by whom. And the law protects James from retaliation.

We also find significant flaws regarding Zack's discussion with Rod. This conversation needed considerable bolstering as well. Zack should have obtained a more thorough statement from Rod and arranged for a follow-up meeting. A second meeting would allow Rod time to reflect on the meaning of the charges and respond thoughtfully to each item. Although Zack appropriately informed Rod that retaliation would be grounds for immediate discharge, we suggest that Zack should have issued this warning in writing as well as verbally. Furthermore, Zack should have told Rod that any discussion of this issue with anyone other than him or the president would violate confidentiality and be grounds for disciplinary action.

Once the investigation was complete, Zack should have met separately with James and Rod once more to advise them of the outcome. (In this case he met with James and Rod's manager, but not Rod.) If we assume that Rod completely denied the allegations, then the investigation was inconclusive. As a result James should have been informed of such and thanked again for bringing the issue to the company's attention. Zack was correct in encouraging James to come forward if he experienced any future retaliation or harassment. These actions underscore the company's intolerance for sexual harassment.

Regardless of Rod's guilt or innocence, Zack should have taken additional steps by meeting with Rod and educating him on the company's sexual harassment policies. Zack also should have reminded Rod that retaliation would lead to disciplinary action up to and including dismissal. Moreover, Zack should have informed him that despite the lack of evidence, if sexual harassment had occurred or would occur in the future, such behavior was totally inappropriate and would result in disciplinary proceedings.

Additionally, we identified some side issues that warrant consideration. Zack expressed concern about this case before he began his investigation. Because this was Zack's first gay harassment claim, he felt that he "had to be extra careful with his investigation procedures." The key to properly handling gay harassment cases is to treat them exactly as you'd treat straight harassment cases.

Finally, Zack needed to consider whether these individuals could continue to work together. We suggest that Zack should have asked both men if they felt uncomfortable working together and arranged an appropriate (i.e., not to James's detriment) transfer if requested.

 Either sex may be the victim or the offender in sexual harassment situations. This story also illustrates what we have emphasized numerous times in our other comments: the importance of adopting policies and procedures that minimize the risk of discrimination claims or, at least, maximize an employer's chance of successfully defeating claims, which will undoubtedly arise despite the employer's best efforts.

Zack's investigation of the complaint was cursory, and he failed to probe further when Rod denied the allegations. Sexual harassment complaints are not always easy to resolve. While employees' conduct may sometimes be blatant and may be publicly known or witnessed by employees other than the alleged victim, it is not unusual for a human resources manager to be faced with a situation where there is a complaint, a denial (e.g., the alleged victim's word against the alleged harasser's word), and no witnesses. The issue then becomes one of credibility. Zack could have asked James to come into the meeting after Rod denied the allegations. Such a confrontation may cause the truth to be forthcoming. However, employers need to be careful not to "force" an alleged harassment victim into a stressful confrontation meeting if the victim prefers not to participate.

In a situation where there is still a credibility issue after the investigation, it is appropriate to review the company's sexual harassment policy with the alleged offender. This will ensure that the individual understands that sexual harassment is unlawful and will not be tolerated by the company. The individual should also be advised that should further complaints arise, other disciplinary action, up to and including termination, may be necessary. Moreover, it is important to emphasize, as Zack did with Rod, that retaliatory action by the alleged harasser against the complainant will not be tolerated.

One important task that Zack appears to have neglected is a documentation of his investigation. Such documentation would be a vital weapon in withstanding any potential charges against the company in the event that either Rod or James filed charges.

Because it is unlawful to retaliate against a sexual harassment complainant, employers need to proceed cautiously if the complainant is discharged from employment for other reasons. For example, in this story, James was ultimately fired for poor performance. Thus, it is important to have documentary support (e.g., performance appraisals and probationary notices) in the individual's personnel file to withstand any charges of retaliation, and to refute the employee's likely claim that the alleged performance deficiencies were only a pretext to conceal an underlying motive—anti-gay bias.

Chapter 7

Controversial Beneficiaries

"Insurance companies honor the designated beneficiary regardless of current marital status."

Marlene M. Dennis, CCP, CEBS
Director of Human Resources
McDonnell Douglas Helicopter Company

Blood on Her Hands

Pierre LeCompte whistled his favorite tune from *Phantom of the Opera* as he pushed through the lobby doors that morning. Although it had been nearly a month since his promotion to vice president of human resources, he secretly looked at his business card daily to assure himself he wasn't dreaming.

Pierre was the youngest vice president ever appointed in the French-owned company. His rapid rise through the corporate ranks was no accident. He had excellent mentors and worked very hard to master the English language, assimilate into American culture, and learn the employment laws. Although Pierre still retained a slight accent, he communicated clearly and effectively with both management and the line employees in the factory.

That morning as he strolled through the lobby, he casually noticed three unusual-looking people sitting in the reception area. He checked his watch. It was only 7:45 a.m. Rarely did visitors arrive at such an early hour.

Two of the visitors were frightening-looking women in their early to mid-30s. Both were as large as a pair of Sumo wrestlers and wore angry expressions on their faces. A leprechaun-like gentleman, clad in a finely tailored Armani suit, was sandwiched between them. He continued to pat the hand of the woman on his left, whose nostrils flared with the greater anger.

Pierre breezed past the receptionist on his way to grab a cup of coffee. By using only his eyes and a slight tilt of his head, he communicated silently, "Who *are* those people?"

The receptionist whispered, "Mr. LeCompte, these people arrived here at 7:30 a.m. They are waiting to see you. The woman in the black dress is the wife of Leroy Calhoun, one of our assembly workers. I don't know who the others are."

Pierre looked toward them and smiled. The women glared back. The diminutive gentleman in the Armani suit nodded and responded with a wide grin. "Please, tell them I'll see them as soon as I get settled," Pierre instructed the receptionist.

Pierre walked into his office, hung up his coat, and set down his briefcase and coffee. He reviewed his calendar and observed that he had no meetings scheduled until 9:30. "Good," he thought, "I won't have to change my schedule, and I can give Mrs. Calhoun adequate time."

Since Pierre's secretary had not yet arrived, he took a deep breath and personally went to the lobby to greet the mysterious Mrs. Calhoun and her entourage. As he approached the group, Pierre smiled and said, "Hello, I'm Pierre LeCompte. I understand you wanted to see me. Would you like to come to my office so we can talk privately?" he asked, motioning toward the hallway that led to his office.

Mrs. Calhoun, the menacing woman in the black dress, stood up immediately. Pierre tensed as he felt the floor vibrate from her weight. "I'm Lucretia Calhoun, Leroy Calhoun's wife. This here is my sister, Ruby Mae Watson, and our family mortician, Mr. Tyrone Fogel."

"It's my pleasure to meet you," Pierre responded, shaking their hands. He privately was thinking, "Mortician? What in the world is she doing here with a mortician?" Then he motioned again to the hallway, and said, "If you'll step this way . . ."

While Pierre arranged for them to be comfortably seated on the sofa and wing chairs in his office, he asked, "Would any of you like some coffee?"

All declined.

"Well, then, how can I offer you assistance?"

"We're here to tell you Leroy died this weekend," Lucretia announced.

"Oh dear, I'm sorry," Pierre said, offering his sympathy. "How did this happen?"

"He came home drunk as a skunk and abusive as hell," Lucretia scowled, "so I shot the damn SOB, dead."

Pierre was speechless. While he was trying to formulate a question, Lucretia continued matter-of-factly, "We're here to find out how much life insurance he has and if there's any pension money for me. When Leroy and I got married last June, he told me he had a $30,000 policy. That should cover a first-class funeral and leave me some money to fix up the house."

"Amen," said her sister Ruby Mae, with the undertaker, Fogel, nodding in approval.

Pierre remained silent as he scanned their expressions. The sister furrowed her brow in concern, while the undertaker smiled with obvious delight that money would be available for a grand funeral. Pierre still wasn't sure what to say at that point, but finally managed to ask, "Were the police involved in this matter?"

"Yeah, they were there," Lucretia said. "They took pictures and brought me down to the station, but I'm out on my own recognizance. I just want to know what benefits are due me."

Pierre instinctively knew that Lucretia would not be entitled to any death benefit until she was cleared of any criminal charges. His mind searched for a way to gracefully get them out of his office, without having to tell her that directly.

"Let me check the records for you and verify the benefit amounts," he suggested. "If you'll excuse me, I'll be back shortly."

Pierre calmly left his office. As he headed for the office of the corporate attorney, Jean-Claude Moreau, Pierre felt perspiration begin to bead on his forehead. Fortunately, Jean-Claude was at his desk. Pierre felt instant relief knowing that he would not have to face the trio alone. "With this group," he shuddered inwardly, "I not only need legal counsel, I probably need a bodyguard, too."

"Jean-Claude, *mon ami*," Pierre began in French, and quickly briefed his colleague of the unusual predicament.

As they checked the records together, they discovered that Leroy's benefit had, indeed, been $30,000. Unfortunately, when he changed jobs from supervisor to assembly worker two months ago, Leroy's benefits were reduced to $10,000. Furthermore, the profit-sharing plan contained only $1,500.

"Mrs. Calhoun is going to be one unhappy lady," Pierre said.

"Unhappy is an understatement," Jean-Claude said, pointing to the line on the document that indicated the beneficiary. "Look here."

Pierre blanched. Leroy listed his ex-wife, Velma, as the beneficiary. The same was true for the profit-sharing plan. A further check on the records showed that Leroy had listed Lucretia as his current spouse and added her to his health benefits. However, he had failed to change the beneficiary on his life insurance policy to Lucretia.

Jean-Claude returned with Pierre to the office where the group eagerly awaited the news. Using the utmost diplomacy, the two men explained the situation. However, even Henry Kissinger himself could not have mollified this group.

Lucretia's face grew more intense with anger. Then she raised her fist and shouted curses toward the ceiling as though addressing Leroy's ghost, while Fogel's spirits dropped like yesterday's party balloons. Finally, after about five minutes of Lucretia's histrionics, the two sisters stomped out of Pierre's office with the deflated undertaker following meekly behind.

Although human resources professionals deal with complex and difficult situations on a daily basis, it seems inconceivable that we could be hurt or even killed in the normal course of conducting business. However, one only has to read the newspapers to know that society is changing and workplace violence exists. Thus, it's our obligation to maintain our own safety as well as the safety of those around us. We think Pierre's actions were irresponsible in this case.

Pierre should have taken some precautionary measures to more effectively gauge the situation. He could have requested that the receptionist assess the purpose of the trio's visit. Once he knew their intentions, Pierre should have called the factory to determine if Leroy was at work. Alternatively, Pierre could have pretended to have a busy schedule, playing for time until he obtained more information. He also could have alerted security and had them available if needed.

After safely extricating himself from the meeting, Pierre's biggest error in judgment was *returning* without taking appropriate precautions. Having an attorney at his side might save him in court, but would be no defense against a gun if Lucretia had decided to bring one along.

Before returning, Pierre easily could and should have alerted company security, called the local police to alert them, and then listened to their assessment of this group's potential for violence. At a minimum he could have advised the receptionist to prepare to call the police if it appeared that there was an altercation.

Furthermore, to avoid any potential negative reaction to the bad news, he could have engaged in a number of stall tactics. Such tactics would have enabled him to safely communicate by letter or telephone without exposing the company to liability. Pierre could have indicated, for example, that he was unable to locate the records. He also could have stated that he required a copy of the death certificate to start the process and would have to contact the insurance company to verify the benefits.

Besides Pierre's failure to take appropriate safety precautions in the office, we feel disclosing the beneficiary details to the group was a breech of privacy to the real beneficiary. In doing so, Pierre exposed the company to liability and potentially endangered the real beneficiary.

Pierre was lucky. Through no action of his own he got through the meeting unharmed. His next step, however, should be to document the incident, advise the police of the situation, and consider advising the beneficiary as well.

From a benefits administration perspective, there are some additional considerations. Insurance companies honor the beneficiary designated regardless of the employee's current marital status. Employees who divorce and remarry may not remember to change beneficiaries on policies. In this case, Lucretia is probably out of luck. However, Pierre can minimize a reoccurrence by preparing a checklist to include with all coverages requiring beneficiaries. This checklist could be used whenever an employee wishes to change *any* coverage affecting a beneficiary. For example, someone from the human resources staff could go over the checklist with each employee who asks to change health care dependents.

Also, the company could enclose annual or quarterly notices in employees' paychecks, reminding them to make sure their beneficiaries are current. Moreover, during open enrollment each year (the period when employees can re-enroll or update their benefits, specifically life and health programs), companies should ask employees to review and update any beneficiary designations as well. In this particular case, such a review would prevent a former spouse being awarded survivor benefits even though a new survivor exists.

 It is not uncommon for employees to forget (or fail) to change their beneficiaries on company-provided benefits to reflect their current family situations. Often employees are not familiar with the company's procedures for such matters as changing beneficiaries on life insurance or savings plans or adding dependents to medical and dental plans. Sometimes employees are not even aware that they may need to fill out different change forms for each company benefit. To assist employees in this matter and to avoid litigation by disgruntled children, widows, and others, it is prudent for employers to communicate the company's benefit plan. The company should provide information about benefit procedures in the company handbook and remind employees to

review designated beneficiaries on their various beneficiary forms annually.

Some employers and their insurance companies are sued by persons who believe the company is responsible for their misfortune in not being designated on the beneficiary form. Ultimately, in order to succeed in being recognized as the "rightful" beneficiary, the non-designated beneficiary would probably have to prove one or both of the following: that it was the intent of the employee to designate that individual and that the company had represented to the employee that he/she had done what was necessary to effectuate the necessary change in beneficiary, or that the company had been negligent in failing to honor the employee's express intent. Generally, if successful, such a beneficiary would receive only the benefits of the policy at issue and would not be entitled to punitive or emotional suffering damages.

A final note: did Leroy really *forget* to designate Lucretia as his beneficiary?!

Relief or Grief

Victoria Morrow, the benefits manager, was scheduled to meet with Minnie McManus, one of the staff surgical nurses. Minnie arrived promptly, and Victoria offered her some coffee.

"No thanks. I just came off my shift, and I'll never sleep tonight if I have a cup so late in the afternoon," Minnie said.

Victoria smiled warmly and said, "So how can I help you, Minnie?"

"I just want to clarify a few things about our benefits."

"Which benefits are you concerned about?" Victoria asked.

"It's my understanding that our health insurance will pay for an abortion whether it is medically necessary or elective. Is that correct?"

"Yes, that's correct, Minnie," Victoria confirmed. "We are one of the few organizations that pay for elective abortions."

"That's what I thought," Minnie said. "I'm glad we do, because I'm going to require the procedure. However, I need to know if I'm eligible for one of our other benefits."

"Which one?" Victoria asked compassionately.

"I'd like to know if I can take bereavement leave, following the procedure. Generally we get a week if it's next of kin, don't we?"

Victoria tried to mask her astonishment, although the thoughts running through her mind were, "Bereavement leave? For an elective abortion? Are you nuts?" Out loud she replied, "Minnie, bereavement leave is normally reserved for the death of a person, which usually involves a funeral or some type of memorial service. It generally doesn't cover an unborn fetus."

"Well, would you provide it if someone miscarried, say at six or seven months?" Minnie countered.

Victoria was stumped. The issue had never come up. "I don't know, Minnie, we haven't had to test our policy in that way, although you do raise an interesting point. There certainly would be real grief involved, but I don't know if the grief period would fall under bereavement leave. I would imagine that any grief or recovery time needed after the miscarriage probably would wind up being covered under our disability plan."

"Well, let me tell you, Victoria, my grief will be no less real than someone who had a miscarriage," Minnie said, as her voice cracked and her eyes welled up with tears. "Right now I have three children and my husband just lost his job. When I found out yesterday that I was two months' pregnant, he told me he just couldn't deal with the pressure of another child and would divorce me if I had it."

"Have you considered all your options?" Victoria asked.

"You tell me. Do I have any other real options?" Minnie asked bitterly. "Our disability policy is limited to three months, and I don't know how I could physically handle this pregnancy even if I decided to carry the baby to term. I'm 46 years old. It's likely that at my age the pregnancy will be risky. I probably wouldn't be able to work up to the last minute as I did with my other three children. It wouldn't surprise me if I ran into complications and had to stop working by the second trimester. If that happened, I'd be without income for several months. We just can't afford that!" Minnie sobbed.

"And, as far as giving the child up for adoption," Minnie continued tearfully, "forget it. That would kill me. So in order for me to stay sane about this whole thing, I have to have the abortion. But, believe me, it was a very hard decision. I feel like I'm grieving already."

Victoria was deeply moved. She could understand Minnie's dilemma but felt that her situation was beyond the scope of the bereavement leave policy. If she allowed Minnie to use the benefit, it would set an unusual precedent.

"Minnie, I can appreciate how you feel, but I don't think bereavement leave is the appropriate benefit to meet your need. Let me offer you some alternatives. Obviously, your choice is a difficult one and one that is causing you pain. Let me suggest that you consider taking advantage of our EAP—that's our employee assistance program. This program provides confidential counseling at no cost to you. Another alternative is for you to use your medical benefits for psychological counseling that is reimbursed at 50 percent. I think the critical issue here is that you get whatever help you need."

Minnie dried her tears. "I know I can't afford to pay for the counseling through our health benefit—at least not now. I didn't realize we could use the EAP for this type of thing. You're right, I do need help. Can you help me make arrangements?"

"Absolutely," Victoria said. "I'll be glad to help in any way I can."

The purpose of bereavement leave is generally to arrange for and/or attend funeral or memorial services. Since we assume there would be no such service in this case, we all agree that bereavement leave is not the appropriate benefit coverage. To clarify the intent of such policies, some companies use the term "funeral" leave instead of bereavement leave.

Some of us feel that the company should eliminate its bereavement leave policy and provide sick leave or personal leave for such situations. And, since abortion is a medical procedure, perhaps Minnie should discuss an appropriate medical disability with her doctor, considering her emotional condition.

Victoria demonstrated compassion and was wise to refer Minnie to the employee assistance program for counseling. Clearly Minnie was distraught and not in an emotional position to make such an important decision. However Victoria should *not* have engaged in speculation or hypothesizing about benefits coverage with Minnie. An early EAP referral might have resulted in the development of additional alternatives that Victoria hadn't initially considered, thus avoiding further debate about the bereavement coverage.

Victoria took unnecessary risks by openly speculating about benefits with Minnie. She may have given Minnie ideas that might ultimately cost the company more money than by simply agreeing to bereavement leave. On the other hand, re-engaging Minnie in the discussion *after* an EAP referral would have given Victoria time to consider all the options and/or seek additional advice from other experts.

Finally, some of us feel the company should reconsider the length of this type of leave, as it appears excessive based on typical bereavement practices.

It's a wise human resources manager who recognizes his/her limitations when it comes to dealing with some employees' personal problems. One of the great advantages for companies that have employee assistance programs is that the company can offer its employees free or low-cost counseling for personal problems, thus relieving human resources from playing the role of psychologist or from becoming too intimately involved in an employee's personal life.

We commend Victoria for her sensitivity in recognizing that the bereavement leave, even if extended to Minnie, would not solve her underlying problems. Under the circumstances, a referral to the EAP seems like the appropriate solution.

The request for bereavement leave for an elective abortion is a new one on us. We are unaware of any case on point. One potential legal issue that comes to mind in this context is the requirement for employers to reasonably accommodate an employee's religious beliefs. For some employees, it is a tenet of their faith that life begins at conception, and the death of an unborn child as a result of miscarriage, stillbirth, or abortion may be just as tragic as the death of a living child, thus justifying a bereavement leave. It would not be unreasonable for a company to adapt its bereavement policy to such situations, but that is a policy matter, not a legal obligation. The company would also need to be sensitive to the precedent that granting bereavement leave for an abortion would create.

Chapter 8

Flaming Frauds

"A company should clearly communicate its philosophy regarding the consequences of workers' compensation fraud."

Charles F. Weiss, SPHR
Senior Vice President - Chief Administrative Officer
Pacific Enterprises

The Mysterious Malingerer

"Hi, Clyde, what can I do for you?" Bennett Rutowski, the human resources manager asked.

"I'd like to request a medical leave. My doctor tells me I have a brain tumor and he wants to send me out of state to a hospital where he knows some specialists," Clyde said. "So I'm going to have to leave for a while and have the operation there. The doctor said I'll probably need to be off about eight to 10 weeks."

"I'm sorry to hear that, Clyde," Bennett said sincerely. "Where's the hospital located?"

"California," Clyde responded.

"How soon do you need to have this surgery?"

"Next week."

"Okay, I'll make arrangements for your leave. You, of course, understand that you'll have to deal directly with the insurance carrier to get approval for payment on the surgery," Bennett informed him.

"I've already begun the process," Clyde said.

Clyde had worked for the small processing plant as a supervisor for the past eight years. He was well liked and well respected. Bennett was concerned. He knew that Clyde was a widower, struggling to raise two teen-age boys.

"Who in your family will be there to help you?" Bennett asked.

"My sons will be coming along with me."

"Will you have one of them call me when you're out of surgery to let us know how you're doing? They can call collect," Bennett said.

"Sure."

The following week, Bennett got a call from one of Clyde's sons, Harry. Harry told Bennett that his dad was doing well and expected to return to work in two weeks.

"Two weeks! That's terrific!" Bennett exclaimed. "Can you tell me the name of the hospital and what room your dad's in? We'd like to send some flowers."

"I really don't know his room number," Harry said.

"Well, what's the name of the hospital?"

"Mount Sinai," Harry responded.

Bennett's assistant, Brian, called the hospital to get the information. Brian reported that the hospital had no record of Clyde as a patient. "I checked all over the hospital and probably spoke to nearly a dozen different departments. There is no record. I even called the person who schedules the surgery, and Clyde wasn't on the list." Brian said. "The billing department doesn't have him registered, either. Don't you think that's strange?"

"Sure do," Bennett remarked, tapping his pencil on his desk. "I sure do."

The next day, Clyde called the office. "Hi, Bennett," Clyde began. "My son told me you wanted to send flowers. That's real nice, but really— don't bother. I'm all right, you just can't call me because there's no phone in the room. And Harry couldn't tell you what room I'm in because they keep moving me. First I'm in recovery, then intensive care, then here."

Bennett's antennae began to rise. "But you *are* at Mt. Sinai, aren't you?"

"Oh, yeah. It's a great hospital," Clyde confirmed.

"Well, so how are you doing?"

"To be honest, they told me that the tumor's malignant and that I probably only have a year to live," Clyde said softly.

"Oh, Clyde, I'm really sorry. Is there anything I can do?" Bennett offered politely, despite his feeling that Clyde was scamming him.

"There's nothing you can really do. I just ask that you keep this confidential. I don't want anyone at the plant to know I'm dying," Clyde said gravely.

"Of course, I won't tell anyone. By the way, where are your boys staying?"

"They're at the Calastoga Motel in town," Clyde answered.

Bennett informed Brian of his latest discovery. Brian verified that the boys were indeed at the hotel, but Brian could not get a verification of Clyde's stay at the hospital.

A few days later, Clyde called Bennett again. "Just wanted to let you know, I'll be discharged tomorrow."

"Five days after brain surgery? That's amazing! By the way, how come you're not registered with the hospital?" Bennett asked.

"Oh, I worked something out with the doctor."

"What doctor?"

"Dr. Ozwald Sampson," Clyde said.

"Can I call the doctor?"

"What for?" asked Clyde.

"I'm concerned about you. I'd like to know what's happening," Bennett answered.

Subsequently, Bennett attempted to locate Dr. Sampson. There was no listing for the doctor in the telephone directory in the city where they were supposedly staying. There was also no Dr. Ozwald Sampson registered with a license to practice in the state of California.

Bennett grew concerned. He wanted to get to the bottom of things and began a quiet investigation among Clyde's co-workers and the staff in the plant.

About a week and a half after his surgery, Clyde showed up at the plant. He staggered into Bennett's office with his head wrapped in bandages. When Bennett saw him he said, "Are you okay? I hope you didn't drive."

"No, of course not. My son dropped me off, but he'll be back in a little bit. I wanted to talk to you and explain what's going on," said Clyde. "I just need to make sure you didn't tell anyone in the plant that I'm going to die. Also, I want to start back to work next week."

"Look, Clyde, we keep all employee medical information confidential, and I'm truly sorry about your condition. But before I can have you return to work, I need a medical release from your doctor."

"Why?" asked Clyde.

"Because that's our policy."

Clyde started to shift in his seat and looked uncomfortable. "What do you mean?"

"Well, obviously you're an incredible individual. You had brain surgery and a tumor removed. Then, in less than a week, you're discharged from the hospital and drive halfway across the country. Now you're back home and want to start work next week. That's a remarkable recovery. I assume that you've been referred to a surgeon here to follow up on your care."

"Yeah," Clyde affirmed.

"Fine, can you give me his name?"

"I've got it written down at home. I don't remember." Suddenly, Clyde behaved as though he were dizzy and having double vision. "I'll call you tomorrow and tell you."

The next day Clyde called. "Look, Bennett, I'm very embarrassed, but this whole thing has been a sham."

"Oh, is that so?" Bennett remarked, although he was not surprised. During his investigation, Bennett had discovered that Clyde had collected between $3,000 to $5,000 from the other employees. Clyde had told them he needed money for surgery because insurance would only pay for part of it.

"Look, Bennett, this whole thing just snowballed. I was looking for a little sympathy, and one lie led to another. I just can't deal with it anymore," Clyde admitted.

Bennett suggested to Clyde that he come in and discuss the situation in person. After Bennett gathered all the facts, he provided some alternatives. Bennett explained to Clyde that he was in a very responsible position as a supervisor and that his recent actions had destroyed his credibility. Thus, Clyde would be removed from his position as supervisor. However, Bennett recognized that Clyde had been a model employee up to that point, so he offered him two choices. Clyde could accept a demotion and continue with the company, or he could resign. Clyde opted to resign. Subsequently, Bennett assisted him by arranging for interviews with other employers. Fortunately for Clyde, another organization employed him shortly thereafter.

Bennett is the person who needs brain surgery in this case! Bennett could have completely avoided the entire situation if he had required medical certification *before* granting the leave of absence. Even under the Family and Medical Leave Act, Bennett had a right to require such proof up front.

Certainly his company should consider requiring pre-certification for hospital admissions. This action directs the service provider to investigate the proposed procedure. They typically assess the length of stay as well as determine whether services could be performed at the same quality level at a more efficient, less costly location. If Bennett had purchased these cost-saving services, Clyde would not have been allowed to continue the charade.

Human resources staffs routinely call upon health care practitioners. These practitioners will verify and monitor the progress of treatment for certain individuals if the legitimacy of the illness may be questionable or the nature of the claim is costly. In the latter case, such monitoring is entirely appropriate. Many companies may decide to purchase case management services (i.e., a registered nurse who works with the patient and the physician to determine the most cost-effective health care delivery).

Bennett was correct to request a physician's release before allowing Clyde to return to work. Without such a release, Bennett would expose the company to substantial liability and possibly workers' compensation problems by allowing someone who was not well to return to work.

However, Bennett failed miserably in other aspects of this case. The majority of us feel that Bennett should never have given Clyde the option of demotion and retention as an employee. Clyde lied on numerous occasions, obtained company disability benefits fraudulently, and violated his supervisory trust by taking money from his subordinates under false pretenses. He should have been terminated and not permitted to resign. The company also had a strong case for contesting unemployment and COBRA (Consolidated Omnibus Reconciliation Act) benefits.

Perhaps the most problematic and unfathomable of Bennett's actions were his efforts to help Clyde secure another job. Bennett's implicit (and probably explicit) endorsement to prospective employers could result in severe negative consequences. His actions not only tarnish the company's reputation but may also expose the company and perhaps himself to liability if Clyde engages in such conduct at the new employer.

Employers may require medical certification from their employees requesting medical leave, whether the leave is requested pursuant to the company's own disability leave policy or the federal Family and Medical Leave Act of 1993 (FMLA). (A large number of states also have family and medical leave laws.) In this story, had Bennett requested Clyde provide him with appropriate documentation regarding his need for medical leave, the sham may have been exposed a lot sooner—and the company may have been able to retain a good employee and avoid a lot of problems.

When an employee requests a medical leave, such a request generally triggers consideration of the FMLA. In general, the FMLA requires private employers of 50 or more employees to provide eligible employees with unpaid leave of up to 12 weeks during any 12-month period. This covers the employee's own serious illness, as well as the birth or adoption of a child or the care of a seriously ill child, spouse, or parent.

The FMLA recognizes that employers must be able to plan and adequately staff their organizations. For a serious medical condition that is based on foreseeable planned medical treatment, employees must make a reasonable effort to schedule the treatment so as not to unduly disrupt the operations of the employer. For serious medical conditions that require treatment, employees are required to give 30 days advance notice before the date on which the leave would begin, or if treatment is in less than 30 days, such notice as is practicable.

To prevent employee abuse of leave for serious health conditions, the FMLA authorizes employers to require medical certification of the medical condition. This certification should include the following: a statement by the employee that he/she is unable to perform the functions of his or her job; date on which the serious health condition commenced; the probable duration of the condition; the appropriate medical facts within the knowledge of the health care provider regarding the condition; and, if an intermittent leave or reduced schedule is required, the date and duration of treatments required. If an employer doubts the original certification from the employee, an employer may require, at its own expense, a second opinion from a different health care provider chosen by the employer. If there is a conflict between the first and second medical opinions, a third opinion may be required by the employer, at its own expense, from a health care provider designated or approved jointly by the employer and the employee. The third medical opinion will be considered final and binding. An employer may require subsequent recertification from the employee on a reasonable basis and require a fitness-for-duty certification that an employee is able to resume work.

An employee who fraudulently obtains an FMLA leave from an employer has no job restoration and maintenance of health benefits protection under the FMLA.

One final note: we would caution employers against assisting a former employee in finding another job when it knew that the former employee had perpetrated a fraud against the company and his co-workers.

A Grievous Act

"Alma, there's a call for you on line two," Keith said.

When Alma picked up the line, Keith heard her scream and drop the phone. He raced over to find out what was wrong.

"Alma, what is it? Are you okay?"

"My mother . . . she's been in a car accident," she sobbed. "I've got to catch a plane to Houston. They've taken her to the hospital and she's in critical condition."

"Of course, Alma, leave right now. I'm so sorry about your mother," Keith said, putting his arm around her to comfort her.

Alma quickly gathered her belongings and left immediately. Two days later Alma called from Houston to tell Keith her mother had died. She would not be returning to work for the next five days. Keith told her not to worry and to take care of her personal business. Her five days' bereavement leave would cover her absence.

The following day Sam Sutton, the human resources manager, received a surprising telephone call.

"Sam Sutton speaking," he answered.

"Mr. Sutton, this here is Mortimer Hazelwood. You don't know me, sir, but I think you oughta know something about that connivin' Alma Florent workin' out there in your shipping department. You see, Alma done told her boss that her mama got killed. Truth is, her mama ain't dead. Alma's lied."

"I see, Mr. Hazelwood. And how do you know that?" Sam asked, wondering where this was leading.

"Cause she put me up to callin' her at the office and pretendin' like her mother got in a car wreck. Well, there weren't no wreck 'tall. She made the whole thing up so we could take off for 'Vegas.

"I'll tell you, you have to watch out for that Alma," Mortimer rattled on, "she's damn slick. Why, she even printed up prayer cards to prove to ya'll that there was a funeral. Only problem is, she decided to give me the heave-ho and took off with my cousin, Cecil, instead. Now that she's gone and taken up with Cecil, I'm hoppin' mad. So I figured I'd fix her good for leavin' me high and dry."

Sam was trying to digest what he was hearing and asked, "So you're saying that her mother is alive and there was never a car accident?"

"You got it!" Mortimer confirmed.

"And who can verify that for us?" Sam asked.

"Well, call her sister, Laura-Lynn. I can give you the number," Mortimer offered.

Sam took down all the details, pulled Alma's file, and gave Alma's boss a call. "Keith, I got a peculiar call today from Alma Florent's supposed boyfriend. He tells me Alma's mother's death is a hoax. Do you have any reason to believe this?"

"I can't believe that," Keith assured Sam. "When she found out her mother was in a car accident, that woman dissolved into tears and became as limp as a tomato plant during a Texas drought. She's called several times and could barely talk through her sobs. Why would someone be so cruel?" Keith questioned skeptically.

"I don't know," Sam said, "but I'm going to check it out. Let me have her department file, so I can see if there's anything else in there that might give me a clue."

Both files listed the closest relative as Alma's sister, Laura-Lynn Holbrook. The telephone number matched the one that Mortimer Hazelwood provided. Sam dialed the number.

"Hello," a man's voice answered.

"May I speak to Laura-Lynn Holbrook?" Sam asked.

"She isn't here right now, but this is her husband," Mr. Holbrook responded.

"Well, perhaps you can help, Mr. Holbrook. This is Sam Sutton. I'm the human resources manager where Alma Florent works. We understand her mother just died, and we would like to know where to send flowers," Sam fibbed.

"Dead? There's nothing wrong with Alma's mother. We just talked to her yesterday!" Holbrook told Sam.

"So she survived last week's car accident?" Sam asked.

"Car accident? What car accident? Where did you get that story?" Holbrook laughed.

"Alma told us that her mother died in a car accident," Sam informed him.

"Oh boy, she's up to her old tricks again," Holbrook sighed. "Mr. Sutton, Alma has always been the black sheep of the family. We're still trying to get out of debt for the bills she's run up on us. She stole my wife's driver's license and credit cards. Then she charged up a bunch of stuff and withdrew cash to support her cocaine habit. The woman can lie like a sailor. She's nothing but a thief and a junkie. Right now there's a warrant for her arrest for credit card fraud in Galveston."

"Do you have your mother-in-law's phone number?" Sam asked.

"Can't help you there. She's just moved to Topeka and has been staying with different friends until she gets settled," Holbrook said apologetically. "We only hear from her every two or three weeks, but I'll have her call you, if you'd like."

Sam thanked Holbrook, but wasn't satisfied. He had to find solid evidence to snare Alma before she returned to work. If Alma was really lying, he didn't want to drag this out. "Need to play detective . . . how can I verify the boyfriend's story?" Sam thought as he thumbed through his papers to prepare for his next appointment.

When Sam's eye fell on a vendor's business card, a broad smile crossed his face. "That's it! The printer!" he said aloud and jumped up to get the yellow pages from his bookshelf. "She must have hired a local printer to make up those phony prayer cards. Maybe we'll just get lucky . . . ."

Indeed, Sam's hunch played out. On the 14th call, he struck gold. "Yeah, we got an order from an Alma Florent about three weeks ago," the printer confirmed. He located the order and read the copy to Sam. "It said October 1, death of Mary Florent, survived by Alma Florent and Laura-Lynn Holbrook, interred October 5. Interment October 5, by the Gerasi Mortuary in Houston, Texas."

"Hot dog!" Sam thought. But he couldn't resist asking, "Didn't you think it was strange that she put in an order three weeks before her mother's death?"

"Yeah, we asked her about that," the printer said. "She told us her mother had been on a respirator for several weeks and that they planned to pull the plug on October 1 if there wasn't any improvement. She asked us to schedule the job, and she would call us if she needed the cards. As a matter of fact, we heard from her a few days ago, and she told us to run the job. Seemed to make sense to me, although I must say it was a first for us."

"Could you fax us a copy of the order as well as the prayer card?" Sam asked. "We need it for our records when we send flowers."

"Sure, no problem. I'll get it right to you," the printer responded.

Sam supplied the fax number and then called Houston information. "Could you give me the telephone number of Gerasi Mortuary?" he asked.

"I'm sorry, sir, but we have no number for that listing," the operator informed Sam.

"I knew it!" Sam grinned. But to really make sure, he called the public library and asked the librarian to check her sources for any mortuaries in Houston that sounded anything like "Gerasi." The research librarian found nothing close to the Gerasi name.

Sam informed Keith of the evidence and told him to box up Alma's personal belongings from her desk and have her report to human resources when she returned for work the following Monday. When Alma arrived in Sam's office, he told her he was aware that she had fabricated her mother's car accident and death.

Alma denied his allegations and said, "How could you be so cruel! I am still grieving. It took all my strength to come back to work today. This is nothing but mental harassment. You'll hear from my lawyer about this!" she charged.

Sam quickly doused Alma's fire when he produced photocopies of the printer's order for the prayer card and the evidence that no Gerasi Mortuary existed. Alma sat limply in her chair as he informed her that she was terminated for falsifying funeral leave. He handed her a box containing her personal belongings, informed her she would be escorted out, and buzzed his secretary.

Then a deputy from the Galveston sheriff's office walked in with a warrant in his hand. "Ms. Alma Florent?" he asked.

"Yes?" she said, still dazed over being caught in her bereavement scam.

"We have a warrant for your arrest in Galveston. You'll need to come with me," the deputy informed her.

Alma's world collapsed as the officer handcuffed her and discreetly escorted her through a side door. Sam saw them off and shook his head. Somehow, he never expected that his role as human resources manager would bring him so close to police work.

Sam must enjoy playing detective. Is his last name Spade, by any chance? On balance, Sam did a good job of handling this investigation. While it is easy to disregard anonymous callers, Sam very appropriately listened to details offered by the phone caller and verified the information. However, we think he was probably over-zealous in some of his methods of inquiry, particularly his request for the printing company's records of Alma's order. Sam's actions could be considered as infringing on the employee's privacy. Nevertheless, we support his decision to terminate Alma based on falsification of bereavement leave.

A better use of Sam's time and resources might have been to use internal investigative services, if available, or to commission an external source to verify the situation. As a human resources manager, Sam should have focused on counseling Keith, Alma's boss, about dealing with the upcoming confrontation with her, rather than single-handedly resolving the situation. The idea here is to train managers to handle human resource matters of this type, rather than to do their work for them. With Sam's actions, it's not surprising that HR gets tagged as the "company cops!"

Sam's sense of civic duty apparently compelled him to inform the Galveston police about Alma's whereabouts. However, it was poor judgment to blend that initiative into Alma's termination for falsification. Sam could have contacted the Galveston police after her termination, thereby avoiding her workplace arrest.

Finally, once the decision was made to terminate Alma, Sam should have selected a more appropriate procedure for handling the removal of her personal belongings. Given Alma's propensity for falsification, it would more prudent to grant her the opportunity under supervision to remove her belongings rather than having Keith do so.

 Human resources managers undoubtedly wear many hats. But just as human resources managers should avoid the risk of becoming an *agent* of the police (see, *Deadbeat Dad*), they should also resist the temptation to overplay the Sherlock Holmes/private investigator routine. Employers need to proceed with caution, being mindful of privacy rights of individuals, when investigating matters concerning employees.

While it turned out that Alma was lying, Alma's boyfriend may just have easily been lying when he reported Alma's scheme to Sam. Sam's actions aptly illustrate how an overzealous investigation can create a potential risk of liability for invasion of privacy when an employer, without authorization from the employee, begins calling individuals, making personal statements—possibly untrue statements—to those individuals. Similarly, human resources "investigators" may damage the reputation of persons they inquire about, and this may lead to libel or slander claims, for which both the manager and the employer may be liable.

Back in the Saddle

Emily reviewed the fifth workers' compensation claim submitted by Dakota Hornsby during his two-year tenure with the company. "Gosh, I could probably set my clock by this guy," she groaned.

Dakota was one of the company's custodians. His first claim involved a back injury sustained while replacing a light bulb in a ceiling fixture. Dakota indicated that the twisting and stretching motion pulled his back. He was off for two weeks and then placed on light duty for the next two weeks. Three or four months later, he claimed he hurt his back while tightening some bolts in the boiler room. That time he was off for four weeks. All his claims involved soft-tissue, lower-back pain, which were certified by a physician.

It seemed that every three or four months Dakota would injure himself and require a period of recuperation. Emily realized that she had little alternative but to process his claim. This time Dakota allegedly pulled his back while painting the ceiling and required three weeks off for bed rest and light activity.

About a week later, one of Dakota's fellow custodians, Miller Hanson, knocked on her door.

"Excuse me, Emily, could I see you for a moment?" Miller asked.

"Sure, come in," Emily said. "How can I help you?"

There was a long pause. Emily waited patiently and then finally asked, "Is something wrong, Miller?"

"Well, I just don't think it's right," Miller began.

Emily continued to smile and nod her head, encouraging him to express his concern. Again, Miller grew silent.

"Miller, whatever it is, I'll try to help you. What don't you think is right?" asked Emily.

"I hate being a snitch, but I think Dakota's been sandbagging you about his back injuries," Miller informed her contemptuously. "I don't think it's fair that the company has to pay for his recreation."

"I've pretty much known that all along, but just try to prove it," Emily thought bitterly. Then she addressed Miller, "What makes you think he's 'sandbagging' us, Miller?"

"Well," Miller replied, "he was telling all the fellows that he was getting ready to ride in a rodeo next week. And Emily, I can lay you odds he won't be flat on his back at home. I'll bet you you'll find him up there riding and doing it on the company's nickel. It must be nice to get extra paid vacation."

Emily knew she shouldn't jump to conclusions, but this was wonderful news. She tried to contain her excitement. "I see," she responded with perfect composure. "Do you happen to know the name of the rodeo and where it's going to be held?"

"I'm not exactly sure," Miller responded. "But I know he belongs to some association that plans all these events. It shouldn't be too hard to find out. I just don't want him to know it was me that told you."

"I'm not sure I can promise you that. If what you say is true, we may end up in a legal battle over this. If that's the case and I'm deposed by his attorney, I may have to tell them if I'm asked," Emily said earnestly. "I can promise you this: I won't volunteer my source."

"Well, what's wrong is wrong," Miller said. "I guess if he finds out it was me, then he does."

Emily thanked Miller and began her investigation. She called security and briefed them on Miller's allegations. They located the city and date of the upcoming event and drove to the site armed with a video camera. Sure enough, as Miller had predicted, Dakota was there, listed in the program as Rider Number 23.

The security officers enjoyed the rodeo and waited anxiously for Dakota's appearance. As soon as the announcer called for Rider Number 23, the security officer started taping. Moments later, Dakota broke out of the chute atop the black stallion, Wild Diablo. The security officer got excellent footage of Dakota spurring the horse and clinging to the rope, while the bucking bronco tossed him wildly about. As Dakota held for his eight-second ride, the security officer zoomed in on his face and panned to his body. Finally, he captured the number 23 pinned to Dakota's back. The officers found it equally gratifying to obtain the extra footage of Dakota grinning ear to ear as he received the trophy for third place.

Emily was ecstatic when she viewed the footage. She contacted corporate counsel and began proceedings to deny Dakota's claim and terminate his employment for falsification of a claim. Although Dakota's attorney initially tried to appeal the workers' compensation claim, once the company informed him of the video, he dropped the case. When confronted with the evidence, Dakota made no effort to fight the termination.

Abuse of workers' compensation can significantly drain a company's bottom line as well as negatively affect employee morale and loyalty. Hats off to Miller! If he had not come forward, the company may have continued to pay Dakota's claims.

Dakota's work group had knowledge of the cowboy's scam. If he continued to successfully defraud the company, this could perpetuate the belief that "If he can get away with this, so can I." Unchecked, such thinking can spread rapidly and create other fraudulent claims. The major lesson in this case is to clearly communicate the company's philosophy concerning the consequences of any type of fraud and implement preventive strategies.

Regarding Emily's actions, we commend her reaction and response to Miller; it was close to perfect. She exhibited good listening skills, provided a supportive environment, and demonstrated patience, which helped Miller deliver a difficult message. Along with her listening skills, Emily used good open-ended questioning techniques during their discussion. She didn't pressure Miller or lead him into answers he might have anticipated she was seeking. Any less skill may have resulted in Miller's leaving without overcoming his obvious reluctance to inform on a co-worker.

We also credit Emily for controlling her desire to express her long-held suspicions to Miller. Such an admission would be clearly inappropriate and possibly defamatory, particularly if the allegations ultimately proved false or inconclusive.

While we do not see any invasion of privacy in this case since security conducted the filming in a public forum, one must also be aware of such issues. Thus, Emily should have consulted an attorney *before* sending security to the rodeo. Furthermore, in complicated legal proceedings, advice from attorneys in advance will help increase chances that chain-of-custody and other evidentiary issues don't preclude using a videotape in court.

Many of us think that Emily should have been more proactive in this case. She should have acted on her suspicions sooner by having her workers' compensation insurance carrier investigate Dakota's claims. If she had, perhaps the problem would not have persisted for two years. Insurance carriers employ investigators for just this purpose. Moreover, many companies require pre-employment physical examinations. This procedure typically narrows the possibility of paying for pre-existing conditions through workers' compensation.

Additionally, the company might consider adopting and publishing a confidential informant "hot line." This would make it easier for civic-minded employees to alert their employer about fraudulent activities and goldbrickers like Dakota.

Today many employers are plagued with meritless workers' compensation claims. While most workers' compensation claims are legitimate, the proliferation of false claims has become a national crisis and costs employers unnecessary expenditures in insurance premiums, not to mention excessive absenteeism of the malingerers and loss of productivity. In some instances, insurance carriers and employers are driven to undertaking defensive tactics such as surveillance, as illustrated in this story, in an effort to expose the false claim.

Employers are often concerned about invasion of privacy claims when it comes to videotaping employees. Federal and state legislation is evolving in the area of workplace monitoring and employers need to ascertain the legality of videotaping in certain circumstances on their work premises. However, in this instance, the videotaping did not take place on company property—it took place in public, at an event where many individuals may have been taking photographs or videotaping, and where Dakota certainly had no expectation of privacy. Thus, he could not successfully claim that the company invaded his privacy.

While employers may not retaliate against employees for asserting their rights under workers' compensation law, it is not unlawful for an employer to terminate an employee who has falsified a claim.

Larceny or Lunacy

Doug Markham thumbed through the sales printouts with the skill of a weaver. "Territory 6 looks good . . . Territory 7's doing great . . . look out Territory 8, you've knocked them out of town!" he exclaimed. Then he turned to Territory 9. "Whoa, mama, have we gone to sleep here?" Sales were nearly zero for the month.

Kashra Rushdi was in charge of Territory 9. Doug leaned back in his chair and tapped his pencil rhythmically on the armrest. He mulled over Kashra's history during the past few months. Doug had been working with Kashra each month attempting to identify problems and giving him tips to improve sales. Obviously, his periodic phone calls and gentle nudging weren't doing the trick. Lately, it even seemed as though Kashra was trying to dodge his phone calls.

It didn't make sense to Doug. Doug had a reputation for being an effective sales manager whose ability to train staff had won him a number of awards. Although their product was highly technical, Kashra was bright and well educated. Plus, with his Middle Eastern background, Kashra should be kicking sales through the ceiling, since his assigned territory catered to Middle Easterners. Doug just couldn't understand why sales continued to plummet.

"Maybe I need to shoot some life into him," Doug said to himself. "I'll go out and ride with him for a day or two and see if I can motivate him." This time when he dialed Kashra on his car phone, Doug finally connected.

"Kashra, this is Doug. Which parkway am I catching you on?" he asked.

"Actually, I'm stopped at a light on Main," Kashra replied.

"Listen, I've just gone over last month's sales report for your territory, and I think we need to get together," Doug suggested. "I'll drive up the coast and catch you on Tuesday."

"Oh, you don't have to take the trouble," Kashra said. "I'm doing just fine. I'm loaded with appointments for the next two weeks."

"That reminds me," Doug said, "I haven't received your call reports in three weeks."

"Really? I don't understand," Kashra said. "I send them every week. Maybe there's a problem with the mail."

"Well, how about faxing the copies to me?"

"The copies . . . ?" Kashra stumbled.

"Yes, you know, the call reports are in multiple pages. You keep copies for yourself, don't you? You need them for tax purposes, I would suppose," Doug reminded him.

"Oh, yes, yes, of course," Kashra said. "I'll fax you the copies when I get home."

"But I still want to come up and spend some time with you," Doug persisted. "I'm glad you're so busy. I think it would be good for us to catch up on things."

"This really isn't a good week. I have relatives visiting," Kashra responded.

"Well, I'm only going to be with you during your scheduled appointments. I promise I won't keep you out in the evenings," Doug assured him. "I'll be up on Tuesday and meet you at the district office at 7:30 a.m.—unless, of course, you have an appointment scheduled sooner than that," Doug joked.

Kashra realized that Doug was not going to take no for an answer and agreed to meet him Tuesday. When Doug arrived at the office, he waited until 8 a.m. for Kashra.

"Oh, sorry I'm late, Doug. I felt a little queasy this morning, so I got a slow start," Kashra apologized.

"Gee, that's too bad. I hope you're feeling better, Kashra. Would you like me to drive?" Doug offered sincerely.

"Oh, no. I'll be okay," Kashra said weakly. "I took an antacid."

The two of them got into Kashra's car and pulled out of the parking lot and onto Main Street. They were in the middle of discussing one of Kashra's prospects when suddenly Kashra slumped over the steering wheel and the car began to veer into the next lane of traffic.

Startled, Doug grabbed the steering wheel, turning it to the right while pushing Kashra's lifeless body back into his seat, and quickly pulled the car back into position. Then he kicked Kashra's feet out of the way to reach the brake. Eventually, Doug maneuvered the car to the berm, eased it to a stop, and turned off the ignition. He tapped Kashra lightly and asked him if he was okay, but got no response. Terrified, Doug called 911 from the car phone for an ambulance. The emergency squad arrived within four minutes.

As the paramedics approached the car, Kashra suddenly bolted upright. "I really didn't want you to be here," he blurted out. "I'm very anxious about this, so I thought if I pretended to have a heart attack you would leave me alone."

Doug was speechless and stared at Kashra incredulously. His thoughts were interrupted by a paramedic tapping on the car window. Although Doug was still shaken by the highway episode as well as confused by Kashra's untimely confession, Doug informed the paramedics that Kashra had somehow miraculously revived. The paramedics checked Kashra's vitals, asked key questions, and then departed as quickly as they arrived.

Doug regained his composure and looked squarely at Kashra. "Kashra, I am here to help you, not to hurt you. That is my job. Do you understand that?"

Kashra nodded in weak acknowledgment. They spent the next several hours over coffee, where Doug used all his knowledge and training to help Kashra reduce his anxiety about Doug's visit. He suggested that Kashra cancel the remainder of his appointments and go home and relax for the rest of the afternoon. Kashra agreed to try again the next day.

The next morning began much like the first, with Kashra arriving a half-hour late for his appointment with Doug. Doug couldn't believe that Kashra continued this passive-aggressive behavior but tried to remain patient. Again, they began their journey on Main Street. This time they entered a ramp that accessed a toll bridge. There were four lanes for the toll gate, and Kashra chose the gate farthest to the left. Once Kashra paid the toll, he got a wild look on his face, turned the wheel to the right, and began to accelerate the car. He sped recklessly across all lanes of traffic and aimed directly for the guard rail.

"Are you crazy?! You're going to drive us right off the bridge!" Doug shouted, and wrestled the wheel from Kashra.

Doug reached his foot to the brake, but couldn't slow the car down quickly enough to avoid smashing head-on into the railing. Both men were jolted forward from the impact. Doug threw the gear into park, ripped the keys out of the ignition, tore off his seat belt, and leaped out of the car. He stood on the walkway and breathlessly balanced himself against the guard rail. Finally, he summoned the courage to look down, and took a big gulp as he stared at the water 80 feet below.

Still breathless and dazed, Doug stared at Kashra who remained transfixed behind the wheel. The police sirens interrupted Doug's thoughts. Doug told them he was Kashra's boss and that Kashra was feeling exceptionally pressured by his visit, which may have contributed to his irrational behavior. While they questioned Kashra, Doug noticed that the impact of the collision had caused the trunk to pop open. When he looked inside, he saw about a four-months' supply of undelivered customer samples crammed in every available corner. "I think I'm beginning to understand why he didn't want me around," Doug murmured and unobtrusively closed the trunk.

The police cited Kashra for reckless driving. Since the car was still operable, the police allowed Doug to drive Kashra home. Doug said nothing to Kashra about the undelivered samples in his trunk. When Doug pulled the car up to Kashra's house, he stopped in front of a two-car garage and opened the door with the remote attached to the visor. There in the right bay of the garage Doug saw boxes of company samples stacked from floor to ceiling.

Kashra said nothing. He meekly opened the car door and walked quietly into his house. Doug immediately called the district office from the car phone. He asked for security to come to Kashra's home so they could document the samples, take pictures, and remove the items from the premises.

A full internal investigation followed, and security learned from Kashra's customers that his samples were never delivered. Security also discovered that Kashra attempted to form alliances with salesmen from other territories. He offered to buy some of their samples in return for a cut of the profits he made from selling the product directly. Through his connections, Kashra could obtain triple the retail price on the street.

The human resources manager coordinated with security, legal counsel, and public relations. They decided against filing criminal charges. If the public were aware that one of their employees was selling their product illegally, it could tarnish their public image. Instead, they chose to end Kashra's employment for poor performance and unauthorized use of company property. Kashra showed extreme remorse for his behavior and told them he appreciated that they didn't file criminal charges.

Kashra's appreciation was short-lived. He took his case to the Equal Employment Opportunity Commission (EEOC), which sued the company on Kashra's behalf for age and ethnic origin discrimination. Not surprisingly,

Kashra conveniently left out a few key facts surrounding his discharge. Thus, when the EEOC investigated the full story, it dismissed the case.

Whoa! Fasten your seat belt! This is an example of lack of timely management follow-up of performance indicators. Where has Doug been for the past several months—asleep at the loom while Kashra was weaving his intricate pattern of deceit? Why didn't Doug deal with Kashra's performance more directly when a trend began to develop? This never would have happened if Doug performed regular audits and gave Kashra an action plan. Both parties should have signed the plan, and Doug should have set follow-up meetings to monitor the results.

Although we support the company's decision to terminate, we feel "termination for poor performance" was a risky choice of words. Unfortunately, "poor performance" often is interpreted as a lack of training in unemployment hearings. Instead, we recommend "theft," "unauthorized use," or "failure to perform the job of which he was capable"—all immediate termination offenses.

We would also advise that the company have a handbook for employees to sign, demonstrating their acknowledgment of the rules. This strategy acts as further evidence that Kashra knew his actions were against the rules. We also suggest that the company review its hiring decisions and determine if something in Kashra's history or during the interview process would have tipped the company off to his behavior problems.

We disagree with the company's failure to file criminal charges. We don't believe the concern about tarnishing the company's public image is valid. Most people recognize that any company may have a bad apple. The public will be more impressed if they perceive that the company has dealt firmly with the situation rather than attempting to sweep it under the carpet. Prosecution also clearly signals to other employees that the company will not tolerate criminal misconduct. It demonstrates that employees who engage in such activities will not only lose their jobs but also face the criminal justice system.

 An interesting issue posed by this story is the company's right to search for and reclaim company property that is in the employee's possession. Federal constitutional prohibitions against warrantless searches and seizures generally apply only to *government* searches. However, many states restrict an employer's right to search such areas as an employee's desk, office, briefcase, and locker. Employers should ascertain the lawfulness of searches in their jurisdiction prior to doing such a search.

In this case, Kashra would likely have an "expectation of privacy" in his garage at home, and it is unlikely that the employer could lawfully drive a truck up to an employee's garage and start loading up boxes, since there is no indication that Kashra consented. Thus, the company might be liable for trespass.

It is understandable that the employer wished to preserve its public image, but this is theft—and that is the province of the police. The company materials would likely be considered to be evidence. Technically, the company would have the right to commence legal proceedings to recover its property or the value thereof but resorting to self-help is always fraught with peril for employers.

This story also illustrates the company playing "good guy" and getting stung—that is, getting slapped with an EEOC charge. To minimize its risk of legal proceedings, the company could have considered having Kashra sign a release surrendering his right to file any charge or suit against the company relating to his termination, perhaps in exchange for the company agreeing not to commence a civil lawsuit against him and a repayment schedule. Releases should always be drafted with the assistance of counsel to ensure they are enforceable.

Chapter 9

Gender Blenders

*"Our competitive position in world markets depends on our ability to use the talents of **all** our human resources."*

J. Barry Bigham, CCP
Director of Compensation
Monsanto Corporation

Pointed in the Right Direction

As Maggie stood in front of the mirror to give her hair a quick spray, she saw Georgia enter the rest room and walk toward one of the stalls. Maggie smiled in the mirror and gave Georgia a wave to say hello.

"Hi, Maggie," Georgia said. "How are ya doin'?"

"Trying to keep my hair from frizzing today," Maggie grinned. "The humidity is a killer."

Georgia walked into the stall and closed the door. While Maggie finished touching up her make-up, she heard a thunderous flow of water. Startled, Maggie scanned the row of sinks to see if there was a leak, but found no running water. Then she turned toward the stalls and began checking each. When she peeked in the stall next to the one Georgia occupied, she noticed that Georgia's feet were facing the commode rather than pointing toward the door.

"Strange . . . ," Maggie thought, as she scratched her head and did a quick calculation. Something didn't seem quite right. Georgia's feet were not only aimed in the wrong direction for someone who would be sitting, but they were also a considerable distance from the commode.

When Maggie heard a flush, she raced back to the sink area and pretended she was still primping. Georgia came out of the stall, smiled at Maggie, washed her hands, and went on her way. Maggie was perplexed. She knew that some women preferred to avoid sitting on a commode for sanitary purposes. However, even if they used the camper's squat, their feet pointed forward. "Well, maybe Georgia straddles backwards," Maggie considered and decided to test it out.

Maggie entered a stall and stood facing the commode. She attempted to straddle the commode and noticed her feet. They were placed along side of the commode, not a foot or so away as Georgia's had been.

A cold chill ran up Maggie's spine as all sorts of possibilities ran through her mind. The idea that Georgia may be using the ladies' rest room for an opportunity to satisfy a voyeuristic obsession frightened Maggie. Then she worried, "What if she's a *he* waiting for an opportunity to rape one of us?"

Maggie decided not to jump to any more irrational conclusions and enlisted several of her female co-workers to observe Georgia's bathroom trips. They agreed to follow Georgia unobtrusively to the bathroom each time they saw her headed that way. Maggie instructed her toilet troop to verify the direction of Georgia's feet and assess whether the splash of her stream hit at high-dive or low-dive velocity. After a week or so of observations, all confirmed that Georgia's feet pointed toward the commode and that the tone of her tinkle exceeded the normal feminine range. They agreed—it was time to complain to human resources.

Carl Lehman, the human resources manager, listened to the complaint. He, too, was concerned for the women's safety and began an immediate investigation. First Carl checked the employment records. Georgia listed herself as Georgia Louise Cranston, female. Then Carl had security run a police check to determine if there were any convictions for sex crimes for any man named George Louis Cranston. He received information that there was a felony conviction for an individual whose name was George *Lionel* Cranston. The conviction was not for a sex crime, but for breaking and entering. Although the physical description was close to Georgia's, it did not match perfectly. The age and height disparities were sufficient to convince Carl that the company's Georgia was not the same person as the convicted felon.

Carl decided to call in his boss, Jordan Waverly, from corporate employee relations. Together they worked out a plan. They decided to confront Georgia directly with her co-workers' complaints. Carl and Jordan were both present during the initial interview.

"Georgia," Carl began, "several of your co-workers are raising questions about whether you are using the proper rest room. We want to make sure the women in this facility feel safe and comfortable. We don't want to get into any of your lifestyle choices right now, but if you are a man, you need to be using the proper rest room."

Georgia sat quietly for a few moments and then explained, "I am currently undergoing a sex change. So far I've taken the hormones, have begun to develop breasts, and am having electrolysis for hair removal. The doctor says I must dress like a woman and behave like a woman for a full year. After that period of time, if I still want to go forward, he will perform the necessary surgery."

Carl and Jordan were not expecting this response. They both sat silently for a few moments, and then Georgia continued. "If you would like to talk to my doctor to verify this, I will be happy to give you his name. He can explain all the medical information."

"I think that would be very helpful," Carl said. "Are you sure you don't mind?"

"Absolutely not," Georgia responded. "As a matter of fact, I'm relieved this has come out in the open. This is an awkward time for me. There are still parts of me that don't look quite womanly, and I'm sure it's raised questions. At least now, people won't stare and wonder."

"We will do everything possible to protect your privacy, Georgia," Carl assured her. "After we talk with your doctor, we'll decide on an approach that is acceptable to everyone."

Carl called Georgia's doctor. The doctor very openly talked with Carl and confirmed that Georgia had been taking various drugs and hormones to prepare her for the procedure.

"Which rest room should we have Georgia use?" Carl asked directly. "Is she a man or a woman?"

"Well, physiologically, Georgia's a little bit of both at this time, so she could use either," the doctor replied. "However, it's important for her psychologically during this process to take on the role of a woman, and using the women's rest room is really part of that whole process. If there is any way possible for you to allow her to continue to use the women's rest room, it would help her through the adjustment period."

Carl shared his findings with Jordan. "Well, we can't tell everyone in the plant about her medical condition. That's confidential," Jordan stipulated. "Perhaps we can find a way to handle this without revealing too much. Let's meet with Georgia again."

During their meeting with Georgia, Carl told her that he had discussed her case with her doctor. "Georgia, your doctor told us it was important for you to take on the role of a woman. We want to help you make that transition by allowing you to continue to use the women's rest room. However, it upsets your female co-workers when you stand while using the commode. So, if you want to continue to use the women's rest room, then you will need to use it like a woman. Is that acceptable to you?"

"No problem," Georgia said.

"We also need to respond to your co-workers' complaints," Carl continued. "We don't intend to call in all the employees, only the women. We want to explain to them that we investigated your case and received a medical opinion that you are entitled to use the women's rest room. We don't intend to go into any more detail than that. Is this acceptable to you?"

Georgia agreed, and the company held a meeting with the female co-workers. As Carl promised, he supplied limited personal information, but assured the women they did not have to fear for their safety. He explained they had fully investigated the case and that medical opinion indicated that Georgia had the right to use the women's rest room.

At the end of the meeting Georgia turned to Carl and Jordan. "I can't tell you how much I appreciate the effort you went through for me. You were so sensitive to my feelings. I know this probably wasn't easy for either of you, but I want you to know I never expected two men to respond with such open minds. I'm proud to be part of a company that cares so much for its employees."

Ten months later Georgia underwent her surgery. Upon recovery, she returned to work and continued her employment. Her co-workers fully accepted her as a woman, and she adjusted to her new role without further problems.

 Our competitive posture in world markets will depend on our ability to use the talent of *all* our human resources. We must find ways to accommodate the needs of our people, even if a need appears to be unique to some. Burdening our economy with human resources whose talents lie wasted will cost us money, jobs, and our ability to compete at home and abroad.

Fortunately Carl and Jordan recognized this need. Their handling of this case is an example of stellar employee relations. They exhibited a rare level of compassionate understanding. Most males may feel threatened by a person like Georgia and cannot understand why anyone would want to do what she did. Many women are understandably concerned as well. Is Georgia a man or a woman?

We have observed men who, when confronted with a transsexual undergoing the change, react in stereotypical ways to what a man should be and look like. Perhaps they lack the self-confidence and security in themselves and their maleness to be as compassionately understanding as Carl and Jordan. In these cases, male employees typically do not want a "Georgia" in the men's room. The female employees are also often uncomfortable and unwilling to accept him/her in the women's room. To solve this problem many companies use a neutral rest room (e.g., in the medical facility), until she completes her surgery.

There is a delicate line between satisfying the unique needs of people and adversely affecting the performance of others. In this case, we believe that Carl and Jordan handled the situation in an exemplary manner. They displayed great sensitivity and didn't overreact. They also involved Georgia in working out an approach to deal with the situation and remained sensitive to the confidentiality of the information regarding her medical condition. Finally, they recognized the need to respond to the co-workers' complaints. And congratulations to the employees who became involved in the resolution. We applaud them for being tolerant and understanding. Let's hope that someday *their* unique needs can be accommodated with the same aplomb.

Our only suggestion for handling the situation better would be to gain permission in writing, with Georgia's signature, to talk with her doctor. We're shocked that the doctor so readily furnished all of this data.

One of our panel members raised an additional interesting issue. When Georgia filled out her application, do we consider "female" and the name "Georgia" falsification? If we deal with the falsification issue, we need to terminate. If she/he did falsify, and we do not deal with it, we are setting an undesirable precedent for the future.

 With the expanding array of federal, state, and local laws protecting the disabled, many employers are concerned with what conditions/disorders fall within the definition of *disability*. Transsexuals are neither protected by the federal laws prohibiting employment discrimination nor are they considered disabled under the Americans with Disabilities Act. Gender disorders, transsexualism, transvestism, homosexuality, bisexuality, pedophilia, voyeurism, and exhibitionism are specifically excluded from the ADA's definition of disabilities. Nonetheless, this area remains uncharted waters, and it is conceivable that the Equal Employment Opportunity Commission may at some point view transvestism and transsexualism as being symptoms of an underlying mental or emotional disorder, which would warrant protection as a disability. Moreover, some state and local laws may view gender disorders as protected disabilities. For example, in a recent Washington Court of Appeals case, the court held that transsexualism is a handicap under Washington state law and that a company had violated that law by refusing to let a

transsexual wear feminine clothing prior to her operation to become ana-
tomically female. The court found that the company had failed to accommodate her disability when it fired her for wearing a pink pearl necklace
after having advised her to wear unisex clothing.

This story also illustrates the delicate balancing act human resources
managers are often faced with. Here, Carl was faced with a double-edged
sword—how to address the women's safety concerns and still protect the
confidentiality of Georgia's medical condition. With the increasing awareness and publicity surrounding workplace violence, Carl acted appropriately and swiftly to determine if there was a potential safety problem
under the circumstances.

Although Georgia gave verbal approval for Carl to speak with her
doctor, Carl could have further reduced the company's risk of liability by
securing a written authorization from Georgia. Most physicians would
probably require a written authorization in any event.

Carl also was prudent in limiting the information he provided to the
female employees in the company and seeking consent from Georgia before addressing them. By doing so, he reduces the chance of potential liability for invasion of privacy claims. As long as he documents his actions
and statements, his handling of this situation cannot be faulted.

An Unprecedented Predicament

From the time he was 10, Brent tagged along with his dad, Conrad, when he went to work at the track. Car racing was in Brent's blood. He loved the sounds, the sights, the people, and most of all the excitement. He spent his first summers stocking concession stands and working with the track maintenance crew. It didn't matter what he did as long as he could be part of the action. The allure of the people, their cars, and the camaraderie was irresistible to young Brent.

As Brent grew older, he attended more and more track activities related to the administrative end of the business. Eventually Conrad assigned Brent to the press room to help with public relations. This was a natural for Brent. He spent years observing how his dad made all the racers and their sponsors feel special and welcomed.

Each summer Brent helped Conrad welcome the volunteers from the racing association. This dedicated group kept records on the timing and scoring for the season. Their contribution not only kept down expenses but also built positive relations with key members of the association.

Most of the volunteers were men—racer wannabees whose vicarious thrills came from being on the fringe. They all loved high-performance cars. During their time at the track they lived in a special world known only to race car enthusiasts. Brent liked to hang out with some of his volunteer buddies up in the press room.

"These are real men," Brent often thought with admiration. He enjoyed his time with them almost as much as he did the drivers. The volunteers had all the history at their fingertips. They could rattle off facts and figures with the speed of an auctioneer at a livestock market. Brent would sit mesmerized for hours listening to their anecdotes of perilous crashes and unexpected wins.

"Brent," Conrad said one evening as they were getting ready to leave the office, "you know I plan to retire soon."

"Aw come on, Dad, you'll never retire. Besides, you're only 71," Brent remarked. "Look at George Burns! I heard he has himself booked past 100."

"Listen, Brent, I'm serious," Conrad said. "I want to groom you for taking over. I want you to get more involved with the operations and finance end of the business."

Brent loved public relations. He had some experience with operations, but finance wasn't his strong suit. "How about Don and Gerald?" Brent asked.

"Your brothers aren't even a consideration. Don has a thriving vet practice, and I can't pull Gerald away from his dream to be a pro golfer. You have the business in your blood, son. Someone has to take over or I'll have to sell."

"Sell the business?" Brent replied. "No way!"

"Next summer, I'd like to put you fully in charge of operations, and the following summer I'll ease you into finance. How do you feel about that?" Conrad asked.

Brent was stunned. Although Conrad was 47 when Brent was born, Brent always viewed his dad as an ageless human dynamo who would live forever. The thought of taking over the track was the furthest thing from his mind—especially since he was only 24. He graduated from the university only two years ago, but his degree in communications hardly prepared him for the administrative and financial aspects of the business. Even though he had assisted somewhat in the operations area, he always relied on his dad for any key decisions. This would be a big step. The thought was scary, but Brent started to rev up like one of the drivers waiting for the gun.

"Well, Dad, have I ever walked away from a challenge?" Brent asked confidently.

"Of course not, son," Conrad beamed, knowing he had won him over.

"Then, when are you going to print up my business cards with my new title as VP Operations?" Brent grinned.

Conrad chuckled. "Let's celebrate. Call your mom and make reservations at the Tower for dinner."

"Done!" Brent responded.

Brent awaited the next racing season with the same anticipation as a hunter waiting for opening day of deer season. He spent every free moment with his father, asking questions and planning. Sadly, about two months before the season began, Brent's excitement turned to despair. Conrad suffered a severe stroke, which paralyzed his right side and left him unable to speak. Despite Conrad's courageous effort to recover, doctors were not encouraging about his ability to regain his speech or to walk.

So as the full weight of the new racing season fell upon Brent's shoulders, he worried that he was ill-prepared to cope with his new responsibilities. Nevertheless, he had no choice but to charge ahead without his father's counsel.

The new group of volunteers arrived that season full of concern and support for Brent. He felt comforted by their presence and asked Aaron Lewis, the operations manager, to handle the bulk of the orientation. Brent regretted not being able to spend more time with them personally, but his role had changed and he was feeling overwhelmed.

Despite Brent's fears, the track opened fairly smoothly. However, as the season progressed Brent had his share of challenges. The most frustrating incident occurred about three-fourths of the way through the season. One afternoon Aaron knocked on Brent's door and said in an exasperated tone, "Brent, we have a problem with one of our volunteers. I know the season is almost over, but I can't deal with it any more."

"Tell me about it," Brent said, looking up from his desk.

"Do you remember Eddie Foyer?" Aaron asked.

"Sure, I remember Eddie. He was sort of a hippie throwback—but still a pretty cool guy. I met him about eight years ago. First he let his hair grow long. Then the next year he got his ear pierced. Then one year he dyed his hair blonde. The last time I saw him he started wearing these flashy clothes. He sure had some great stories. Now that I think about it, he wasn't here last season, was he?" Brent remembered.

"No, he wasn't," Aaron answered.

"Why not?"

"I don't know," said Aaron.

"Well, anyway," Brent said, "what about him?"

"He's back, but . . . um . . . ," Aaron hesitated.

"I don't remember seeing him," Brent mused. "But then again, I haven't spent much time with the volunteers this year."

"Well, actually you *have* seen him," Aaron responded, "but he's not exactly as you remember him. He's . . . um . . . ," His voice trailed off, groping for words.

"Yes, Aaron, he's what?" Brent asked, making a coaxing gesture with his hand.

"Well, he's changed his clothes again," said Aaron.

"So big deal," Brent said. "He was always a little weird."

"Well, it's more than just his clothes. He's been showing up dressed in high heels, lipstick, and make-up," Aaron finally revealed.

"Come on, you're not serious!" Brent asked incredulously.

"I am, and I don't know how to handle this. You know how the other volunteers are . . . they're a bunch of macho guys. This has them all weirded out. We've suspected all along, but we finally realized who *she* is this week."

"Wait a minute, what do you mean *she*? I thought we were talking about Eddie."

"We are, sort of," Aaron hedged.

"Quit dancing around this, Aaron, and get to the point," Brent said, eager to get to the bottom of things.

"Well, he doesn't call himself Eddie; he says his name is Elise," Aaron answered.

"Elise? Who's Elise?" Brent was really confused.

"That's who he says he is," Aaron explained.

"Does he use the same last name?" Brent wondered aloud.

"Yep," Aaron answered. "Foyer."

"How do you know?"

"I checked the legal waivers. He signs in every day as Elise Foyer when he enters the track," Aaron replied.

"Well, bring him, or her, or whoever down here. Let's see if we can straighten this out." Brent requested.

Brent could not imagine Eddie dressed like a woman. Sure, Eddie was somewhat eccentric, but a cross-dresser? "Come on," Brent thought. "Aaron's got to be setting me up. That Aaron! He's playing a joke on me."

But when Aaron brought Eddie to the office, Brent unconsciously took a step backwards. Then he grabbed hold of himself, forced a grin and said, "Why, Eddie! Welcome back. We missed you last year."

"Excuse me, but my name is Elise. I don't know anyone named Eddie," she responded in a voice that was clearly Eddie's style and inflection, but slightly higher in pitch.

"Sure you're Eddie, I've known you since I've been 16 or 17. I especially remember one of the stories you told me about the . . ,"

"You must be mistaken," she interrupted. "This is my first year here. I've never met you before."

Then Aaron tried his hand at getting Eddie to 'fess up. "Look, Eddie, you remember me—it's Aaron. We've worked together for nearly 10 years. Why are you insisting to be someone else?"

The volunteer would not respond. The room grew silent. They sat there for a few minutes, and Brent tried another approach. "Look, it's none of our business how you choose to live your life. However, would it be possible for you to dress in a more customary fashion and stop pretending to be a woman when you're working here? It's becoming very disruptive."

"Why wouldn't I want to dress like a woman?" she responded.

"Well, first of all, none of the other women around here dress in high heels and dresses. They all wear casual clothes—trousers or jeans and polo shirts. Why not dress like everybody else that works around here?" Brent countered, proud that he had skirted the issue of Eddie's identity.

"Are you telling me how to dress? I was never told there was a dress code around here," she retorted.

Brent was getting frustrated. The volunteers were critical to track operations, and he didn't want to tarnish the relationship with the racing association. It was too late to get a replacement and train someone else. Brent remained patient. "No," he continued, "I'm not telling you how to dress, I'm asking you to consider dressing like the other people who work here—employees and volunteers alike."

"I'm more comfortable dressed like this," she responded stubbornly.

Brent rolled his eyes and glanced at Aaron for help. The two went around and around with Eddie/Elise for over an hour. They tried to convince her that she was dressing inappropriately for a person who worked at the track. Nevertheless, she kept denying that she was ever Eddie and contended that she dressed as any normal woman would.

As Aaron grew increasingly impatient, he shouted, "Just answer one more question for me, Eddie."

She did not respond. And then Aaron remembered and tried again. "Okay, *Elise,* just answer one question for me."

"What?" Elise replied.

"Are those real boobs?" Aaron blurted out.

"Of course they are!" she huffed.

"Look, I can't have all the other volunteers upset over you," Brent interrupted. "There are only two events left for the summer. You can work those, but unless you get your act together next year, don't bother coming back."

Before Brent could say anymore, Eddie/Elise got up from her seat and calmly smiled. "Have it your way," she said, and she wobbled on her three-inch heels out of Brent's office.

Eddie/Elise worked the last two scheduled events and never returned for the next season. The end of the season was so hectic that Brent and Aaron forgot to verify the validity of the signed legal waivers against her ID. Brent worried about fallout from the racing association over the incident, but he never heard a peep. He felt lucky to have escaped the situation unscathed while keeping his cadre of volunteers in tact.

Was Eddie/Elise simply a cross-dresser or a real transsexual? The answer remains a mystery, even today.

So Eddie/Elise did not dress like the other volunteers, couldn't walk in her high heels, and generally bothered the "real men" at the track. We don't know who she really was, nor is that the issue. Since Elise's dress did not cause performance problems or a safety hazard, there was no real basis for Brent's intervention in this matter. Additionally, there was no reason to continue to disrespect Elise's request to be called Elise, rather than Eddie, nor to badger her on the topic for over an hour. It would appear that Brent's motivation was to satisfy his own curiosity, which is not a legitimate business concern. And Aaron's last question, "Are those real boobs?" was outrageous and inappropriate.

Dress or image codes are difficult to enforce. They must be business-related for them to stick. (For example, a marketing officer for a bank needs to look professional at all times even if a client is calling on a "dress-down" day.)

If the organization wants to impose standards of appearance on its volunteers, the standards should be made clear from the start and applied consistently to both male and female volunteers. Consistency is the key. A simple and inexpensive solution might be the introduction of a quasi-uniform for volunteers of either sex—perhaps black or khaki slacks with an organization-issued polo shirt.

It isn't clear if any kind of screening procedures were in place for volunteer workers. If none were in place, the business should tighten up its standards for "employing" volunteers to protect the security of all employees. These standards should be every bit as rigorous as those for employees, including proper interviewing/selection processes, and should focus on knowledge of the operation and racing. In this case, Eddie/Elise would probably have met the standards anyway.

 The first issue here is whether the relationship be- tween the race track and Eddie/Elise would have cre- ated any liability for the race track in the event Eddie/Elise filed some complaint about his/her treat- ment. Employment laws generally do not reach non- employees, such as volunteers. However, like certain misclassified independent contractors, some volunteers may actually be "employees" and an employer/employee relationship may be established for the pur- poses of some federal employment laws. Before engaging in the use of volunteers, employers should consider obtaining legal advice with respect to the risks and advantages of using volunteers. For example, what if the volunteer is injured? Is he covered by the employer's workers' compensa- tion insurance? What if the volunteer steals from the employer or injures a customer? Does the employer's liability insurance cover them?

Another issue presented here is whether Eddie/Elise may have a pro- tected disability. The Americans with Disabilities Act specifically excludes from the definition of disability homosexuality, bisexuality, transvestism, transsexualism, pedophilia, voyeurism, exhibitionism, and gender disor- ders. However, it is conceivable that the Equal Employment Opportunity Commission may view cross-dressing as a symptom of an underlying men- tal or emotional disorder, which would constitute a disability. Moreover, as we stated in our legal commentary in *Pointed in the Right Direction*, em- ployers need to familiarize themselves with applicable state and local laws since some states (e.g., Washington) may view gender disorders such as transsexualism as a protected disability requiring employers to make rea- sonable accommodations to such employees.

Chapter 10

Users & Abusers

"*Even with the intervention of employee assistance programs, people are still responsible for their own actions.*"

Cecil L. Murphy
Director Corporate Employee Relations
The Travelers Companies

Getting a Line on the Trouble

Sally stopped by Cameron's office and lightly tapped on the door. "How are things going?" she asked. "Ever since you've been promoted to vice president of human resources for the retail division, we hardly get to see you."

"Oh, I've been trying to figure out how to solve a problem in the store," Cameron said. "There have been rumors flying that we've got a drug ring in the main store. The trouble is, I suspect that security is in on the deal, so I'm reluctant to involve them."

Sally was a human resources director for the catalog division at corporate. "Security? At what level?" she asked.

"That's the problem. I don't know, and I don't want to take the chance of tipping anyone off."

"Do you think you might want to hire an outside investigator? Maybe get someone to work undercover?" she suggested.

"I've been thinking about it. I don't want to act hastily. After all, no one has really come forward. We're still at the rumor stage, and our budget is stretched as is," Cameron complained.

"I know what you mean. Let me know if you want to brainstorm on this. I'll try to help if you'd like," Sally offered as she turned to leave.

"Thanks, Sal," Cameron said and gathered up some documents on his desk. He had a meeting scheduled in five minutes with a department manager about a workers' compensation case, and he knew it would take him at least seven minutes to walk there. "I'd better get a move on," he thought.

He took the escalator down several floors. When he arrived on the second floor, he suddenly felt a cramp in his lower abdomen and an urgent need to get to the men's room. "Great, just what I need," he grimaced, searching for the nearest public rest room.

He made it to the lavatory just in time. While he was secluded in the stall, he heard the outside door open. Then he heard several male voices. They were discussing something about prices and lines—but from the nature of the conversation, it didn't sound as though they were talking about margins or merchandise.

Cameron emerged from the stall and walked to the sink to wash his hands. There stood four security guards busily engaged in conversation while cutting a line of coke.

"Hey man, you want a snort?" one asked.

"Maybe; how much?" Cameron asked swiftly with a broad smile. "I could use a buzz."

"Fifty," the guard said.

"Let me go get some more cash. I only have a couple bucks on me," he said, drying his hands. "Can you wait five minutes?"

"Not much more than that, man, we're on break," the guard said.

"No problem. I'll be right back," Cameron grinned.

Cameron casually left the rest room, darted into a stockroom, and located the buyer's office. He felt the adrenaline flood his system as he called the police. He told them about the drug situation and where the guards were located. Next, Cameron positioned himself near the rest room, so he could direct any customers away from the site. Then he prayed he wouldn't have another attack of diarrhea.

Since the store was within spitting distance of the police headquarters, they arrived in three minutes. Cameron met them at the door, pointed out the rest room, and let them conduct the arrests.

When the police questioned the security guards, their investigation revealed that several other employees were involved in the drug ring. Later that afternoon, the police returned with warrants for their arrests, and Cameron assisted by having the employees discreetly removed from the store.

When Cameron returned to his office around 6 p.m., he stopped by Sally's office. "How'd you like to congratulate me?" he beamed.

"For what?" she smiled.

"Tell you what," Cameron said, "Let's grab some dinner and I'll tell you all about it."

Cameron was lucky! We all have at least one fall in our laps. But Cameron can't rest on his laurels; this may just be the tip of the iceberg. With four security guards doing a line of coke in the bathroom, major drug problems as well as potential theft may exist.

If the company hasn't done so, it should implement a drug-free workplace program. The program should include pre-employment testing, random testing, and regular testing for security personnel. Also, if the company experiences any economic loss due to theft of merchandise, it

may consider conducting an internal investigation of the security department personnel. If the investigation reveals that additional security employees are involved in the drug ring, the appropriate company authority
should contract with an outside security service for a full-scale investigation.

Finally, the human resources staff should distribute a written policy
regarding illegal drug use at the workplace to all employees. The policy
should state clearly that the company will contact the police if the staff
finds any use of illegal substances in the workplace.

Apart from the primary concern about drugs in this case, one panel
member raised an additional issue regarding Cameron's dinner invitation
to Sally. Given the professional relationship portrayed between them, the
invitation seemed appropriate. However, if Sally was uncomfortable with
the way he asked or the idea of contact outside the work environment,
she should state any objections firmly and directly up-front.

Most employers are not as fortunate as Cameron—he
simply made a pit stop in a public bathroom and
"caught" his employees doing drugs, and then the
police took over.

Drug and alcohol abuse in the workplace has
become a severe problem for employers. The National Institute on Drug
Abuse has reported that between 10 percent and 23 percent of all workers
abuse drugs on the job. As a result of the human and economic costs of
drug abuse on the job, many employers have adopted policies and programs designed to achieve drug- and alcohol-free workplaces.

Companies should establish and enforce workplace policies that
prohibit the use, distribution, or sale of illegal drugs on company premises. When a company is confronted with obvious criminal drug activity,
as illustrated in this story, the police should be called. Remember: employers should not put themselves in the position of appearing to be an
"agent" of the police (see the commentary in *Deadbeat Dad.*)

Split Personality

"Quinn Forrest, human resources," Quinn responded as he picked up his phone.

"Quinn, this is Alice," announced Alice Hanover, the assembly unit supervisor. "I need your assistance again with Caldonia Beecher," she sighed.

"Oh, is she simply 'Cantankerous Caldonia' today? Or do we have the dreaded fire-spewing 'Beecher Behemoth' approaching meltdown?" Quinn joked.

Quinn reflected for a moment. Caldonia Beecher's recent erratic behavior had become somewhat of an enigma. When Quinn first talked with Caldonia during her employment interview, she presented herself as a shy, demure person. He never anticipated that her dramatic moods swings would put the entire unit on alert. One moment she would joke merrily with co-workers. Then, without warning, she would blast a barrage of verbal blows with such force that half her co-workers would run for cover. Moments later, as quickly as it began, her fury would dissipate and she would return to work as though nothing had happened. In the meantime, she left a trail of shell-shocked casualties strewn throughout the unit.

Alice and Quinn counseled Caldonia after the first incident, and again after the second. Caldonia's genuine remorse and her charming manner were bewitching. Both were convinced that she would improve.

"No, Quinn," Alice said, interrupting his thoughts. "This is not the same type of problem. Caldonia told me she hurt her back on the job about a week ago, so we'll need to set her up for a visit with the company medical lab for x-rays and file a workers' compensation claim."

"Oh, I see," Quinn said, a little relieved that he would not have to tend to the walking wounded she often left in her wake. "Send her to the office, and we'll get the paperwork started."

When Caldonia arrived, Quinn's assistant had her fill out a series of forms and waivers. It was company policy that a drug test be administered to anyone who claimed an occupational injury. Quinn's assistant explained the procedures to Caldonia after she completed the forms.

"Ms. Beecher, here is the address of the Lastalon Medical Laboratory. Your appointment is at 1 p.m. tomorrow. They will review your case and then take all the required blood and urine tests as well as x-rays so we can process your claim," Quinn's assistant explained.

The next afternoon, Quinn received an unexpected call from the Lastalon Medical Laboratory. "We've got a problem here, Mr. Forrest," the technician said. "Your employee refuses to take the drug test. What do you want me to do?"

"Put her on the phone," Quinn said, wondering why Caldonia was being uncooperative.

Before Quinn got a chance to say hello, Caldonia began shouting, "What the hell's the deal here? No one ever told me that I had to take a drug test. You people have a lot of nerve messin' with me. This is a bunch of crap! Tell these creeps to keep their grimy paws off of me. What the hell does my backache have to do with drugs anyway?" Caldonia screamed directly in Quinn's ear. This was the first time Quinn was the direct target of the legendary Beecher belligerence.

"Caldonia, I'd appreciate it if you'd control the tone of your voice. There are other people in the laboratory, and you could be disturbing them," Quinn reminded her.

Quinn's unwavering, calm tone seemed to placate her a bit. "I'm just aggravated," Caldonia complained, still somewhat riled. "It's just hard to stay calm when I get so mad . . . but I'll try."

"Caldonia, remember when my assistant gave you those forms to sign? Those forms said that you agreed to take a drug test. She explained that you would be taking blood and urine tests."

"Yes . . . well . . . maybe I just don't remember what she was telling me 'cause my back hurt so bad. I thought the urine test was to see if my kidneys were hurt from my accident," Caldonia claimed.

"Caldonia, a urine test might reveal problems like that too, but we specifically must test for drugs. You signed a form that explicitly states you agreed to a drug test. This is part of our company policy. Now, are you going to take the test so we can help you with your claim?" Quinn asked patiently.

"I suppose," she sulked.

When the lab called with the results, Quinn was informed that Caldonia tested positive for cocaine. Since company policy stated that anyone who tested positive for illegal drugs must be discharged immediately, he called Caldonia to his office and explained the test results.

Caldonia listened politely to Quinn's explanation for her termination. When he finished, Caldonia replied with genuine innocence, "Well, that's just not possible, Mr. Forrest. I have never taken drugs in my life. I don't even take aspirin because of my allergies. Why, I can't imagine what would happened if I ever took cocaine. With my asthma, I'd be dead faster than a fly on a frog's tongue." In a honeyed voice she added, "Tell me, Mr. Forrest, could those lab boys possibly be mistaken?"

"They are very careful, Caldonia, so it's quite unlikely—maybe one in a thousand," Quinn responded, as her beguiling charm began to influence him.

"Well, can I retake the test?" she pleaded, with a credible "I'm-innocent-please-believe-me" expression on her face.

Since barely 24 hours had passed, Quinn acquiesced. "Okay," he told her, "but you will have to pay for the second test."

"That's fair," she smiled congenially.

"Why don't you go down around 4 o'clock today," Quinn suggested.

About 4:15 p.m. Quinn received a call from the lab. "Mr. Forrest, we have another problem."

"What's the matter now?" he asked, feeling his stomach start to tense.

"Ms. Beecher's sample is unusable," the technician reported.

"Can you explain that?"

"It's too cold," the tech stated.

"Too cold?"

"Yes, our procedure is to check the temperature on a urine sample immediately after we receive it," the tech explained.

"And?"

"Hers was well below the acceptable temperature for urine that just left the body."

"But didn't she provide it to you on-site?" Quinn asked.

"Yes, she did. She gave the sample to the nurse when she came out of the rest room," the tech answered.

"So?"

"So, the urine must have come from someone else."

"How do you figure?"

"We don't know for sure. But she has her daughter with her, and she asked if her daughter could use our rest room when they first got here. When we said yes, the nurse observed Ms. Beecher follow her daughter in. So it's possible Ms. Beecher switched her urine for her daughter's. She may have kept it in some type of container in her purse. We can't tell you exactly where it came from. We just know it can't be hers."

"Please tell Ms. Beecher to come to the phone. Tell her I'd like to speak with her," Quinn requested, beginning to feel exasperated with Caldonia's alleged shenanigans.

"Caldonia, you're going to have to go back to the bathroom and provide another sample," Quinn told her.

Clearly irritated, Caldonia asked, "Why, what's the matter?"

"For some reason the sample is unusable," Quinn replied.

"Unusable? What do you mean, unusable?" she railed loudly.

"It's considered a cold sample and it's unusable," he explained. "That means that for some reason it didn't come out of you right there."

"That's ridiculous," she fumed. "It's mine."

"Well, you need to do it again."

"I'm not going to do it again!" she boomed.

"Unfortunately, you have to."

"I won't. I'm coming in to see you tomorrow morning," she blared shrilly and crashed the receiver down.

The next morning Caldonia showed up in Quinn's office as promised. No anger—she was all smiles. When Quinn's assistant directed Caldonia to a seat, she took on an angelic pose. Puzzled, Quinn stared at her, wondering where he was going to begin. But there she sat, casting her spell and looking like *Saint* Caldonia.

Quinn promised himself he would not allow her to con him this time. "Caldonia, is there anything you can think of that would first, cause you to test positive, and second, explain the cold sample?"

"Well, maybe you got my sister instead of me," she offered, in the most plausible tones.

"What do you mean?"

"I have a twin sister," Caldonia stated.

"Did you send your twin sister down to the clinic?" he asked in amazement. "Why would you send someone else?"

"I'm not saying," Caldonia declined.

"What's your twin sister's name?"

"Her name is Caldonia too."

"You two have exactly the same name?" Quinn asked, raising an eyebrow.

"Yes. Caldonia often comes and works for me."

Quinn began to feel as if he were a psychiatrist in session with a severely delusionary patient, but he decided to play along. "Tell me," he asked, "did we hire you or did we hire your sister?"

"You hired me," she stated clearly.

"You're sure?"

"Of course I'm sure," she said, unwavering.

"But your sister works for us, too?" he continued.

"Yes."

"Every day? Every other day? Half days?"

"It varies," she responded.

"Well, then, whose back was hurt? Was it yours or your sister's? Whose urine test was it the first time? And whose test was it the second time? Who screamed at me both times on the phone? Who am I dealing with in the office?" he asked impatiently.

"We switch around a lot. And I'm not going to tell you who was over there at which time and who wasn't," Caldonia held fast.

"You know something, Caldonia, I really don't care. As far as I'm concerned, you're both fired!" he announced, convinced she was wacky. Quinn called security and had Caldonia escorted from the building.

But was Caldonia really more wiley than wacky? She retained an attorney, claiming that her back injury had become disabling. Unfortunately, the company couldn't prove that Caldonia was "under the influence" of cocaine when she sustained her injury because they administered the test well after the actual injury occurred. To avoid a protracted legal battle, they settled out of court for about $8,000.

 The company made three mistakes in this situation. First of all, it is critical that any policy regarding drug testing be carefully designed and followed to the letter. Once the company makes a decision to test, it should arrange for the test, preferably the same day. Scheduling the test for the next day was a mistake that only complicated the situation.

Second, Quinn Forrest's decision to allow the employee to take the test again was a serious error. Assuming that a certified lab took and analyzed the sample properly and barring any question about the "chain of custody," retesting was inappropriate. This action casts doubt on the integrity of the first test, sets a precedent for future cases, and would certainly complicate any subsequent litigation.

When using an outside lab, make sure the lab has appropriate procedures for maintaining chain of custody. For example, a good chain of custody procedure divides the original sample into two portions. One portion is tested, and the other is frozen and retained for one year in case of a dispute. Assuming the lab followed this type of procedure, Caldonia's contention would have been groundless.

Finally, the company should not have tolerated Caldonia's previous disruptive behavior. Her supervisor or Quinn should have suggested that Caldonia seek assistance from the company's employee assistance program, if available, during their counseling sessions. Repeated instances of unacceptable conduct should result in termination of employment. She was playing games with them. Employers should not be required to endure disruptive co-workers.

Despite Quinn's mistakes, a number of us feel this company should consider itself lucky to escape with only an $8,000 no-fault settlement. Typically, workers' compensation cases can run to five or six figures, exclusive of attorney's fees. We consider the $8,000 an inexpensive way to rid themselves of an ongoing problem employee!

This story warrants some clarification on the issue of medical examinations, workers' compensation claims, and drug testing as they apply to the Americans with Disabilities Act (ADA).

Not all employees injured on the job will meet the "disability" definition required for protection under the ADA. Work-related injuries do not always cause physical or mental impairment severe enough to "substantially limit" a major life activity. Conversely, many employees may be disabled for reasons wholly unrelated to the workplace.

The ADA imposes restrictions regarding medical examinations. Employers may not require a job applicant to take a medical exam or respond to inquiries about his or her health unless (a) the pre-employment medical exam is requested *after* a conditional offer of employment has been made and (b) the employer requires the examination of all entering employees in the same job category. The ADA requires that any examination of an employee must be "job-related and consistent with business necessity."

A medical examination of an employee may meet the requirement of job-relatedness and business necessity if such an examination is required to determine if the individual can perform the essential functions of the job or to determine what accommodation might enable the individual to perform the essential functions of the job. Generally, if an employee has an on-the-job injury that seems to affect the employee's ability to perform the essential job functions or the employee wishes to return from a job-related disability leave, then a medical exam or "fitness for duty" exam would most likely meet the "job-relatedness and consistent with business necessity" requirement.

To further confuse the subject, a pre-employment drug test is *not* considered a pre-employment medical exam under the ADA, and an employer can test an employee for illegal drug use even if the test is not job-related and consistent with business necessity. However, a blood alcohol test is considered a medical examination and can only be required in conformity with the ADA—it must be job-related and consistent with business necessity. Again, aside from ADA considerations, employers should ascertain the status of state and local drug testing laws before developing or implementing a workplace drug testing policy.

An employee or applicant who is currently engaged in the illegal use of drugs is *not* disabled under the ADA. On the other hand, drug users who have been rehabilitated, or who are participating in a supervised rehabilitation program *and* are not currently using drugs, or who are erroneously regarded as engaging in the use of illegal drugs, are protected by the ADA.

Unlike the ADA, some state and local laws treat drug abuse as protected disabilities even if the affected person is not recovered or in a treatment program. Employers are well advised to check the law in their state or locality before making any employment decisions based on known or suspected drug abuse of an employee (or an applicant).

Dead Drunk

"Human resources, Nick Richards," Nick responded when he answered his phone at 7:30 on Monday morning.

"Nick, it's Nancy," said the general manager. "I've got some bad news. We found out late on Friday that we didn't get the contract on the Elerbee Bridge with the state. That means we'll need to start layoffs beginning next Monday. I've got a list of all the effected employees that need to be notified. Can you get the process started today?"

Nick was not surprised by the phone call. Their business lived and died by state and federal contracts, so he was always prepared. "Of course, Nancy. How many employees are we talking about?"

"Thirteen to be exact."

"Okay, send your secretary down with the list," Nick said. "I'll take care of the rest."

"Thanks, Nick," Nancy said and clicked off the line.

Nick began the paperwork. On Wednesday, he arranged to notify all 13 employees of the layoff. He indicated the layoff would begin at the end of business on Friday.

As soon as Derrick Lazurby, an engineering drafter-designer, received his notice, he informed his supervisor that he had a doctor's appointment the following morning. Derrick indicated he expected to return to work by noon. The next day, Derrick presented his supervisor with a letter from the doctor. The letter certified that Derrick was a chronic alcoholic and required immediate sick leave.

His supervisor was shocked. Derrick had never exhibited any clues that he might be an alcoholic. He rarely missed work, and although his performance was hardly stellar, it certainly was satisfactory. "I'm sorry to hear this, Derrick," his supervisor said sincerely. "Would you like me to make arrangements for you to enter a treatment center? I don't know if you are aware, but the company can arrange for you to go to the Betty Ford Center."

"No thanks," Derrick replied.

"Well, what type of treatment are you going to receive?" his supervisor asked.

"None, I'm just going to stay home."

"I don't get it—don't you want to recover?"

"You don't have to get it. I'm not going to any stupid rehab center," Derrick stated adamantly.

Derrick's supervisor presented the information to Nick. As Nick listened to the supervisor's explanation and reviewed the doctor's letter, warning signals went off. "I find the timing of Derrick's appointment curious," Nick thought. "I wonder whether it's mere coincidence that it occurred immediately after learning of the layoff, or just a clever move on Derrick's part? And his refusal to seek help is very strange. Something is just not right here."

Although Nick assumed the doctor's certificate was valid, he suspected that Derrick may be attempting a goldbricking technique. If Derrick was placed on sick leave prior to the date of layoff, he would be removed from the layoff pool. That meant he would be eligible for full pay for a minimum of eight weeks and avoid the reduced salary provided by unemployment compensation.

On the other hand, if Derrick's alcoholism was legitimate, Nick felt an obligation to ensure that he receive help. Nick briefed Skylar Arnold, his outside legal counsel, on the facts and asked for assistance.

"Can't we at least require him to check into a rehabilitation center to secure treatment?" Nick asked.

"I'm afraid not," Skylar advised him. "We can't handle this any differently than if it were an appendectomy."

Nick was livid. "So you're saying that we let this guy go home and drink himself to death!"

"Sad, but true, Nick."

"Look, Skylar, I don't think it's the same thing. Right now he's on the company's sick leave. We pay for that, not an insurance company. Why can't I tell him that our policy assumes that if you're sick, you seek treatment? If you don't seek treatment, we don't pay."

"I don't think that would be prudent," Skylar maintained. "He could open up a whole legal can of worms that you don't need."

The whole situation smelled foul to Nick, but he deferred to Skylar. Derrick remained on paid sick leave for eight weeks. Subsequently, the company's long-term disability policy continued to cover his case for nearly six more months until he finally died. To this day, Nick is uncomfortable with the handling and outcome of the situation. He feels that he should have ignored the attorney's advice and interceded with a demand that Derrick seek treatment. If he had, perhaps Derrick would be alive today.

Unfortunately, Nick and Derrick's supervisor were a day late and a dollar short with their help for Derrick. We question the supervisor's statement that there were no prior indications of alcohol abuse. It is truly rare that someone in Derrick's advanced stage of decline would not manifest some detectable signs. More often than not, it is easier for management to ignore or avoid such situations—particularly when absenteeism and performance are not serious issues—than to engage in constructive confrontation.

An employee assistance program may have prevented this situation by training Nick and Derrick's supervisor to identify and intervene at an earlier point when Derrick may have been more open to help. The program may also have made self-help available to Derrick and trained co-workers in identifying and referring substance abusers. Nevertheless, given the situation, Nick could have required a second, independent medical evaluation. This action would have determined whether Derrick was really ill or attempting to fraudulently collect disability benefits.

It appears that the policies and procedures of this company contributed to the creation of this situation. First, prior notice of layoffs always creates the potential for such problems as sabotage and fake disabilities. A safer practice is layoff notifications and immediate termination.

Second, the company should immediately change its eligibility for disability. Disability benefits should end with *notification* of termination. Such a policy avoids employee temptations to fraudulently obtain benefits as they go out the door.

Most employee benefit policies today do not permit human resources or a corporate official to dictate the actions or treatment of employees. If on-the-job performance is deteriorating, they are allowed to intervene and declare certain expectations and set certain goals. But in this particular case, if the physician certified that Derrick was "totally disabled" from performing the primary duties of the job for a period of time and is unable to perform any similar job for which he was reasonably qualified, then Derrick would be eligible (under most company benefit plans) for long-term disability coverage.

The attorney in this case would need to consider any precedents by examining past management actions regarding other disabled participants in the company's benefit plans. If the company established certain guidelines setting forth management's ability to intervene and direct treatment, then they may have been able to dictate a course of treatment. Moreover, Derrick would be considered disabled under the Americans with Disabilities Act. Thus, under provisions of this act, Derrick would be afforded "like" consideration as other individuals at this company.

We would advise Nick that he should not take responsibility for Derrick's behavior. Derrick's doctor may have suggested treatment; we'll never know. Derrick's death is his own responsibility. Even with interventions such as EAPs and independent medical evaluations, people are still responsible for their own actions. Nick and the company provided help and tried several times to get Derrick to accept the help. Nick needs to let go and, for the future, concentrate on ensuring that managers and employees are fully aware of the EAP and other company assistance.

Perhaps the thorniest employee relations issues arise in the context of physical and mental problems, especially when the disability is alcoholism. Intertwined with an employer's sick leave, short-term disability, and long-term disability programs are a plethora of laws with overlapping and concurrent provisions applicable to disabled employees, which have added to the employers' dilemma. To complicate matters further, some employees abuse the laws and policies designed to protect the genuinely disabled, and attempt to use the disability laws as a way to obtain guaranteed job security or compensation when they are not entitled to it.

Nick's quandary illustrates why we advise clients not to announce a layoff in advance. All too often, employees who know they will be laid off just happen to suffer on-the-job injuries and file workers' compensation claims. Other employees have been known to sabotage equipment, disrupt production schedules, destroy computer files, or abscond with customer lists and/or other confidential or proprietary documents in the period prior to their layoff. To avoid these problems, it is generally preferable to provide some pay in lieu of notice.

Finally, employers who anticipate large layoffs should consult with counsel as to their obligations under the Worker Adjustment and Retraining Notification Act (WARN) or similar state "plant closing laws." Mass layoffs and facility shutdowns often trigger the application of such laws.

Alcoholism is a protected disability under the ADA (and usually under state disability laws) warranting reasonable accommodation. However, the decision to lay off Derrick and the other 12 employees was made before the company knew Derrick was disabled. The layoff was based on business needs, and was not a pretext to discriminate against Derrick because of his alcoholism. Reasonable accommodation does not equate to guaranteed job security rights. Based on the facts of this story, had Derrick been laid off on the scheduled date in the same manner as the other 12 non-disabled employees, it is unlikely that Derrick could successfully sue the company for unlawful discrimination.

Chapter 11

Outrageous Liars

"Sound employee relations require the utmost in integrity. Be consistent and human in your approach."

Bob Forbes
Personnel Executive
Chrysler Corporation
(Powertrain and Acustar Division)

The Mistletoe Incident

"Honey, who just pulled up in the driveway?" Marianne asked her husband, Chuck, as she was clearing away the evening dishes.

"I don't know, I'll check," he said, walking out to the driveway. He didn't recognize the car, but spotted his secretary, Darlene, in the front seat next to a man. Although he thought it was peculiar that she was wearing sunglasses at dusk, Chuck was more surprised to see her sitting in a car parked in his driveway.

Chuck walked around to the passenger's side, and Darlene rolled down the window. "Hi, Darlene, what brings you here at 7:30 on a Sunday evening?"

"Chuck, this is my husband, Alvin. He wanted to meet you," Darlene said.

Chuck nodded hello and was still trying to figure out what was going on when Darlene said, "Chuck, would you mind getting in the back seat? I need to tell you something."

Chuck thought the whole scene was strange. However, Darlene had worked for him for several years and was a good secretary, so he obliged her request. As he got himself comfortable, he said, "Okay, Darlene, what do you need to tell me?"

"Chuck, it's not so much what I need to tell you, it's what I need to tell Alvin. I wanted Alvin to know that you and I have made love in your office at least seven times since I've worked for you. He's suspected it, and I can't live a lie. I just wanted him to know that I love him and that he has nothing to worry about. It was just a fling."

Chuck was dumbfounded. "Are you crazy, Darlene?" he shouted. "Why are you doing this? We have never made love in my office. For God's sake, this is the most insane thing I've ever heard. I'm getting out of here right now."

Alvin never said a word. He just nodded as Darlene told her story and drove calmly off after Chuck jumped out of the car. When Chuck walked in the house, Marianne was waiting. She saw the look of shock across his face.

"What wrong, Chuck? Who were those people?" she asked, concerned.

"Sweetheart, sit down. You are not going to believe this," he told Marianne, easing her to the couch while he himself was still shaking. He told her about Darlene's accusations and said that he was going to meet with the president first thing in the morning to get this straightened out. He could not figure out what motive Darlene would have to make such claims, but he was going to get to the bottom of it.

As he promised Marianne, Chuck immediately reported the incident to the president. The president called in the human resources manager, Brad Denver, and explained the situation.

"Okay," Brad said, "let's call her in and see if we can figure this out."

Brad and the president met with Darlene. "Darlene, Chuck told us you stopped by his house last night with your husband and then accused Chuck of having sexual relations with you. Is that correct?"

"Yes," Darlene acknowledged.

"Could you tell us just how and when this happened in the office?"

"Well, Chuck has a couch in his office and a lock on the door. We just locked the door during lunch and did it on the couch. Although sometimes we made love on the floor, or in his chair, or on his desk," she said.

"Did Chuck ever force you to have sex or threaten you in any way?"

"No."

"Well, then why did you decide to bring your husband over to Chuck's house?" Brad asked.

"I just wanted him to know the truth," she said.

Brad was perplexed. None of this made sense. "Chuck said you were wearing sunglasses last night. Why were you wearing sunglasses at night?"

"I'm more comfortable that way," she commented.

Brad noticed that her make-up was applied rather heavily that day. "Darlene, is that a black eye I see?"

"Yes," she said.

"How did you get that black eye?"

"Alvin gave it to me," she replied.

"Before or after you visited Chuck's?"

"Before."

Brad decided to call Chuck into the president's office. Both Brad and the president left the room so Chuck and Darlene could discuss the incident between themselves. Brad hoped they might be able to find the truth.

After about 10 minutes, Brad and the president returned to the office. Chuck faced Darlene and said, "Darlene, are you willing to admit that what you just told the president and human resources manager is not necessarily true?"

"Yes," she acknowledged.

"Do you want to tell them the real reason you came to my home?"

Darlene turned to Brad and the president. "Look, my husband is very jealous. He kept insisting that I was having an affair, which I wasn't. Then he said he was going to find out the truth by beating it out of me. That's when he punched me. Finally, to save myself, I made up a story about Chuck. I was afraid Alvin was going to kill me."

At this stage, Brad and the president weren't sure whom to believe. Then Brad suggested, "Look, we don't know who's telling the truth here, but I think we really need to find out. Chuck, would you be willing to take a lie detector test to clear her initial allegation?"

"Absolutely," Chuck responded.

The test determined that Chuck never had sexual relations with Darlene. However, another piece of information surfaced during the exam. When Chuck was asked if he had ever had physical contact with Darlene, Chuck said, "Well, just once. It was during our Christmas party two years ago. We all had a few drinks and were feeling pretty happy. There was mistletoe, so Darlene and I kissed. It wound up to be a little more passionate than we both expected and maybe I kind of copped a feel in the process—but only once and never since."

Brad and the president dismissed the Christmas incident as inconsequential. However, they could not condone Darlene's behavior. Brad explained to Darlene that lying about Chuck's behavior could have cost Chuck his job and was a serious offense. Even though she may have thought her reasons for fabricating the story were legitimate, the company could not accept her actions, and Brad discharged her.

Darlene filed a sex discrimination claim with the Equal Employment Opportunity Commission. The EEOC investigator argued that Chuck was never punished for his behavior of kissing and fondling her, but she was discharged for lying. Therefore, the company demonstrated sex discrimination.

After considering the alternatives, Brad decided the case was not worth fighting and rehired her. He was careful, however, to place Darlene in a different department where she would not have regular contact with Chuck.

We all agree that the company handled the matter too hastily and that Darlene's termination was far too severe. On the other hand, her false charge of sexual harassment was, indeed, a very serious offense. This charge could have damaged Chuck's reputation as well as the company's. However, Darlene also seemed to be a woman in a great deal of personal trouble. Certainly what she did was wrong, but her actions also appeared to have been a desperate cry for help. As an alternative to termination, we first would have counseled her and then placed a stern warning in her file. The warning would state that any further false allegations of harassment would be grounds for immediate termination.

Second, we would arrange for her to get help through the employee assistance program (EAP). The EAP should be able to evaluate her personal issues (i.e., beatings from her husband) and refer her to the proper medical and/or community services. This counseling should be a requirement of continued employment.

Finally, we would recommend transferring her to another department, to a job that fit her skills. This would allow her to get a fresh start, since she and Chuck would most likely be uncomfortable continuing to work together.

However, we disagree on the relevance of the mistletoe incident. Some of us feel that Chuck should be re-educated on the company's sexual harassment policy and given a severe written warning as documentation to his file. Others of us consider this a non-issue. Chuck and Darlene's actions were consensual, happened long ago, and were never brought forward as a claim by Darlene. Thus the incident lacked relevance to her current allegations. Furthermore, obtaining the information through a lie detector test was questionable (see legal comments).

Regardless of how we view Chuck's guilt or innocence on the mistletoe matter, Chuck and Darlene should be put on notice that they may not discuss any aspect of the case with co-workers. This warning should be verbal as well as written. It should indicate that disclosure would be inappropriate and grounds for disciplinary action up to and including termination.

There are a few other items that deserve mention. All employees are accountable for their behavior on the job and at company-sponsored functions. They should be mindful of their actions, especially if they consume alcoholic drinks. To prevent future "mistletoe mishaps," the company should consider changing its policy about allowing alcohol at company-sponsored events.

Also, it was ill-advised for Brad and the president to leave Chuck and Darlene in a room alone together to "discuss the incident between themselves." This action may have had negative consequences. Either Darlene or Chuck may have been threatened, bought off, physically hurt, or further harassed by the other.

One of the issues in this story concerns the use of a lie detector test in the workplace. Federal and state laws regulate the use of lie detector tests on applicants and employees.

Brad most likely subjected Chuck to a lie detector test illegally under both federal and state laws. Except in limited circumstances, the Employee Polygraph Protection Act of 1988 generally prohibits private employers from using lie detector tests for screening applicants or testing current employees. An employer may test an employee if the employer reasonably suspects the employee's involvement in workplace theft or some other incident causing economic loss to the employer. Moreover, under the Employee Polygraph Protection Act, an employer is prohibited from making employment decisions such as termination, disciplinary action, promotions, or denial of employment, solely on the basis of a polygraph test result. In a workplace theft investigation, the employer may request that an employee submit to a lie detector test if (a) the employee had access to the property allegedly stolen, (b) there is reasonable suspicion to believe the employee was involved in the theft, and (c) the employee is given a written statement as to the reason for testing certain employees.

Employers need to remain mindful of state and local polygraph/lie detector laws, which may be more restrictive than the federal law. For example, while some states limit themselves to merely regulating the licensing of polygraph examiners, other states, such as Delaware, Hawaii, Massachusetts, Michigan, Oregon, and Rhode Island, prohibit all use of the polygraph in private sector employment.

Some employees have successfully sued their employers on the grounds that polygraph testing violates privacy rights under the U.S. Constitution and some state constitutions, or for invasion of privacy, defamation, and intentional infliction of emotional distress.

We also question the wisdom of rehiring the employee after she falsely accused her manager of criminal and illegal activity, especially since it is clear that she was not discriminated against because of her sex. Nothing in the story even suggests that the Christmas kiss was unwelcome by Darlene. Moreover, that single episode is probably time-barred in any event.

The Foibles of Fraternizing

"What's wrong, Leanna? Why do you look so blue?" Chad asked sympathetically.

Leanna managed to force a smile. She had just returned from the doctor with some bad news. "The doctor tells me I have endometriosis plus some other stuff."

"Oh wow," Chad said. "What's the prognosis?"

"Well I have to have an ovary removed, which probably cuts my chances for having children by 50 percent. And since Harry and I broke up, I don't even have any potential prospects on the horizon—and my clock is ticking," she moaned.

"I'm sorry, Leanna. I know you feel scared, but from all that I've read about the new laser technology and advances in infertility, your chances are probably much greater than you think," Chad said encouragingly.

"You're so sweet, Chad. Thanks for being such a caring friend as well as a terrific secretary," she said, smiling.

Chad had been the human resources department secretary for nearly a year now. He was certainly an anomaly for an industry where men only did "men-type things." But Leanna was pleased with his performance. She took a lot of flack from the others for hiring a male secretary, but Chad was the fastest typist and most efficient secretary she had ever known.

Later that afternoon Victor McGrane, her colleague in the benefits department, popped his head in her office. "So how did it go at the doctor's?" he asked.

Leanna had been invited to dinner the week before by Victor and his wife, Marge. They were considerably older than Leanna and had offered to help her get established when she first moved to town. She viewed Victor as a mentor and Marge like a mother, so she felt comfortable confiding in them about her physical problems. "Not wonderful, Victor. I guess I have to have the surgery after all. I'm just wondering what I'm going to do. With Harry out of the picture, by the time I establish another meaningful relationship, I'll be too old to have any children. Although I could consider artificial insemination . . . but the thought of not knowing the full background of the donor makes me uncomfortable," she rambled.

"Look, you're just feeling down right now. Once you have your surgery behind you, you'll figure out a way," Victor assured her.

"You know, Victor, you'd be a perfect donor," she joked. "If I could find someone like you, I'd be thrilled. You're healthy, intelligent, honest, tall, and best of all, Methodist. Who could ask for anything more!"

Victor tossed his head back and laughed. "Leanna, I never know what you're going to say next! Tell you what—Marge has a cousin who's about your age. I'll tell her to arrange a casual dinner for the four of us. I think you'd like him."

"Excuse me, Leanna," interrupted Chad, who had been waiting patiently for a break in their discussion. "Your interview is here. Are you ready to see him?"

"Yes, certainly, Chad," Leanna responded and turned to Victor. "Go ahead and arrange that dinner, Victor. I'd like that a lot."

❦ ❦ ❦

Leanna's surgery was successful. Several weeks later she invited her friend, Dan Jones, to join her for dinner in Old Town. Dan was the computer support representative from the human resource information systems department. Although they had different bosses, they often worked together on projects and had become fast friends. He gained her confidence with his competence and won her friendship with his sense of humor. He had helped her keep her sanity through system crashes and other crises, so his fun-loving attitude was the perfect antidote for Leanna's lingering post-op depression.

Chad seemed to like Dan as well. He often called Dan in to help whenever he had a sticky problem with his software, since Dan was the software support guru for the department. As they finished up the day's business before heading off to dinner, Dan confided in Leanna that he thought Chad purposely messed with his system to create glitches that required Dan's personal attention.

"Come on, Dan, why would he do that?" Leanna asked incredulously.

"Well, don't you think he's a little weird? After all, how many guys do you know who are male secretaries?" Dan asked.

"No, I don't think he's weird. He's the best secretary in the business," she said firmly.

"Well, if he's such a great secretary, why does he keep doing stupid things to his computer to get me to come in and fix them?"

"Just what are you getting at?" Leanna asked, getting annoyed. Although Dan never told her directly, she had heard through the grapevine that Dan received a number of gifts and romantic messages from Chad during the holidays. Dan claimed that Chad left him a box of candy with a signed note saying, "You are my dream, my desire, my enigma. I celebrate the thought of you!" However, since Leanna never saw the note, and Dan never mentioned it to her directly, she chose to ignore the whole matter as office gossip.

Dan danced around Leanna's question with a half-answer. "Oh, he just leaves weird stuff for me."

Leanna saw her opening, and pressed, "So what did you do about it?"

"I just told him, 'Chad, I'm had, I'm had; I'm not interested,'" Dan laughed.

Leanna wasn't sure whether Dan was telling the truth or exaggerating. Sometimes it was hard to tell if he was serious. He loved to tease her because she was a good sport. She thought he may be pulling another one of his "GOTCHAs," so she decided to change the subject and avoid being the butt of one of his jokes.

As Leanna and Dan were packing up to leave the office, Chad leaned in and casually asked, "Where are you two off to tonight?"

"Oh, we're going to cruise a few spots in Old Town," said Dan. "Do you want to come along?"

"Sure," Chad said, as his face lit up. "Let me run these copies and I'll meet you in the parking lot."

As Chad took off, Dan elbowed Leanna mischievously. "See what I mean?" he grinned.

Leanna contorted her face and shook her head with an "I've-had enough-of-your-nonsense" look.

The three took off for Old Town in Dan's car. They had a wonderful night listening to music, eating, and drinking beer. At the end of the evening, they all piled into Dan's tiny car to return to the company parking lot where Leanna and Chad had left their cars. As Dan put his keys in the ignition, she noticed a grimace on his face and saw him look in his rear-view mirror at Chad who was sitting in the back seat. "Cut it out, Chad!" Dan demanded sharply.

Leanna looked in the back seat at Chad who was giggling, but she couldn't see anything unusual. "I said knock it off," Dan repeated, raising his voice several tones louder. "Try that on Leanna and see if she thinks it's funny," he added sarcastically.

The three drove back to the company parking lot in silence. Leanna couldn't figure out what the rift between the two fellows was all about, but she thought the sun roof would blow off any moment from the tension. As soon as Dan stopped the car in the lot, Chad jumped out of the car, slammed the door, and raced to his car. Then he sat in his car and glared at Leanna and Dan. Dan turned to Leanna. "Did you see what was going on?"

"No, I couldn't see anything," she said.

"Well, let me show you what he was doing," Dan said angrily. He got out of the driver's seat and sat in the back. Then he pushed Leanna's seatback slightly forward and thrust his foot through the crevice between the seatback and the seat. She felt Dan wriggle his toes under her fanny and inch seductively toward her privates. "Okay, okay, I get the picture," she said, feeling her face flush.

"I kept hinting that he was gay. You thought I was kidding," Dan said.

"Okay, so what if he is," Leanna said defensively. "He's still a great secretary."

"Look, it's dark. I'll walk you to your car," Dan offered. Dan could see from the corner of his eye that they remained under Chad's surveillance. While Dan stood at Leanna's car, he told her of all the times that Chad had expressed his romantic interest in him. Then he explained how he tried to gently rebuff Chad's advances without appearing homophobic. Dan explained that he had asked Chad to join them this evening for a specific purpose. Dan wanted Chad to understand that he liked him as a person, but that he had no desire to develop a gay relationship.

Things were starting to make sense to Leanna. Between the grapevine and some other incidents, Leanna suspected that Chad was gay, but she had no first-hand knowledge. He never discussed his sexual preference, and she never asked. He was not especially effeminate, and she never considered his sexual preference an issue. Her first real inkling that he might be gay came when she overheard him at Christmastime poring over catalogs with the other secretaries. He had selected a dress for Marla and said, "Oooh, don't you think this little number would be just darling on you?" But beyond that discussion, Chad behaved very businesslike.

❦ ❦ ❦

Over the next several weeks Chad's attitude toward Leanna grew progressively negative. He'd do his work begrudgingly, grab papers from her hands, and keep all conversations to a minimum. Leanna was startled by his behavioral changes. She was going to discuss how to handle the situation with her boss, Phil Portman, but Phil beat her to the punch.

"How have things been going with you and Chad these days?" Phil inquired.

"Frankly, not great," she replied. "Chad's been behaving strangely ever since Dan and I took him to dinner with us a couple weeks ago. I think Chad is somehow jealous of my friendship with Dan. I'm not exactly sure how to broach the subject. I just don't think it would be appropriate to impose my personal feelings. What do you think?" she asked.

"Well, actually, Leanna, Chad came to me yesterday with a complaint about you," Phil said.

"A complaint? What kind of complaint?"

"He claims you've been sexually harassing him."

"What!" Leanna exclaimed.

"He says that you've been asking him on a daily basis to be a sperm donor for you," Phil said seriously.

"What?" she repeated. Her eyes widened and her mouth gaped.

"That's what he said."

"Now you don't believe that, do you?" she asked incredulously.

"Chad says he's not the only one you've hounded—that you've asked Victor too," Phil reported.

"Oh, geez, Phil, that was in jest. Why in the world, in this day of AIDS, would I go to a gay guy to be a sperm donor? That's absurd," she said.

"Well, Chad claims that because he's been denying you, you're giving him a hard time on the job and he can't deal with the stress. He says he can't face you. He indicated that the work environment is so hostile, he can't come back. He's been in therapy the past few weeks over this and is under a doctor's care for ulcers."

Leanna found the whole ordeal baffling. Could it be that Chad created this nonexistent romantic triangle so he could have a scapegoat to blame for his own disappointments? His motive became clearer when the company received a threatening letter from Chad's attorney. The letter indicated that Chad would go to the newspapers if the company didn't settle for three-quarters of a million dollars in damages. The company responded that Chad was welcome to share his story with the media, but if that were the case, they would countersue for defamation. Eventually the company agreed to settle the case by paying for his therapy charges if Chad would agree not to sue for further damages. Chad accepted the offer and settled for under $1,000.

 This story contains the unfortunate element of a manager who suspects a problem, but fails to pursue because of a misguided sense of privacy and an attempt to be politically correct. When Dan implied that Chad was making unwelcomed advances, Leanna should have addressed the issue head-on by following the standard procedure for investigating a sexual harassment claim.

Furthermore, when Chad's interactions with her soured, affecting his performance, Leanna should not have waited a week to discuss his behavior. She should have addressed the situation much sooner and documented their discussion. At a minimum, she should have indicated that she provided a counseling session with him regarding his performance and set up an action plan for improvement.

Leanna diminished her credibility by becoming so personal with her co-workers. It was inappropriate to discuss her medical conditions at the office. There must be certain lines of demarcation between personal life and business. This fact came back to haunt her when Chad filed his sexual harassment claim.

Dan showed very poor judgment as well by asking Chad out on the town. Human resources professionals should know better. Unfortunately, too often we don't take our own advice. When line managers do something like this, we lecture them about what they should have done. We're great at assigning guilt, but don't always recognize the human frailty in ourselves.

 The brave new human resources world of the '90s is sure to produce many variations on the sexual harassment theme—and this story is probably not as unique as it appears. It also shows that even well-informed

and conscientious managers may not be able to forestall claims from all employees who feel aggrieved and highlights the importance of adopting policies and procedures designed to minimize the risk of such claims and maximize the chances of prevailing in those suits that cannot be avoided.

As this story shows, either sex may be the victim or the offender in sexual harassment situations. One of the subtle issues here is whether Dan had a claim against the employer for tolerating or permitting a sexually offensive work environment. Once Leanna was aware that Chad's conduct had become "unwelcome" to Dan, warning bells should have gone off. It would have been prudent for Leanna to have conducted (or caused) a prompt investigation at that time, followed by prompt and appropriate corrective measures to prevent the sexually offensive or hostile environment. Indeed, if Leanna had moved quickly to defuse the situation and made it clear that Chad was the offender rather than the victim, the company's interests would have been better served than by her passive reaction approach.

While the information Dan provided about Chad's unwelcome advances toward him may have been told to Leanna as a friend, as a human resources manager, once she was aware if it, the company was on notice that there was a possibility that Chad was sexually harassing Dan. In a hostile environment context, the employer will be liable for the offensive conduct of workers if the employer knew or should have known that a sexually offensive or abusive atmosphere existed.

This story also raises another sticky business issue that employers are increasingly faced with today: what to do in situations where a disgruntled employee is attempting to extort money from or "get even" with an employer by filing unmeritorious charges. One arrow in the employer's quiver not mentioned here is the possibility of securing a release from the employee.

Chapter 12

Potpourri

"Carefully consider different social conventions and practices whenever counseling or disciplining employees from other cultures."

John D. Faure, SPHR
Human Resources Manager
Medaphis Corporation

Holding the Bag

Eve looked around the cabin of the tiny company plane. The prop was taking her to Tulsa, but dropping off the other passengers at another stop in between. There she sat with the other five passengers, crammed in the cabin like carpoolers in a Ford Escort.

One of the executives sat on the special seat. It was in a separate area located directly behind the pilots, and it faced the outside door. This seat doubled as a passenger seat and a toilet. The small area could be closed off with two privacy curtains, one to screen off the cockpit and the other to screen off the cabin. Eve, who was newly promoted to senior engineer, was a highly competent but very shy and private woman. She eyed the potty seat nervously, silently praying that she would not have to swap seats during the flight. All the other passengers and pilots were male.

Although she purposely limited her fluid intake that morning, just as the plane took off, she began to feel a slight urge. She checked her watch. The normal flight time to the first stop was two hours. "I guess I can hold it," she thought.

When she began to feel extra pressure, she leaned over and tapped Randall, the executive who occupied the potty seat. "Excuse me, could you ask Andy how much longer it will be before we arrive at our first stop?"

"Andy says that we've run into some head winds. It will be about another hour," Randall shouted over the roar of the engine.

Eve managed to nod and smile, trying to mask her discomfort. Then she pictured the layout of the tiny rural airport where they would dropping off the other five passengers. She knew the airport contained nothing more than a short strip and some outbuildings. Usually a company car stood by to whisk away the passengers and then the plane would take off immediately.

"I know," Eve thought, "I'll just ask Andy to wait a moment, and I'll relieve myself behind one of the outbuildings. There is no way that I'm going to use the plane potty with the pilot so close that I can blow in his ear." She winced slightly when some turbulence bounced her and her bladder uncomfortably about.

As the plane approached what appeared to be a speck of a runway, she grew eager with anticipation. Then her heart sank. Just below, she saw several farmers buzzing around in their crop dusters over the fields.

"Great, just what I always wanted to do, moon a group of Kansas crop dusters," she sighed to herself.

To add to her pain, there was no car waiting. So the plane delayed its takeoff until it could unload the other five passengers. Although the next five minutes seemed like an hour, the car arrived and the plane was off to its next stop, this time to refuel. Eve knew that the refueling airport had full rest room facilities and was only 10 minutes away. "I can hold off, as long as Andy sets this plane down real smooth," she thought, crossing her legs even tighter.

Then, over the drone of the props, she heard Andy shout back to the cabin, "I've got good news, Eve. We've got some tail winds now, so I won't have to stop to refuel. We're going directly to Tulsa. We should be there in 45 minutes."

"Forty-five minutes! I'll explode," Eve nearly cried. She finally conceded that her situation had become critical.

"Andy, I need to use the bathroom, and I need to use it now," she announced urgently.

"Fine, be my guest," Andy responded nonchalantly.

Eve attempted to pull the privacy curtain between herself and the pilots, but it got stuck halfway across its track. She tugged and tugged. Finally Andy turned around in his seat to try to help her. No luck. The co-pilot was talking to the tower at Tulsa, so he was unable to assist. The curtain was jammed and would not budge. In total desperation she lifted the lid of the commode. There she saw that the seat was composed of a plastic rim with a large plastic bag attached.

"If I can't go to the mountain, I'm going to bring the damn mountain to me," she decided, and ripped the plastic seat and accompanying bag right out of the commode. Then she took it into the cabin and closed off the other privacy curtain between the potty seat and the cabin. Finally, with perspiration dripping from her forehead, she relieved herself. And oh, how she relieved herself!

With her physical needs met, Eve could relax and turn her attention to hygiene concerns. "Now, what am I supposed to do with this?" she speculated, as she stared at the circular plastic toilet rim with the bag still attached. "I certainly am not going to put this back in the commode and have Andy clean up after me. He'll know it's mine. I'm too embarrassed," she worried.

Eve carefully removed the plastic bag from the seat rim. Although the bag had nearly two cups of liquid, she had room to twist around the top of the bag and tie it securely into several knots. Next, she scouted around the cabin and found another plastic bag. She placed her bag inside the empty one, tying off the outer bag as well.

Eve knew that a consultant would be waiting at the airport to meet her. The last thing she wanted to do was greet him with one hand while holding a bag of urine in the other. So, ever the resourceful professional, she emptied some of the folders from her briefcase and tucked her extra bag inside. When she arrived at the airport, she greeted the consultant with a smile and told him she needed to make a quick trip to the rest room. There she dumped her extra baggage, washed her hands, and went on her way.

When Eve returned to corporate, she informed her boss, John Jones, that she would no longer be flying on the corporate plane. "Unless you arrange to have more private rest room facilities, I feel that I need to fly on a commercial carrier."

"That would be highly inconvenient, uneconomical, and inefficient. You know that some of the towns where we have sites are not accessible by commercial carrier. You'd have to fly to a major city and rent a car. That would not only add to the cost, but probably take an extra day of travel time," John pointed out.

"You knew when you took this job that your key responsibilities required travel out in the field," John reminded her. "If you can't do the job, we'll have to transfer you to another position. And, you realize, we might have to cut your pay if we can't find an equivalent position."

"We'll see about that," Eve said. Then she went to human resources to plead her case.

The human resources department knew that the company was in the process of buying a new plane with private rest room facilities. They expected delivery of the aircraft within the next six months. Consequently, they suggested to John that he accommodate Eve in the interim, since the problem would go away.

He agreed and Eve was satisfied.

 In the words of Bill Clinton, "We feel your pain." As in broader societal issues, the resolution of this case is based on the company's willingness and ability to do something about it. Most enlightened employers

frequently make a conscientious effort to accommodate the individual and personal needs of their employees. We feel John, her supervisor, took a very narrow view of the problems.

Virtually all human resources executives have made exceptions or accommodations for one or more employees. They have often gone beyond the legal requirements of accommodating employees who have temporary or permanent disabilities. Such provisions may include helping to arrange for or subsidize the cost of evening or weekend child care when the employee's job requires him or her to be out of town. Alternatively, management may reduce the frequency of travel by combining trips, teleconferencing, and/or bringing the "client" in rather than going to the client. Another example is when an employer pays for first-class seating on commercial flights because the employee's size makes it uncomfortable or impossible to ride in coach. A company may also arrange for travel by car or train due to an employee's fear of flying. Additionally, a company may buy and install special ventilation equipment based on a person's unusual sensitivity to common chemicals in the office air. Further accommodations may include work-at-home and job-sharing arrangements. The list is as long as it is varied.

As companies decide how to deal with matters of accommodation, it is prudent to consider some key factors. Is the request reasonable or outlandish? For example, we feel it would be unreasonable for Eve to request *separate* rest room facilities. The unisex bathroom is a standard in transportation and at many special events.

Second, what are the cost-benefit tradeoffs of making the accommodation? In Eve's case, the potential "benefit" is keeping a competent, female engineer happy and productive.

Next, the company must consider the potential precedents set by the accommodation. Would other employees view the accommodation as fair and reasonable, or simply as favoritism and "oiling the squeaky wheel?" Also, are there other available alternatives? In this case, the options should not have been limited to either Eve's flying commercial carrier or suffering like everybody else. Instead, these considerations should have been expanded to such alternatives as:

• Rearranging work and travel schedules; combining trips to reduce frequency of required travel

• Repairing or replacing the plane's privacy screens with something more effective

- Strategically placing rented "porta-potties" at those remote landing strips frequented by the company aircraft

- Allowing Eve to pay for some of the extra cost associated with commercial air travel

- Encouraging Eve and others to speak up when "nature calls," while displaying a sincere willingness to accommodate the specific situation, such as a layover at a stop for an extra few moments.

By carefully considering all the options in these and similar cases, human resource executives and management have an opportunity to maintain or increase productivity as well as demonstrate excellent employee relations.

 This story illustrates the importance of employers knowing that they have rights too. As long as the company did not discriminate against Eve because of her gender and did not subject her to disparate treatment, it is unclear what claim she could have against the company. The pilot of the plane could have just as easily been a woman, and the modest manager could have been a man.

"Modesty" generally will not rise to the level of a protected disability. Thus, we doubt the company had any legal duty to accommodate Eve. If we had been consulted by a client regarding this problem, we would have suggested that Eve deal with the inconvenience and save expenses until the new company plane was available. An employer has a legitimate interest in minimizing its travel expenses and maximizing the productive time of its employees.

While John might benefit from sensitivity training to avoid the possibility of claims from other aggrieved employees, in this situation, if he carried through with his plans to transfer Eve to another position due to her unwillingness to abide by standard company travel policies, we doubt the company would have liability.

The Graveyard Shift

Eleanor Swasey's role as night administrator for Metro Hospital was never dull. The job was full of unusual and unexpected events. However, the evening of August 16 seemed eerily quiet and mundane.

When Eleanor completed her rounds of the nursing units, she pulled out her stack of paperwork and hummed softly to herself as she reviewed the files. The telephone interrupted her thoughts.

"Good evening, Eleanor Swasey speaking," she answered, noticing it was about 9 p.m.

"Mrs. Swasey, this is Albert Dietrich of the Dietrich Funeral Home calling. The Daily family has requested that we handle the Mavis Louise Daily case. She expired late this afternoon. We expect to arrive at 10 o'clock this evening. Could you arrange to complete the paperwork and release the body to us by that time?"

"No problem, Mr. Dietrich," she responded pleasantly while goose bumps danced up and down her arms. She dreaded the trip to the hospital morgue. It always gave her the heebie jeebies. Unfortunately, Metro's morgue did not resemble its TV counterpart. It was not a brightly lit room housing a library of bodies that were neatly catalogued, shelved, and masked behind shiny steel refrigerator doors. No, the bodies in Metro's morgue looked more like a mass of general-admission concert fans camping in sleeping bags the night prior to an event.

The morgue was so creepy that Eleanor never went in alone. She always brought an assistant and a flashlight with her on her journey. On that particular evening, she asked Sonya to join her. When they entered the dimly lit room, she shivered slightly as the blast of cool air enveloped her. She could see the outline of several bodies secured in bags and lying on gurneys. The two women began to flash their lights on the identification tags attached to each of the bags.

The first tag listed Zelda Pinsky. "Nope," Eleanor said to Sonya. Then Eleanor thought she heard an unusual noise. "What's that?" she whispered, grabbing Sonya's arm tightly.

"It's nothing, Eleanor. Dead bodies sometimes move and make noises. Ignore it," Sonya advised her as she pried Eleanor's fingers from her arm.

Eleanor continued to the next body. "There it is again. Do you hear it?" she asked.

"Really, it's nothing. Don't worry," Sonya repeated.

Eleanor was insistent. "I am telling you, I heard something."

Then Eleanor moved to the next gurney and shined the flashlight where the tag should be. The light revealed a pair of high-top tennis shoes extending from the pant legs of a white uniform.

"AAHHHHH!" Eleanor screamed, jumping back and crashing into several gurneys. The impact sent the corpse-laden gurneys rolling in all directions as if they were runaway shopping carts scattering in a parking lot on a windy day.

Then, the tennis-shoed body sprung up to a sitting position. Summoning all her courage and clinging tightly to Sonya for support, Eleanor shined the light toward the face.

"Hi, Mrs. Swasey. Didn't mean to scare you," the body said. "It's me—Fletcher."

"Fletcher, is that really you?" she asked, holding her hand to heart. She felt as though she were about to go into cardiac arrest.

"Yes," he answered.

"What are you doing in here?" she shrieked.

"Just taking my break. This is the coolest, quietest place in the hospital, and I thought I'd take a little snooze," Fletcher said. Fletcher was Metro's only night orderly.

By this time Eleanor's emotions had switched from fear to anger. "Fletcher, don't ever let me find you in here again. You know you are not authorized to come in here. Since when does M-O-R-G-U-E spell "Employee Lounge?" You nearly gave me a heart attack. Get out of here right now!"

"Yes, ma'am," Fletcher obliged, springing off the gurney. "But could I just get my dinner before I leave?"

"Your dinner? Isn't it in your locker?" Eleanor asked.

"Well, no, ma'am, I like to pack my own soft drinks and sandwiches, and they need to be refrigerated," Fletcher answered.

"So, we have a cooler in the employee lounge for that."

"Well, I never use the lounge," Fletcher explained. "I usually keep my dinner in here."

"In here?!"

"Yes, in the refrigerator here. You know, the one where the organs are held for the medical school."

"Oh, God, Fletcher," Eleanor moaned. "How can you be so macabre?"

"Macabre?" he asked innocently, clearly missing her point.

"Never mind. Yes, get your dinner and get out of here. And if I ever find you in here without authorization again, I'll write you up. Now go!" she ordered.

Fletcher grabbed his lunch and fled the room. As soon as Fletcher left, Eleanor and Sonya exploded with laughter and dashed to the rest room to avoid any further mishaps.

 Although we probably all chuckled through this rather ghoulish incident, this is no laughing matter. As the night administrator, Eleanor is responsible for ensuring proper employee conduct as well as the safety and health practices of the hospital. We feel she treated the matter too lightly.

Fletcher should not use the morgue to refrigerate his lunch or as a lounge to catnap with cadavers. When Fletcher put his dinner in the refrigerator with the organs held for medical school, he risked contamination of the organs as well as his lunch. Moreover, Fletcher is an orderly who has regular contact with patients. His actions show total disregard for their welfare. Sound practice suggests that the hospital maintain controls for entering and leaving the morgue and coming into contact with patients. Also we suggest improving the lighting in the morgue. If there is concern about heat from the lights, we're sure there are alternative solutions. One should not have to identify bodies using a flashlight.

Eleanor should discuss with Fletcher his motives and rationale for using the morgue as his private lounge. There may be more here than meets the eye. For example, why doesn't he want to eat with co-workers? Could there be strife among the staff? Then, Eleanor must ensure that Fletcher understands the safety, health, and patient service issues. If Eleanor needs to revise the policy for authorization to the morgue then she should meet with the entire staff to explain the new policy, its purpose, and when it will take effect.

At a minimum Eleanor should have documented Fletcher's file, indicating that she coached and counseled him, to record the event. Alternatively, she could impose the hospital's progressive discipline practice or policy. For example, if this was the first offense, then Fletcher should receive a formal verbal warning. A second offense would be a letter of reprimand outlining the specific consequences up to termination if he continues this practice.

We are also concerned about the effect of Fletcher's antics on the hospital's image. If someone leaks Fletcher's shenanigans to the general public, the hospital would have a public relations nightmare. We dare say that Eleanor would find herself more than nearly wetting her pants if she saw his story flash on the 11 o'clock news!

Employees should be told to stay out of the morgue—it's already difficult enough to determine sometimes if one's employees are dead or alive!

Black Magic

Conchita fled from the processing center as though pursued by the devil himself. Screaming and babbling incoherently, she bulldozed through the glass entrance doors to the human resources office and raced for the first available office. There she found Jeff Fenton, the service center's human resources manager, deeply absorbed with his budget projections. The moment she rounded the corner and tore into his office, Conchita broke his concentration. Her face was ashen and her body trembled. As she leaned against the wall to catch her breath, Jeff jumped up from his seat and dashed to assist her.

"What's wrong?" he asked, ushering her toward a chair.

"No habla Ingles, señor," Conchita choked between her tears.

Once Jeff realized she couldn't speak English, he raised his index finger in the air. "Un momento. No problema." Then he motioned for her to sit down and smiled reassuringly as he attempted to leave his office. On his way out, Conchita reached up, grabbed his jacket sleeve, and with both hands latched onto his arm like a python preparing for dinner.

Because she seemed so frightened, he tolerated her vise-like grip and maneuvered one foot on the threshold of the doorway so he could stick his head out into the hall. He called down the corridor to the office next to his, "Amy, please come to my office! I have an employee who doesn't speak English and she's nearly hysterical. Hurry. Please!"

"Be right there," said Amy, the employment recruiter, who arrived in less than 15 seconds.

"What is your name?" Amy asked Conchita in Spanish.

"Conchita Hernandez," she responded, still clutching tightly to Jeff's arm.

"Why are you so upset?" Amy asked.

"When I came to work today," Conchita stuttered in Spanish, "I . . . I . . . I . . . saw the work of the evil spirits."

"What evil spirits?" Amy asked, as she provided a continuous translation for Jeff.

"There was a voodoo doll on my desk. I think it could be the work of Santeria!" Conchita sobbed.

"What does she mean?" Jeff asked.

"I'm not sure. Like black magic, I guess," Amy offered.

"Why would someone do this?" she said to Conchita.

"I don't know," Conchita cried, "but they are trying to put a spell on me."

"Did you bring the doll with you?"

"No. I wouldn't touch it," Conchita cowered. "I thought it might hurt me."

"Why do you think it will hurt you?"

"I don't know. I'm just scared that it could," she sputtered.

"Well, don't worry," Amy consoled her. "We'll find it and get rid of it for you. If you'll let go of Jeff's arm, he'll go to your work station and take the doll off your desk. Then we'll try to figure out what this is all about."

"You won't leave me, will you?" Conchita asked fearfully.

"Of course not, I'll stay here with you," Amy reassured her. "But you'll have to tell us where your desk is located."

Finally, to Jeff's relief, Conchita relaxed her grip on his arm and told them the location of her work station. As Jeff rode the elevator to the floor where Conchita worked, he rubbed the circulation back into his arm. When he reached her work area, Jeff spotted Conchita's desk. On top he saw a small doll with red hair lying across a china plate. As he got closer, he noticed that the doll also had a red bow wrapped around its neck and five different-colored stick pins piercing its heart. The doll's left arm had been crudely amputated and placed alongside the body. Then Jeff noticed a tiny brown paper bag. He opened it and found a granular substance that appeared to be salt with a sprinkling of spices. Next to the bag was a partially burned candle and three pennies.

He removed the entire display and brought it back to Amy's office. Then he called Lupe Braga, another employee. Jeff knew Lupe was familiar with the rituals of Santeria. He explained what happened and asked for her help.

When Lupe reviewed the display she asked Jeff, "Does this woman, Conchita, have red hair?"

"Yes," Jeff responded.

"Ah, I see," Lupe mused, as she continued to view the remainder of the display.

Jeff waited nervously for her assessment. "Well, Lupe, don't keep me in suspense. What's this all about?"

"Well," Lupe began, "first of all, the red hair tells me the doll represents Conchita, since Conchita has red hair. The red ribbon is associated with a particular saint. This one happens to be Saint Barbara. That means the person who cast the spell is asking for the help of Saint Barbara to make the spell work. The three pennies represent an offering—it's more or less a payment."

"What about the five pins in the heart?" Jeff asked anxiously.

"I'm getting to that," Lupe assured him. "Each pin is a different color and represents five different saints. The red one is, of course, Saint Barbara again. I can't remember exactly which saints the other colors represent. The pins suggest that whoever cast the spell wants to inflict pain on Conchita by doing some damage to her heart. I don't think we're talking a death-type thing, maybe just sort of break her heart. The salt and spices in the bag are designed to sour or spoil Conchita's life. And the arm was ripped off as a kicker. It can pretty much be interpreted literally. They'd like to break her arm."

"Wonderful," Jeff said sarcastically. "So, what about the candle?"

"Oh yeah, I forgot. Sorry," Lupe apologized. "It's typical to light a candle when you pray to the saint. It's all part of the deal. They go through a prayer or incantation, and then they blow it out when they're done."

"Boy, they sure didn't give me guidelines for dealing with voodoo when I was in graduate school," he sighed, as he considered his alternatives.

Jeff wondered not only *how* he was going to handle this situation, but also just *what* it was he was going to handle. "I suppose this is probably some form of harassment," he thought. "But how am I going to identify who the harasser is? Certainly no one is going to come forward and admit doing this."

To Lupe he said, "Right now I've got to get Conchita calm and somehow counteract the effect of this whole thing."

"Well, if I can be of any help . . . ," Lupe offered.

"You know what, Lupe? I think you can. Here's what I'm thinking . . . ." Jeff described the creative plan he'd come up with to Lupe.

He asked Lupe to relieve Amy of her hand-holding duty so Amy could return to her office where she and Jeff could talk. When Amy arrived, Jeff briefed her on the Santeria display and its meaning. "Look," Jeff said, "Conchita doesn't really know what all these symbols mean. I'm going to tell her human resources has much greater power than Santeria— that we can counteract any spells. But before I do, I'm going to need some supplies. Can you get me some *Super Glue*, red construction paper, a candle, and some sugar?" Jeff asked.

"Sure," Amy said. "I have some birthday candles from our last party, and I'll run down to the lobby drug store and get the rest."

"Great," Jeff said. "In the meantime, I'll tell Conchita we're working on our spell."

When Amy returned with the items, she said, "I got everything but the sugar. All I could find were five *Equal* packets by the coffee machine."

"That will work," Jeff said as he assembled his materials. "Can you cut out a red heart about one inch in diameter from this paper, Amy?"

"Yep."

Amy and Jeff conferred on a few other details and then walked into his office where Lupe sat with Conchita. Conchita cringed, hiding her head in Lupe's shoulder when she saw Jeff carry in the doll on the plate.

"Don't worry, Conchita, we're going to get everything all fixed up," Jeff promised, as Amy translated.

"First of all, we're going to fix your heart." He removed all the pins from the heart, made a circular motion with his arm, and dropped each one symbolically into the trash can. Then he held up the red heart made of construction paper. "Here is your new heart, Conchita. It's full of love and happiness," Jeff said, smiling. Then he glued the heart to the doll's chest.

Next, he picked up the bag of salt and spices. He held it about five feet above the trash can and emptied it slowly, allowing the white stream to fall into the waste basket as Conchita stared transfixed at the grainy powder.

"No more salt to sour your life," Jeff said with authority, dusting off his hands. Subsequently, he tore open each packet of *Equal*, taking great care as he poured the contents into the small brown bag. "Instead, Conchita," he said, "your life will be filled with sweetness and joy."

Then he picked up the mutilated arm and applied some glue. "With this glue, you will be stronger than before. You will be able to fight off anyone who wishes you harm," Jeff continued. He held the arm tightly against the doll's body and lifted it with both his hands above his head. Then he turned in a circle three times, waiting for the glue to set.

Now Jeff focused on the coins. With utter contempt, he spouted, "These three cents show the weakness of the enemy who cast the spell. Our company power is much stronger," he added, as he flipped a

Kennedy half-dollar high in the air, catching it as it fell. He ceremonially shined the coin on his sleeve and placed it on the plate next to the doll.

Finally, Jeff lit the candle. He and Amy began to wave their hands over the flame as they chanted, "Hocus pocus, ishka pishka, kick this evil spell in the kishka!"

Then he told Amy to tell Conchita to blow out the candle. When she blew out the candle, Lupe, Amy, and Jeff clapped their hands and congratulated her. Relief washed across Conchita's entire body. She was all smiles and thanked them for helping rid her of the evil.

When Conchita returned to work that morning, she was completely productive. She remains a productive employee with the company and has experienced no further harassment. It seems that word quickly spread through the office that nobody better mess with human resources. They have some strong magic of their own!

Although we found this story amusing and initially applauded Jeff's creativity, on reflection we feel that he was very lucky, indeed. It may not have ended so happily.

Most of us view this incident through the cultural perspective of Judeo-Christian tradition and ascribe Conchita's beliefs to silly superstition. However, for her they are deeply felt beliefs about the nature of good and evil. A mistake in the use of symbols could have been damaging psychologically to her and perhaps would have made things worse.

Furthermore, if Conchita encountered bad fortune or if she experienced further harassment from the practitioner(s) of Santeria, the company might be exposed to liability. Conchita and others may accuse the company of misleading her into a false sense of security and well-being. It could be argued that the company failed to take direct, appropriate, and realistic actions to determine the source of the harassment and put a stop to it.

Moreover, if this case had taken place in an international branch of a company, there would be additional considerations. If other native employees learned about the incident, they might construe Jeff's actions as condescending and mocking traditional native beliefs.

Perhaps Jeff could have achieved the same results by suggesting alternatives to Conchita. She could consider getting an antidote for the evil spell from someone familiar with Santeria (such as Lupe or someone Lupe might recommend). Another somewhat unconventional approach might have been to call in a native shaman or priest to perform the exorcism. The company would then have been perceived by the employees as respecting traditional beliefs rather than demeaning them. We would still encourage Jeff and Amy to seek a resolution through more conventional means.

 Visions of *Workforce 2000*. As most employers know, these situations are not something to be dealt with in the future—their time has already arrived. Issues concerning workplace diversity will be an everyday challenge to today's human resources professional.

As time goes on, employers will be faced with different and unfamiliar cultural and religious practices of their employees. Human resources will need to develop heightened sensitivity to reduce the risks that they will inadvertently offend people and discriminate against them. However, while employers are obligated to reasonably accommodate an employee's religious needs, an employer is not required to permit an individual to utilize his/her religion to harass a co-worker.

Many companies have been providing or are considering diversity training for their employees. While these programs may have the positive benefits of improving teamwork and productivity, they are not without risks and must be done in a professional and expert manner. In at least one case, female employees successfully sued their employer partially based on statements their managers made at a diversity training session—which helped the women prove management bias!

Schwarzenegger-Phobia

Valerie fanned the phone messages in her hand, studying them with the intent of a high-stakes poker player. "I don't think I can bluff my way through this round. Maybe I'll just fold and wait to see if I get dealt a better hand the next time," she thought, wishing it were that easy.

She was the lone ranger of human resources, covering a vast territory of satellite sales and remote service centers for the company. The human resources staff was so sparse that she often felt like a piece of taffy, stretched and pulled into fibrous strands. Her advice and opinions were in constant demand. Although Valerie preferred to offer prevention strategies, she was unfortunately recruited more often for cleanup detail. From the looks of today's messages, Valerie suspected she would be relegated to mopping up management mishaps.

As she reviewed her phone messages again, she thought, "What is it—a full moon tonight?" They all spelled trouble. Before she got the pleasure of selecting one for response, Valerie's secretary buzzed her office.

"Valerie, Jerry Bailey's on the line. He sounds awful—says it's an emergency. Something about an employee, Ravi Pental," her secretary said.

"Hmmm . . . I wonder what could be the problem," Valerie thought. She'd been working with Jerry for the past three months. Jerry was one of the best-trained managers in the customer service group.

Ravi Pental was one of Jerry's service representatives who was having performance problems. It seemed that Ravi had a difficult time following instructions. He liked to do things his own way, which resulted in serious data entry errors.

Valerie counseled Jerry on coaching techniques to help Ravi achieve success. Jerry took Ravi through all the appropriate steps. At Valerie's urging, Jerry documented all of his coaching discussions with Ravi. The documentation demonstrated that Jerry provided additional training and prepared detailed development plans to assist Ravi, who was also having some difficulty with the language (Ravi had been raised in India).

After each session Ravi behaved as though he understood Jerry's expectations. He'd do fine for a few days but then would lapse into his own ways, ignoring standard procedures.

Jerry made it very clear to Ravi during each counseling session that there was a time limit on performance improvement. If Ravi couldn't demonstrate sustained improvement, he would lose his job. When the deadline arrived, Ravi fell short of performance expectations.

When Jerry called Valerie for counseling about how to terminate Ravi, she gave him explicit instructions. She was surprised to be hearing from Jerry—especially with a call tagged "emergency." Jerry was not the type to cry wolf or overreact.

"Hi, Jerry. What's wrong?" she asked with grave concern.

"Valerie, I have Ravi in another office," Jerry said. "I told him he was being terminated for poor performance and he went bonkers. I don't understand it. I must have told him on four occasions that if his performance did not improve he would lose his job. He'd just smile and say that he'd do better. Val, he's normally this mild-mannered, smiling little guy—somewhat thick headed maybe, but not hysterical. When I told him, he turned white as a sheet and scampered under the desk. He's in there now cowering and crying and chanting something in Hindi. I don't know what to do here," Jerry lamented.

"Let's not panic, Jerry. I'm sure that there must be some explanation," Valerie offered. "Now tell me exactly what you said to him in the interview."

"I did what you told me to. I told him that today was his final opportunity for improving performance. I showed him the computer printout, which listed his errors. I told him his error rate fell way below standards, and then I told him his services were no longer needed by the company and he was being terminated. We would mail him his final pay, which included pay for today."

Valerie couldn't find any real fault with his procedure. "And you're sure you told him during the other counseling sessions that he would be losing his job if he didn't meet production standards?" she asked.

"Yes," Jerry confirmed.

"Well, everything you did sounds okay to me, but let's see if I can find out what his problem is," Valerie suggested. "Do you think you can get him to come to the phone?"

"I'll try, but I don't know."

A few minutes later Ravi came to the phone.

"Hello." Ravi sobbed.

"Ravi, this is Valerie Morris, in the human resources department. I understand that you're very upset about losing your job. Did Jerry tell you during your counseling sessions that you would be fired if you didn't perform to company standards?"

"Yes," Ravi moaned.

"Are you surprised that you no longer have a job with us?"

"Nooooo," he whined.

"Well then, Ravi, why are you so frightened and upset?"

"Well . . . Jerry . . . said the company was going to terminate me," he wailed.

"That's right Ravi, you *are* being terminated for poor performance."

"But I just made mistakes. I didn't mean to. Why are you going to kill me for a few mistakes?" he cried, clearly terrified.

Valerie put her hand up to her mouth. "Poor Ravi," she thought. Then she asked him, "Why do you think we are going to kill you?"

"When Jerry counseled me he only said I would lose my job. He never said you would terminate me," he whimpered.

Valerie did everything to contain her laughter. "Ravi, let me explain. In this country, when we say *terminate,* we mean end your employment. We do not mean we will kill you. This is a civilized country. We don't kill our employees for poor performance," she said. "Although sometimes we'd like to," she thought to herself.

"Oh, bless you, Ms. Morris. Thank you for explaining. I am so relieved. I thought my children would have no father," Ravi sang out with joy.

"And bless you, Ravi," Valerie thought. "You made my day!"

While this may be a humorous incident, it illustrates two very important points. Human resources professionals tend to use the word "terminate" alone when the proper usage is "termination of employment." Termination is a harsh word even for an employee whose primary language is English—"separation" is a better choice. It is understandable that the employee was terrified!

Secondly, managers should carefully consider different social conventions and practices whenever counseling or disciplining employees from other cultures. For example, Jerry should have asked Ravi to explain his understanding of their discussion at the end of each counseling session. Using this technique, Jerry would have known if he had communicated effectively. As we go forward into the next century (*Workforce 2000*), our workforce will become increasingly diverse. Managers and supervisors need to develop a heightened sensitivity toward cultural as well as language (both direct and implied) differences. We suggest that the company provide some hands-on training to demonstrate how people of different cultures interpret what we consider normal or even mundane.

Finally, we think Valerie handled the situation very well. She remained calm, asked the right questions, and did not jump to conclusions.

What can we say? Employment-at-will—'til death do us part!

About the Author

*"**O**ur company repeatedly contracts with Dr. Fried. She's a nationally recognized compensation consultant and professional speaker who always underpromises and overdelivers."*

Pat Alcorn
President
Management Perspectives, Inc.
(An association management firm and speaker's bureau)

Biography

N. Elizabeth Fried is president of N. E. Fried and Associates, Inc., a national management consulting firm located in Dublin, Ohio. The firm was established in 1983 and specializes in compensation and expert testimony. It serves clients from small, entrepreneurial businesses to *Fortune 500* companies.

Fried received her Ph.D. from The Ohio State University and her Certified Compensation Professional Designation from the American Compensation Association (ACA). Additionally, she is listed in *Who's Who of American Women* and *Who's Who of Emerging Leaders in America*. Fried, a vibrant and entertaining professional speaker, incorporates magic, humor, and surprise in her presentations to human resources and general business groups. She has also entertained audiences with her wit and humor on more than 100 radio shows and a dozen television interviews, including CNN's *Sonya Live!* and *Working Women*.

Fried conducts ad hoc compensation research and is a nationally recognized authority on secretarial grading practices and retention bonuses designed to maintain key employees during acquisitions, mergers, and divestitures. She has been quoted widely in such national publications as *The Wall Street Journal, Chicago Tribune, Washington Post, USA Today,* and *Ms. Magazine*. A prolific writer, she is frequently invited to contribute to professional journals and trade publications. She has written for such publications as ACA's *Technical Perspectives in Compensation, BNA's Compensation and Benefits Guide, HR Magazine, Journal of Compensation and Benefits, Journal of Staffing and Recruitment, Warren Gorham Lamont's Compensation Guide, B&C Solutions,* and *Human Resource Executive*. Most recently she co-authored *Developing Statistical Job Evaluation Models: An Approach to Building a Job-Worth Hierarchy,* an ACA "building blocks in total compensation" booklet. She wrote her first creative work, *Outrageous Conduct: Bizarre Behavior at Work,* in 1991.

Fried teaches two certification seminars for ACA, one on quantitative analysis and the other on job analysis, job evaluation, and job description writing. She also served as adjunct faculty at Franklin University from 1979 to 1986, where she taught a comprehensive course in wage and salary administration.

An active big sister to 12-year-old Yolanda Lorenzo for four years, Fried completes her third year on the board of the Franklin County Big Brothers/Big Sisters Association, currently serving as its vice president of public relations.

Fried is available as a keynote speaker for management and professional meetings and conventions. Please contact Alexandra Fuller at **614-766-9800** for scheduling and fee arrangements.

Compensation Resources

*"**M**y compensation research is highly specialized, technical, and quantitative. **Sex, Laws & Stereotypes** was a creative outlet for addressing broader employee relations issues."*

N. Elizabeth Fried, Ph.D., CCP
President
N. E. Fried and Associates, Inc.

Surveys & Reports

N. E. Fried and Associates, Inc. is a compensation consulting firm and produces ad hoc surveys and reports. The following reports are available to companies and can be ordered directly from the firm. Call **614–766–9800** for more information.

Secretarial grading Practices: 1993 Update N. E. Fried and Associates conducted personal interviews with 478 American Compensation Association (ACA) members about their secretarial grading practices. This survey includes data on job evaluation plans, secretarial title options, exemption issues, union status, shorthand requirements, classification control, manager/secretary team transfers, software usage, recruitment and retention strategies, alternate career path options, and training and development programs. The complete report also includes an extensive review of the literature; sample job description packages, which can be tailored to organizations of varying sizes; key criteria for differentiating among secretarial levels and methods for selling both management and job incumbents on a job-content evaluation system. New this year is the inclusion of an analysis of progressively complex software skills for word processing, spreadsheet, and data base programs as well as an expansion of the creative practices section. This comprehensive 106-page report is available for $295 (US) PREPAID, including postage and handling. (614) 766–9800

Survey of On–Call Pay Policies investigates on-call and beeper premium policies among 50 companies nationwide from 12 different industries. The study reveals that 60% of the companies maintained policies, which varied widely both within and between industries. Surprisingly, the study also found that approximately 23% of the companies maintained special on-call pay arrangements for exempt employees along with their traditional nonexempt policies. The *Survey of On–Call Pay Policies* assesses the following: (1) Are premiums paid to exempt or nonexempt employees who either carry beepers or remain on-call for prescribed periods? (2) When employees are called in, are they paid a guaranteed minimum and at what rate of pay? (3) When does the "clock" start and end? Portal to portal or upon arrival and departure to and from the job site? (4) Is mileage reimbursed for traveling to and from the job site? The report is available from N. E. Fried and Associates, Inc. Price $59 (US) PREPAID. (614) 766–9800

Stay bonuses: Compensation Arrangements Designed to Hold Key People During Acquisitions, Mergers, Divestitures, Liquidations, and Bankruptcies, Vol. II is Fried's second report on retention bonus strategies. It is based on personal interviews with corporate executives and compensation professionals. **Volume II** contains **20** new case studies. In an easy-to-read format, she succinctly distills many hours of discussion into a brief summary that includes key criteria on each case. This unique report describes the circumstances surrounding the proposed sale, acquisition, merger, liquidation, or bankruptcy as well as the company's plan for achieving its objective. It concisely presents a variety of business issues that are resolved with practical and creative compensation arrangements. This 15-page executive summary is available for $180 (US) PREPAID, including postage and handling, from N. E. Fried and Associates, Inc. **Volume I,** which contains **14 case** studies, has been reprinted and is again available for $120 (US) PREPAID. Both reports can be ordered as a set for $225 (US) PREPAID, allowing a $75 savings. (614) 766–9800

Abortion to Wrongful Termination

"*I*t takes a light-spirited approach to make complex topics 'night-stand' reading."

Brian C. G. Settle
Vice President of Personnel
The Methodist Medical Center of Illinois